The Best of
The Hudson Valley
and Catskill Mountains

AN EXPLORER'S GUIDE

The Best of
The Hudson Valley
and Catskill Mountains

AN EXPLORER'S GUIDE

JOANNE MICHAELS &
MARY-MARGARET BARILE

Fourth Edition

The Countryman Press
Woodstock, Vermont

Dedication
To all the people in our lives who have
supported, loved,
and believed in us through the years.
We have been very fortunate in our families
and friends.

ISBN: 0-88150-490-4
ISSN: 1533-6867

Maps by Mike Henkle
Text design by Glenn Suokko
Cover design by Bodenweber Design

Published by The Countryman Press
P.O. Box 748, Woodstock, VT 05091

Distributed by W. W. Norton & Company, Inc.
500 Fifth Avenue, New York, NY 10110

Printed in the United States of America

10 9 8 7 6 5 4 3 2 1

A Note to the Reader

No entries for any of the establishments appearing in the *Explorer's Guide* series have been solicited or paid for.

Please note two things: The prices cited in the book are those available at press time in 2001; they do not include the state and county rooms and meals taxes, which vary from 6 to 8 percent. We have tried to note the addition of a 15 percent gratuity where applicable. Increases are possible.

Smoking: Most bed & breakfasts are now smoke-free, and several have nonsmoking rooms, as do larger restaurants. If this is of importance to you, ask when you call for reservations.

For Families: The crayon symbol points out establishments we feel are especially appropriate for and interesting to children. Please use your judgment when deciding where to take very young children.

Handicapped Access: The wheelchair symbol appears next to places that are partially or fully handicapped-accessible.

Pets: The dog paw symbol appears next to lodgings that accept pets (with prior notification) as of press time in 2001.

Don't Miss: Throughout this guide, our author's choices for must-see attractions are highlighted with gray shading.

Prices: The price rating system is simple. For entrées in the *Dining Out* and *Eating Out* sections:

$ means $15 and under
$$ means $15–25
$$$ means above $25

For inns and bed & breakfasts (per person):

$ means $80 and under
$$ means $80–$100

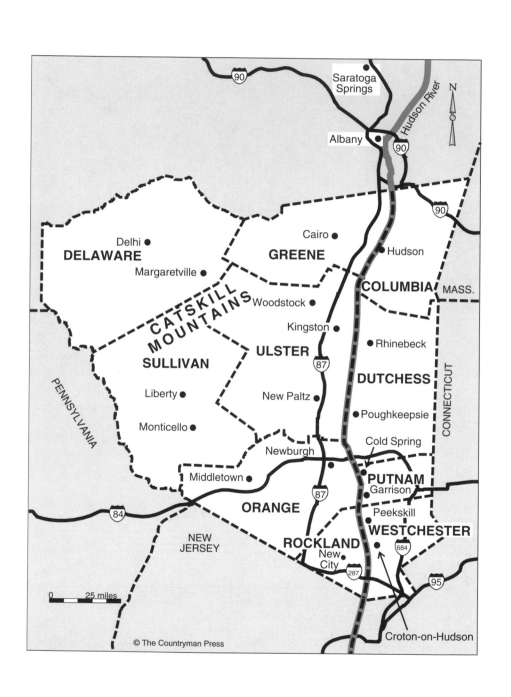

Contents

List of Maps

Acknowledgments

It is never possible to thank everyone who helps a book of this kind come to life; for every person we mention, there were a dozen more behind the scenes who answered questions, sent out brochures, provided suggestions, and opened their homes. The following people who travel the Hudson Valley gave us their recommendations from their frequent excursions: Bruce Moor, Nancy Michaels, Lynne Turk, Alicia Silver, Gail and Alan Paley, and Sheryl Woods. We appreciate their input. Joseph Puglisi traveled to far-flung parts of the Hudson Valley to take photographs of the sights. Sarah Phillips assisted in the research and spent hours on the phone tracking down the necessary information for this edition.

Many people gave us their opinions and the names of their favorite spots, based on years of growing up and living in their respective towns. They probably didn't realize at the time how helpful they were. These friendly folks got us off the beaten track, where we discovered restaurants, back roads, and a fishing hole or two that we probably never would have found on our own. So this book, aside from being what we hope is the very best guide to the area, is also a valentine to all the people in the Hudson Valley and Catskills.

Introduction

Although we were certainly not the first travelers to recognize the beauty of the Hudson Valley and Catskills, we are proud to say that we have remained at the forefront of reminding people that some of the most beautiful scenery in the world is, literally, at their back doors.

Our guidebooks have brought hundreds of thousands of people to this region through the years, and while we've heard from readers when this restaurant didn't live up to its expectations, or that shop wasn't open for business, we've never heard anything but praise for the beauty of the Catskills and Hudson Valley.

When people think of these regions, many imagine mysterious mountains where Rip Van Winkle slept away the years, or lush valleys where bobcats roamed, or even brash hotels where the entertainment and the food never stopped. True, these are part of the region's story, but after traveling tens of thousands of miles on back roads and main roads, in snow, fog, sun, and rain, we know the real story: Nowhere else on earth can you enjoy the same beauty, the same history, that you can find here.

And because there is so much to see and do here, we chose to include only what we considered the "best"—whether it was food, inns, views, or history. At historic sites or places of interest we looked for unusual exhibits or special events. In the case of restaurants, inns, hotels, and B&Bs we looked for distinctiveness, quality, cleanliness, and courtesy. Farm stands, whether large or small, had to show pride in their produce. We traveled the area in all seasons, talked to hundreds of people, and visited every historic and cultural site. In a very few cases, if we couldn't experience a place ourselves, we talked to experts whose judgment we relied on to ensure that you are getting the recommendations of the "best" people as well.

We know that there are many different types of travelers, so this book offers a large number of places for visiting and dining. We have tried to select a wide variety of sites in order to please people of all ages, all backgrounds, all purses. Some places are free, others expensive, but all are the best.

We have to emphasize, however, that dollar ratings often change between the time this book was written and the time it appears in your bookstore. We also must point out that lunches may cost considerably less than dinners, that single lodging rates may be higher or lower, depending on the establishment, and that special rates are available for some historic sites. Please accept the numbers as guides only. If a site or

Bannerman's Castle, on Pollepel Island in the Hudson River, Orange County

restaurant does not appear in this book, this omission does not reflect a negative review. Perhaps we didn't know about it, or it may recently have opened, or we might just have missed it. Tell us about it, so that future editions of this guidebook will be as complete and as accurate as possible. Suggestions and complaints should be sent to us care of P.O. Box 425, Woodstock, NY 12498.

All the sites included in this book are within a day's drive of New York City, and many are a few hours by car from Boston and Philadelphia. The book is arranged by county, beginning with the counties on the west side of the Hudson River, heading north to Albany and Saratoga, and continuing south of Albany on the east side of the Hudson. You can plan a day trip or a weeklong vacation, as the spirit moves you. You can be where the action is or utterly alone. You can eat crunchy apples and creamy goat cheese, hike, canoe, or just take a walk. The climate is temperate and the views are extraordinary.

Many places of interest are seasonal, as are the outdoor activities, but there are sites open year-round throughout the region. Summer events in particular are often held rain or shine, but we strongly suggest that you call ahead and check on schedules before taking a long trip. We have listed the tourism departments for each county and, in some cases, region; web sites are noted whenever possible.

The Hudson Valley and the Catskills have something to please everyone, and we hope you set aside plenty of time to explore our favorite region. But remember to send us your suggestions—we want you all to enjoy your visit to our home.

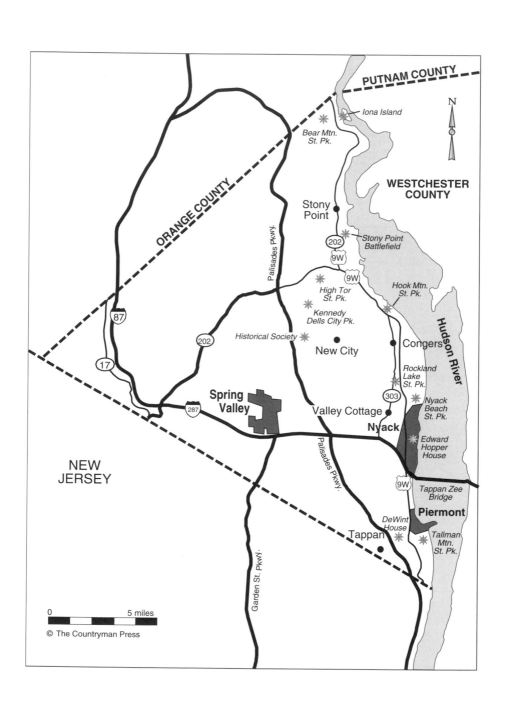

PUTNAM COUNTY

Iona Island

Bear Mtn.
St. Pk.

ORANGE COUNTY

**WESTCHESTER
COUNTY**

Stony
Point

202
9W

Stony Point
Battlefield

9W

High Tor
St. Pk.

Hook Mtn.
St. Pk.

Kennedy
Dells City Pk.

Palisades Pkwy.

202

Historical Society

New City

Congers

Hudson River

87

Rockland
Lake
St. Pk.

17

303

Nyack
Beach
St. Pk.

287

**Spring
Valley**

Valley Cottage

Nyack

Edward
Hopper
House

Palisades Pkwy.

9W

Tappan Zee
Bridge

**NEW
JERSEY**

DeWint
House

Piermont

Tappan

Tallman
Mtn.
St. Pk.

Garden St. Pkwy.

0   5 miles

© The Countryman Press

I. Rockland County

Only 176 square miles in size, Rockland County packs a lot into its area. It seems that everywhere you look in Rockland there is a park, from the tiny vest-pocket squares of green in towns and villages to the great spaces of Bear Mountain. Only 30 miles north of New York City, Rockland has saved from development many of its forests, wetlands, mountains, and historical sites. Wealthy patrons, civic leaders, and citizen activists joined forces to prevent Bear Mountain and High Tor from becoming a prison site and a quarry, respectively. Today the fruits of those early environmental battles are seen and enjoyed by all. Hundreds of miles of hiking and biking trails wind through estuarine marshes, along the Hudson River, and up and over dramatic peaks. Lakes and streams teem with wildlife, and plant lovers will delight in the explosion of color and scent that marks the spring wildflower season. Stony Point Battlefield, the mountaintop meadow where American troops defeated the British Redcoats, is almost as it was more than 200 years ago. In small towns and villages throughout the county, houses have been preserved with such care and such a sense of history that visitors feel as if they have stepped back in time. While touring Rockland you will hear again and again the names of those who made history and are still remembered in ceremonies and festivals throughout the county: George Washington, Benedict Arnold, John André, and even Captain Kidd!

GUIDANCE
    Rockland County Tourism (845-353-5533 or 1-800-295-5723), 10 Piermont Avenue, Nyack 10960; www.rockland.org.

GETTING THERE
    Rockland is accessible from the New York State (NYS) Thruway; watch for the Nyack and Bear Mountain exits.

MEDICAL EMERGENCY
    Nyack Hospital (845-358-6200), North Midland Avenue, Nyack

VILLAGES

Nyack. Located off the NYS Thruway; follow signs to the village. First settled by the Nyack Indians, who moved there from Brooklyn, Nyack soon became home to the Dutch, who began to farm the region. When steamboats arrived, making river travel easier, Nyack became a center for shipping and boatbuilding. The town is now known as an antiques and arts center, home to dozens of shops that offer the finest furniture, jewelry, crafts, and artwork.

To see Nyack's charming architectural heritage, begin at South Broadway near the **Nyack Public Library,** one of the libraries built with funds from the Carnegie Foundation at the turn of the 20th century. Next to the library is a Queen Anne–style house, with a tower and fine shingle work. Heading north, at 46 South Broadway **Couch Court** is an unusual late-19th-century building that sports a towerlike cupola. The **Presbyterian church** was built in 1838 in the Greek Revival style, in which columns and symmetry were used in an effort to capture what was considered the ancient purity of Greece. Down the street a little farther look for the **Tappan Zee Theatre,** built when movies were silent and vaudeville shows were the rage. Across the street the **Reformed church** has a clock tower that dates back to 1850. On Burd Street a plaque on the bank tells a little of the history of Nyack. On North Broadway you'll see the **Congregation of the Sons of Israel,** founded in 1870. The **Hudson Valley Children's Museum** (845-358-2191), 21 Burd Street, is a hands-on museum for small hands where kids can explore art and science up close. A side trip down and around Van Houten Road (it turns into Castle Heights) runs past riverfront homes and offers a magnificent view of the Hudson. Continue your drive up North Broadway, passing magnificent mansions and lovely 18th-century homes, to **Hook Mountain State Park.**

The village of Nyack (845-353-2221 for information) sponsors special events throughout the summer and fall, including arts and antiques street fairs, a Halloween parade, and other happenings.

Tappan. The local government here was the first in New York State to establish by ordinance a historic district, with the result that a walk down Main Street in Tappan will reveal many 18th- and 19th-century structures. The **Tappan Library,** a frame house dating from the mid–18th century, boasts a restored colonial garden. John André was imprisoned in the **Yoast Mabie Tavern,** built in 1755, although Washington's instructions were that André be treated civilly. Just beyond the tavern look for the **Killoran House,** a town house built in 1835 with the bricks taken from a dismantled church. In the middle of Main Street, where it meets Old Tappan Road, the village green was the site of the public stocks and the liberty pole, depending on the mood of the townspeople at the time. The nearby **Reformed Church of Tappan** stands on the site where André was tried and convicted of spying. Although André requested that he be shot as a soldier, the tribunal ordered him hanged as a spy, since to do otherwise would have been to cast doubt upon his guilt. In the nearby burying grounds you will find many old tombstones.

Farther up the road is the **Demming-Latelle House,** best known as the home of the man who manufactured the first canned baby food.

TO SEE

Edward Hopper House and **Hopper House Art Center** (845-358-0774), 82 North Broadway, Nyack. Open Thursday through Sunday noon–5. Donation suggested. The American realist painter Edward Hopper was born in Nyack in 1882 and as a youth spent much of his time in the village. Several of his paintings feature local landmarks, and he taught painting classes at the house, which was built by his grandfather. When he died in 1967, Hopper was buried in the Oak Hill Cemetery. His boyhood home was rescued from demolition not long after his death, and today it is a community arts and cultural center. Exhibits include works by Hopper and other American painters, and concerts are given in the gardens of the Hopper House each summer. The site also sponsors a local garden tour.

HISTORIC HOME

DeWint House National Shrine (845-359-1359), 20 Livingston Avenue, near Oak Tree Road in Tappan. Open daily year-round, 10–4. Free. Constructed in 1700 of Holland brick and sandstone, the DeWint House boasts the pitched roof and tile fireplace common in well-to-do Dutch homes of the period. Although the house is important architecturally, it is best known as George Washington's headquarters and as a shrine to Washington's participation in the fraternal organization known as the Masons. It was also here that Washington—after refusing to commute the sentence—stayed the day the British spy Maj. John André was hanged. It is recorded that Washington asked that the shutters to his room be closed, the same shutters that cover the window today. When the house was purchased by the Masons, the owner said family tradition held that several of the items in the house were there at the time of Washington's visits, including a hat rack, andirons, and a flintlock gun. Today the house offers a look into Washington's day-to-day life during the war, along with the story of his participation in the Masons. A small carriage house museum also contains period artifacts and exhibits, and trees around the site have been marked with identification tags. Don't miss the largest weeping willow tree in the country—34 feet in circumference and almost 150 years old. A self-guided walking tour of Tappan is also available at the carriage house.

HISTORIC SITES

Camp Shanks WWII Museum (845-638-5419), South Greenbush Street, Orangeburg. Open April through October, Saturday and Sunday 10–3. Free. This site was the processing center for more than a million soldiers who shipped overseas from the Piermont Pier to Normandy. Now a small museum, it tells the story of military life at the camp through exhibits and a visit to a barracks.

✍ **Historical Society of Rockland County** (845-634-9629), 20 Zukor Road, off New Main Street in New City. Open Tuesday through Sunday; hours of the gallery and house vary with the season, so call for information. Admission fee. This society offers both history and art to visitors, along with year-round special events. Changing exhibits in the gallery feature works by local and other artists. The house is well known for its demonstrations of open-hearth cooking. Special events may include a folklife festival, house tour, and jazz festival. The shop offers a large selection of local publications and maps.

Rockland Center for Holocaust Studies (845-356-2700), 17 South Madison Avenue, Spring Valley. Open Sunday through Thursday noon–4; closed on national and Jewish holidays. Free. Visitors to this small museum will be humbled and moved by powerful images of the Holocaust and the strength shown by its survivors. A permanent exhibit examines the history and effects of the Holocaust, while videos and artwork bring home the personal horrors of this period. There is a research library for public use.

✍ **Stony Point Battlefield** (845-786-2521), located on Park Road, off Route 9W, Stony Point. Open mid-April through October 31, Wednesday through Saturday 10–5, Sunday 1–5. Closed Monday and Tuesday, except Memorial Day, Independence Day, and Labor Day. Free, but a fee is charged for special events. When George Washington felt he had to demonstrate that American troops were determined to stand up to the superior British forces in the Hudson Highlands, he sent in Gen. "Mad Anthony" Wayne to prove the point. In July 1779 Wayne led the elite troops of the Corps of Light Infantry in an attack on the British at Stony Point. During a midnight raid the Americans routed the British from their beds and challenged their reputation as an invincible fighting force. A self-guided walking tour of the battlefield takes visitors through a wildly beautiful park where remnants of British fortifications still survive. Trails are marked with plaques explaining the battle, and you will pass the 1826 Stony Point Lighthouse; used for more than a century to aid ships on the Hudson, it was restored in 1995. The museum offers a slide show that depicts events leading up to the battle and is accompanied by exhibits and original memorabilia illustrating the tactics and strategies that brought victory to the Americans. Dogwoods bloom along the paths, and special events, like military encampments and holiday celebrations, are held in spring.

TO DO

BICYCLING
Both **Bear Mountain State Park** and **Harriman State Park** offer a number of challenging bike routes. However, both of these areas can get

extremely congested on weekends. You might want to try **Rockland Lake** and **Tallman State Park,** which have paved bicycle paths. Another option is **Nyack Beach State Park,** located off Route 9W with access from Broadway in Upper Nyack. This park runs along the river, and the paths are flat with fine views of the Hudson. **Hook Mountain State Park** also has biking paths with scenic views of the Hudson. To get there, go east North Broadway in Nyack; the park is located at the end of the road.

FARM STANDS AND PICK-YOUR-OWN FARMS

Even though Rockland County is small, you can still discover some terrific outlets for local fruits and vegetables. For additional information, call 845-638-5800.

Cropsey Farm (845-634-1545), 230 Little Tor Road, New City. Open daily year-round, Cropsey Farm is a fully stocked stand that has a holiday shop.

Dr. Davies Farm (845-268-7020), Route 9W, Congers (open year-round), and Route 304, Congers (open May through November). You can pick your own apples in fall and then select from a wide variety of berries, pumpkins, plums, and other goodies at the farm stand.

Duryea Farms (845-356-1988), 101 Ackertown Road, Monsey. Open April through October and again in December. Pick your own plump, red strawberries, juicy apples, and orange pumpkins in-season; select a local tree at Christmastime.

Fellowship Community (845-356-8494), 241 Hungry Hollow Road, Chestnut Ridge. Organic fruits and vegetables sold Friday only, 2–4.

Martin Litchult Farm (845-357-0995), 77 South Airmont Road, Suffern. Open September through April. Vegetables and fruits, but don't forget to sample the fresh-pressed cider.

The Orchards at Conklin (845-354-0369), South Mountain Road, Pomona. Open year-round. This farm has been in business since 1712. Today you can harvest your own fruits on weekends (10–5) and pick a pumpkin at Halloween.

Schimpf Farms (845-623-2556), Germond Road, West Nyack, has a roadside market from mid-July through October.

Van Houten Farms (845-735-4689), 12 Sickletown Road, Pearl River, is open April through November with fruits, vegetables, and holiday greenery.

Van Ripers Farm (845-352-0770), 121 College Road, Suffern, is open until Thanksgiving. You can pick raspberries in-season or select from a wide variety of fruits, vegetables, and bedding plants.

FISHING

The state parks allow fishing, but you will have to check with them for their individual regulations and restrictions. Fishing is also allowed in the Ramapo River, which has a long trout season. Route 17 has parking areas, and the waters north of Ramapo are considered good fishing spots. On Route 202 near Suffern watch for the Mahwah River and the parking areas along its bank. Minisceongo Creek has good fishing from the Rosman Bridge upstream to the Palisades Mountain Parkway Bridge.

HIKING AND WALKING

Almost every park has hiking trails that wind through the woods or over mountains. Some unusual trails, set up to commemorate the American Revolution, also provide ways to get to know local history. The 1777 Trail, the 1777 E Trail, and the 1777 W Trail—known collectively as the **Bicentennial Trails**—are all under 3 miles in length. Located in Bear Mountain and Harriman State Parks, the trails are accessed from Route 9W, 1 mile north of Tomkins Cove. Look for the diamond-shaped white blazes with red numbers. This is also the starting area for the **Timp-Torne Trail,** a 10-mile hike that offers spectacular views down the Hudson River all the way to New York City. The trail ends at the Bear Mountain Lodge.

The shorter **Anthony Wayne Trail**—a 3-mile loop marked with white blazes—can be found along Seven Lakes Drive in Bear Mountain State Park, near the traffic circle. Another popular trail is the **Pine Meadow Trail,** which begins at the Reeves Meadow Visitors Center on Seven Lakes Drive.

If you want to climb Bear Mountain, take the **Major Welch Trail** from the Bear Mountain Inn (see *Lodging*).

Buttermilk Falls Park, in Nyack, has trails from the parking lot to the falls themselves, lovely in early spring.

     Kennedy Dells Park, Main Street, 1 mile north of New City (watch for signs), was once part of film producer Adolph Zukor's estate. Along with hiking trails, there is also a trail for people with disabilities.

Dutch Garden, at the County Office Building, New Hempstead Road, New City, is a 3-acre historic site with gardens and paths.

Shorter walks may be taken in **Betsy Ross Park,** Tappan; **Tackamack North** and **Tackamack South Parks,** Clausland Mountain Road, Blauvelt; and along the **Erie Trail,** which runs from Sparkill to Grandview along abandoned railroad tracks. **Mount Ivy,** off Route 202, Pomona, is a rails-to-trails park, with hiking along the old tracks, and a wetlands and nature study center.

GREEN SPACE

Bear Mountain State Park (845-786-2701). Take the Bear Mountain exit off the Palisades Parkway or Routes 6 and 9W. Open daily year-round; parking fee. Part of the vast Palisades Interstate Parks System, Bear Mountain shares almost 54,000 acres with its neighbor, **Harriman State Park.** Noted on maps since the mid–18th century, Bear Mountain has been known as Bear Hill, Bread Tray, and Bare Mountain (presumably

Bear Mountain Bridge over the Hudson River

because of a bald peak). Once the site of Revolutionary War Forts Clinton and Montgomery, the area the park now covers was slated to become the home of Sing Sing Prison until public outcry and political pressure persuaded the state to change its plans early in the 20th century. Since then a parkway system has made the park accessible to the hundreds of thousands who visit each year, and several lakes add to the park's outdoor appeal. Visitors to the park will find a four-season outdoor wonderland featuring a wide program of activities and special events, including swimming, fishing, miniature golf, hiking, boating, sledding, and cross-country skiing. At the **Trailside Museum, Nature Trail, and Zoo,** located next to the Bear Mountain Inn (watch for signs; also see *Lodging*), exhibits and programs describe the Native American, military, and natural history of the area. (There are even mastodon remains!) Open daily 9–5 year-round. Admission is free.

The self-guided trail is the oldest continuously run trail in the country. The short trail also features a unique zoo with wildlife in natural settings, including a beaver lodge (which has been cut away for easy viewing), a reptile house, and trees, shrubs, and plants with identi-fication tags. On into the park visitors may want to bike or drive along the scenic interpark roads or rent a paddle- or rowboat at one of the lakes. (Canoes are subject to an inspection.) Three lakes—Welch, Sebago, and Tiorati—have swimming, picnicking, and other recre-ational areas, and special events are scheduled throughout the year at the Bear Mountain Inn and in the park. In the past there have been winter holiday fairs, orienteering meets, crafts and ethnic festivals, professional ski-jumping competitions, even stargazing nights.

Hook Mountain State Park and **Nyack Beach Park** (845-268-3020). To reach Hook Mountain State Park, take North Broadway, in Nyack, east to the end; follow signs. To reach Nyack Beach Park, take Route 9W from Broadway. Both parks are open daily, dawn to dusk; free. Hook Mountain was once referred to by the Dutch as Verdrietige (tedious) Hook, because the winds could change rapidly and leave a boat adrift in the river. The area was also a favorite campground of Native Americans because of its wealth of oysters. For modern visitors, the park provides a place to picnic, hike, bike, and enjoy scenic views of the Hudson. A hawk-watch is held every spring and fall, and the park is said to be haunted by the ghost of the Guardian of the Mountain, a Native American medicine man who appears during the full moon each September and chants the ancient harvest festival. Nyack Beach is open for swimming, hiking, and fishing; the views of the river are outstanding, and there are cross-country ski trails available in winter.

Piermont Marsh and **Tallman State Park** (845-359-0544), Route 9W in Sparkill, near Piermont, north of Palisades Interstate Parkway, exit 4. Piermont Marsh can be reached through Tallman State Park by following the bike path or from the Erie Pier in the village of Piermont. Admission fee. This nature preserve covers more than 1,000 acres of tidal marsh, mountains, and river and is considered one of the most important fish-breeding areas along the Hudson. Wildflowers, such as the spectacular rose mallow, abound in portions of the marsh, and this is a prime bird-watching locale in all seasons. The area along the marsh is a marvelous place to view the river, and a hike up the mountain offers a spectacular panorama for photographers. Tallman State Park is a wonderful place to spend a summer day—along with its natural wonders, the park has complete recreational facilities, including bike paths, a swimming pool, tennis courts, and hiking trails. There are even some human-made ponds that have become home for many varieties of reptiles and amphibians; ironically, the ponds were to have been part of a tank storage area for a large oil company earlier in the century. Today, especially in spring, the ponds hum with the sounds of frogs and the woods come alive with birdcalls.

Rockland Lake State Park (845-268-3020), Route 9W, Rockland Lake exit, Congers. Open daily year-round, although the Nature Center is closed October through May. Use fee. Another jewel in the crown of the Palisades Interstate Parks System, this popular recreation area is located at the base of Hook Mountain. The lake was once the site of an ice farm, which provided a harvest of pure, clear ice for nearly a century before the advent of modern refrigeration. The park is a wonderful place to explore—in addition to hiking, you can enjoy swimming, jogging, fishing, biking, boating, and golf. During the winter go ice skating on the lake or cross-country skiing and sledding on some of the challenging hills. At the Nature Center you will discover live animals and exhibits, special-events programs throughout the summer, and guided tours along the wetlands walkway (it's about 3¼ miles around the lake). Just outside the center are marked nature trails that run along a boardwalk and contain Braille interpretation stops for the blind and visually impaired. Wildflowers and birds are particularly vibrant during the spring, but there are wonders to discover here any time of year.

LODGING

Bear Mountain Inn (845-786-2731), off Routes 9W, 9A, 9D, and 6, Bear Mountain 10911. ($$) Located in the heart of Bear Mountain State Park, the 77-year-old inn's rustic charm makes it a fine place to relax. The stone-and-wood building complements this panoramic spot, and all of the facilities of the park can be enjoyed as well. There are 60 guest rooms in the inn, all with private bath. This is a large establishment in a public park, so it is best to visit in the off-season when the crowds have disappeared. Open year-round.

Cove House (845-429-9695), P.O. Box 81, Tomkins Cove 10986. ($$) This ranch on 3 acres offers one of the best views of the Hudson River around. There are three rooms; one has a private bath, and two share a bathroom. Open year-round.

The Inn at Clarksville Corners (845-353-5356), 11 Strawtown Road, West Nyack 10994. ($$) This charming historic inn offers three rooms, all with private bath. It's located in a lovely building separate from the Clarksville Inn restaurant (see *Dining Out*). The Palisades Center Mall is nearby.

WHERE TO EAT

DINING OUT

Cafe Portofino (845-359-7300), 587 Piermont Avenue, Piermont. ($$) Open daily for dinner 5–10. Regional Italian cooking is served in a warm, friendly atmosphere by the chef-owner. The daily specials include veal, chicken, fish, and seafood dishes. And save room for dessert; all are homemade.

The Clarksville Inn (845-358-8899), 1 Strawtown Road, West Nyack. ($$) Open daily, except Tuesday, for lunch noon–2; dinner 5–9; Sunday brunch 1–4. This restaurant is situated on a historic property circa 1850. Both Martin Van Buren and Washington Irving spent time here. The New American cuisine is prepared fresh daily by the Culinary Institute–trained chef-owner. A couple of the specialties of the house are New Zealand loin of lamb with goat cheese herb crust and roasted black olive sauce, as well as pan-seared Gulf shrimp and sea scallops in a tomato fennel broth atop cappellini pasta. For dessert don't miss the sinfully sweet chocolate cake.

Freelance Cafe and Wine Bar (845-365-3250), 506 Piermont Avenue, Piermont. ($$) Open daily for lunch noon–3; dinner from 5:30; Sunday brunch noon–3. Right next to Xavier's, this informal eatery is a café at heart, with specialties like coconut shrimp in a sharp mustard sauce, grilled chicken salad with raspberry sauce, and *tiramisu*.

Giulio's (845-359-3657), 154 Washington Street, Tappan. ($$) Open for lunch Monday through Friday 11:30–2:30; dinner Monday through Friday 5–10, Saturday until 11; Sunday 2–9. Fine northern Italian cuisine is served in this 100-year-old Victorian house. There is a romantic candlelit setting at dinner and a strolling entertainer midweek and Friday evening. Sample the Valdostana *vitello* (veal stuffed with prosciutto and cheese in a champagne sauce) or the scampi Giulio (jumbo shrimp sautéed with fresh mushrooms). Children are welcome. Reservations suggested; proper attire recommended.

King and I (845-353-4208), 93 Main Street, Nyack. ($$) Open daily from 11:30. Enjoy the spicy, sophisticated flavors of Thai cuisine at this delightful restaurant. Chicken and vegetarian specialties are offered, and the decor is lovely. Try fried curry paste, shrimp simmered in coconut milk, or twice-cooked sliced chicken. The dishes range in spiciness from mild to dangerous. A unique dining experience.

The Landing (845-398-1943), on the waterfront, Piermont. ($$) Open for lunch and dinner Monday through Saturday noon–10; Sunday brunch 11–3; dinner until 8. This is primarily a steakhouse, and we suggest the aged porterhouse steak, a favorite of the chef. There are also tasty seafood and lobster dishes to be enjoyed, with a view of the park and Hudson River from the dining room.

La Maisonette (845-735-9000), 500 Veterans Memorial Drive, Pearl River. ($$) Breakfast (6:30–11:30), lunch (11:30–3), and dinner (5–10) daily. Within the Pearl River Hilton, this elegant restaurant has a strong local following. The dining room overlooks the golf course, and the relaxing view further enhances the gracious cuisine. Continental and American entrées include mushrooms filled with crabmeat and spinach, broiled tuna on eggplant, homemade bread, and luscious desserts (try the rich chocolate peanut butter pie). Reservations are suggested for dinner.

Marcello's (845-357-9108), 21 Lafayette Avenue, Suffern. ($$) Open for lunch Monday through Friday noon–2; dinner daily 5–9:30. The chef-owner, Marcello, travels to Italy twice each year and brings back new ideas for the continually changing menu. Every dish at this elegant spot is cooked to order, and all pastas are homemade. The seafood ravioli and veal chop with sage are just a couple of the superb house specialties.

Montebello (845-365-6900), 500 Route 340, Sparkill. ($$) Open for lunch Tuesday through Friday noon–2:30; dinner served Tuesday through Sunday 5–10. The Italian cuisine here features pasta, veal, and chicken specialties as well as homemade desserts. On the property is the oldest white ash tree in the United States, believed to be at least 400 years old.

Old '76 House (845-359-5476), 110 Main Street, Tappan. ($$) Open daily, except Monday, for lunch at 11:30; dinner at 5. Located in a restored 1753 sandstone-and-brick house, this restaurant boasts beamed ceilings, fireplaces surrounded by Dutch tiles, and a real colonial atmosphere. (Legend says British Maj. John André was imprisoned here during the Revolution.) The food is American and Continental, and entrées include veal Antoinette, steaks, and seafood.

Pasta Amore (845-365-1911), 200 Ash Street, Piermont. ($$) Open daily for lunch and dinner 11:30–10. There are over 20 delectable pasta dishes on the menu here. One of our favorites is the bowtie pasta with shrimp and vodka sauce. The menu is huge, and there is an array of meat, chicken, and fish dishes as well. The chicken Amore is a popular entrée with local patrons.

Romolo's (845-268-3770), 77 Route 303, Congers. ($$) Open for lunch Tuesday through Friday 11:30–2:30; dinner Tuesday through Sunday at 5. There is a full range of Italian and Continental specialties here. The veal verbena is an interesting dish: veal with prosciutto, asparagus, and mozzarella cheese in a wine sauce. There are nightly salmon specials. This a good spot for fine casual dining.

The Turning Point (845-359-1089), 468 Piermont Avenue, Piermont. ($$) Open for lunch Wednesday through Saturday 11:30–3; dinner Wednesday through Sunday at 6; Sunday brunch at 11:30. Lunch menu served after dinner hours. Relax and enjoy a fine lunch, dinner, or brunch while listening to live music. The restaurant has been a hangout for movie companies, and it is a popular local spot. For dinner, try fettuccine with goat cheese and sliced duck or poached salmon; 15 herbal teas and nearly 20 kinds of beer are listed on the menu. For Sunday brunch, try buttermilk pancakes or French toast. Check the continually changing evening performance schedule—some well-known folksingers have appeared—by visiting the web site: www.turningpointcafe.com.

Wildflower Restaurant at Bear Mountain (845-786-2731), Route 9W, Bear Mountain. ($$) Open Monday through Saturday for lunch at 11; dinner at 5; open Sunday for brunch 11–3, dinner 5–9. Regional American cuisine and views of lovely Hessian Lake and the Hudson Valley. The time to come here is for Sunday brunch, when waffles with ice cream are served. Great lunch and brunch menu.

Xavier's at Piermont (845-359-7007), 506 Piermont Avenue, Piermont. ($$) Open Wednesday through Sunday for dinner at 6; Sunday brunch noon–2:30. An intimate, elegant spot, this is a perfect place for people who enjoy fine dining. Continental cuisine has included roast pigeon with truffle sauce and fettuccine with fennel sausage and white grapes. For dessert, try maple walnut soufflé, the house specialty. Not recommended for children.

EATING OUT

Cafe Dolce (845-357-2066), 24 Lafayette Avenue, Suffern. ($$) Open Monday through Thursday 10:30 AM–10 PM; Friday and Saturday noon–midnight; Sunday 4–9 PM. This European-style café serves cocktails, coffees of all kinds, tea, and light fare in a relaxed yet elegant ambience.

El Bandito (845-425-6622), 27 East Center Avenue, Route 45, Spring Valley. ($) Open daily 11 AM–midnight. Strolling guitar players add to the fun atmosphere at this colorful Mexican eatery, where the portions are generous and the margaritas are first-rate.

Fordy's Broadway Grill (845-358-8114), 83 South Broadway, Nyack. ($) Open daily for lunch and dinner at 11:30. This informal eatery serves an eclectic menu, including Sicilian vegetable sauté over pasta, lobster ravioli, and stuffed clams.

Hudson House (845-353-1355), 134 Main Street, Nyack. ($$) Lunch Tuesday through Friday 11:30–2:30, Saturday until 3. Sunday brunch is served 11:30–3. Dinner is served Tuesday through Thursday 5:30–10, Friday and Saturday until 11, and Sunday 4:30–9. Located across the street from the **Helen Hayes Performing Arts Center,** this building was originally a firehouse in the 19th century and later became the Nyack Village Hall. The chef, a Culinary Institute graduate, features contemporary American cuisine served with an imaginative touch.

Khan's Mongolian (845-359-8004), 21 Route 303, NYS Thruway, exit 12, Blauvelt. ($) Open daily for lunch and dinner noon–11 PM. This is one of the better Mongolian barbecue restaurants we've tried. Choose your own ingredients and sauces and watch while the chef creates your meal right before your eyes. Don't miss this if you're traveling with children.

Mandarin Gourmet (845-352-9090), 212 Route 59, Monsey. ($) Open daily noon–10. The Szechuan, Mandarin, and Hunan specialties are all particularly good.

Temptations (845-353-3355), 80½ Main Street, Nyack. ($) Open Monday through Saturday for lunch and dinner at 11; Sunday at noon. The shop is open late on summer evenings. Those with a sweet tooth won't want to miss this café. There are scores of dessert selections in addition to a wide selection of ice creams, frozen yogurts, cappuccinos, and exotic coffees. The light menu features soups, quiches, salads, and sandwiches.

SELECTIVE SHOPPING

In Nyack

Nyack has many shops that are worth a visit, and an entire day can be spent strolling the shopping district and enjoying the antiques and artwork on view. Most shops are open daily except Monday, but call ahead if you are planning to visit. The following establishments are some of the highlights of the area, but there are many more with some great shopping.

Hacienda Gallery de Artesanias (845-358-0300), 136 Main Street, offers

Browsing for antiques in Nyack

unusual South American and Mexican gifts, clothing, and decorative items.

Hand of the Craftsman (845-358-3366), 5 South Broadway, carries works from more than 200 artists and craftspeople and offers a unique selection of kaleidoscopes and jewelry.

Christopher's (845-358-9574), 71 South Broadway, is a fine gift shop with all kinds of unique items including antiques and dried flowers.

Good Goodies (845-353-9010 or 1-888-25-CANDY), 120 Main Street. Fine chocolates, truffles, and other indulgences.

Hickory, Dickory Dock (845-358-7474), 138 South Main Street. Clocks that tick, clocks that tock—hundreds of selections, so pity the poor mouse.

Liberty Crafts (845-358-3864), 13 South Broadway. Silver and gems, unique clothing, and a bead and findings section to help you create your own wearable art.

MaryGrace's Antique & Country Pine (845-358-3273), 41B North Broadway. Pine and fine antiques from Europe.

My Doll House (845-358-4185), 7 South Broadway, has everything for the miniature doll furniture and doll lover.

Nyack Tobacco Company (845-358-9300), 140 Main Street. For the cigar aficionado, this is *the* place. One of the most extensive selections outside of Manhattan.

Oh, You Beautiful Doll (845-354-6835), 30 North Broadway, specializes in dolls and accessories.

Squash Blossom (845-353-0550), 49 Burd Street, offers Native American jewelry and crafts.

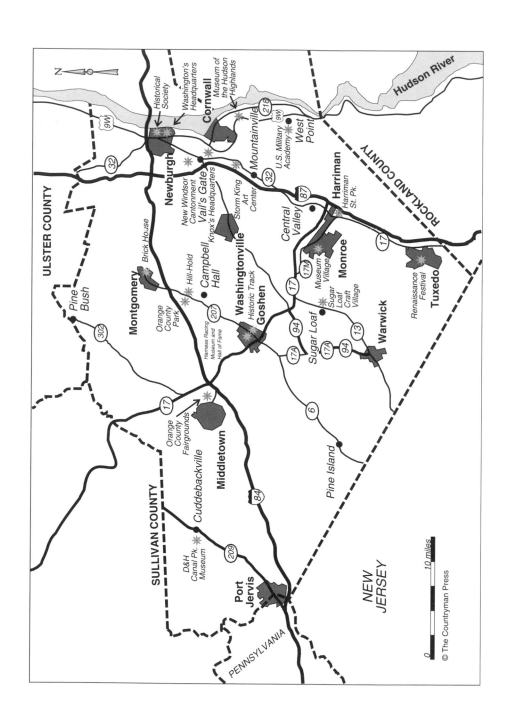

II. Orange County

Visitors are reminded in every village and every park in Orange County that this is a place that cherishes its history. Museums, restorations, and historic exhibits are everywhere, from the Native American displays in the Goshen Courthouse to the collection of military equipment at West Point. You can imagine the life of a Revolutionary War soldier as he waited out the bitter winters in a wooden hut, or watch as a costumed group of interpreters reenacts a battle that helped turn the tide of the American Revolution.

Orange County is also a place where the agricultural heritage of New York is still strong, a place where vegetable farming is a way of life for families and has been for generations. Stop at a farm and take home some just-picked peaches, or join in the fun at the Onion Festival. The Black Dirt area is a unique farming district where some of the best of New York's produce is grown, and a drive through the region in early summer gives new meaning to the word *bountiful*.

GUIDANCE
Orange County Tourism (845-291-2136), 30 Matthew Street, Goshen 10924; www.orangetourism.org.

GETTING THERE
Orange County is accessible from exits 16 and 17 off the New York State (NYS) Thruway, as well as from Route 17, which joins the Thruway at Suffern.

MEDICAL EMERGENCY
St. Luke's Hospital (845-561-4400), 70 Dubois Street, Newburgh; **Arden Hill Hospital** (845-294-4330), Harriman Drive, Goshen.

TO SEE

✏ **Harness Racing Museum and Hall of Fame** (845-294-6330), 240 Main Street, Goshen. Open year-round 10–6; closed Christmas, Thanksgiving, and New Year's Day. Admission fee. Messenger and Hambletonian, pacers, trotters, standardbreds—all call to mind the speed and grace to be found on a trotting track, and the history and color of the sport can be discovered at this unique museum established in 1951. Trotters and pacers (trotters move their right front and left rear legs at the same time;

The Hall of Fame of the Trotter traces the history of the sport.

COURTESY ORANGE COUNTY TOURISM

pacers move both legs on one side at the same time) have long been a part of American history: Such notable figures as George Washington, Abraham Lincoln, and Ulysses S. Grant spent time breeding and racing these swift horses. At the Harness Racing Museum and Hall of Fame the history of the sport can be traced through dioramas, prints, exhibits, and statues displayed throughout the former Good Time Stables building. Galleries contain permanent displays of Currier and Ives prints, famous racing silks, and the amazing Hall of the Immortals, where dozens of small, lifelike statues recall the greatest participants (human and four-legged) in the sport. Restored stalls have full-sized replicas of horses and their equipment, while you can see the sulkies and sleighs the horses once pulled (it wasn't unheard of to drive a horse many miles, then race it, then drive it home to the farm). There is even a room that reproduces the interior of the clubhouse from the nearby Historic Track. The room is so well maintained that you expect to hear the rustle of programs and the voices of members discussing the best bet of the day. There are films and shows in the auditorium, as well as changing gallery exhibits throughout the year.

Historic Track (845-294-5333), located directly behind the Harness Racing Museum and Hall of Fame. The only sports facility in the United States that is a National Historic Landmark, the Historic Track has been hosting meets since the 1830s. Although the Grand Circuit races visit here only once a year, the track is used as a training facility, so you may be able to see pacers, trotters, and a local blacksmith at work no matter when you visit. The track is such a local institution that some of the private boxes have been passed down in families for generations.

✐ **Museum of the Hudson Highlands** (845-534-7781), The Boulevard, Cornwall-on-Hudson; take Route 218 east, turn onto Payson Road, and follow signs. Open year-round but hours vary, so call for times. Donation suggested. Established in 1959 as a children's educational center, the Museum of the Hudson Highlands has expanded its natural history and environmental programs to include such special concerns as returning the bald eagle and peregrine falcon to the Hudson Valley and creating a detailed environmental "reference collection" of animals and plants from the region. Nature trails on the museum grounds wander through forests, glens, and an unusual tall-grass prairie. The museum itself is a wonderful place for parents and kids to get to know the local environment and the creatures that inhabit it. The natural wing, with its high, vaulted ceilings and tall windows, houses an indoor mini zoo, home to local snakes, mice, moles, turtles, owls, and crows, along with taxidermic mounts and a display depicting how local Native American tribes lived before the Europeans came. The Ogden Gallery shows the work of local artists. Throughout the year the museum hosts special events, which include exploration days, workshops, and nature walks. The museum also owns **Kenridge Farm** (Route 9W, Cornwall; 845-534-5506), where visitors can enjoy evening speakers, workshops, and classes, including those for young naturalists.

✐ **Museum Village of Orange County** (845-782-8247), exit 129 off Route 17, Museum Village Road, Monroe (follow signs). Open May through December; hours vary with the season, so call ahead. Special events are held throughout the year; call for a schedule. Admission fee. The daily life of preindustrial America has been preserved and re-created at this fascinating museum comprised of buildings and equipment moved to the site from other parts of the Hudson Valley. Set up like a small crossroads village, the museum is considered to have one of the largest sites devoted to the folk arts of everyday America. More than 35 buildings house crafts, equipment, and agricultural displays. At the blacksmith's shop artisans hammer and pound hot metal into a door latch or horseshoe. The thump-thump of a foot-powered loom comes from the weaver's loft, where you may have a chance to try out the treadles yourself. In the newspaper office the master printer and the printer's devil (apprentice) are composing the weekly newspaper, and in the potter's workshop butter churns and mugs take shape on the wheel. Costumed guides answer questions; photos, prints, and tools trace the history of Orange County. The museum is a favorite place for children, and special events (Weekends on the Green), offered throughout the season, have included fiddling, a children's festival, America's birthday, and more. (For a fun time set even farther back in history, visit the Mastodont, the most complete skeleton of this 11,000-year-old animal in New York State.) Every Labor Day weekend there is a Civil War encampment, the largest in the Northeast, and it includes battles, camping demonstrations, and drills.

Storm King Art Center (845-534-3115), Mountainville. Take the NYS Thruway to exit 16; the center is off Route 32 north, on Old Pleasant Hill Road. Open April 1 through November 15; indoor galleries open mid-May. The sculpture park is open Saturday in June, July, and August until 8 PM, with an admission fee charged from 5 to 8. Call regarding special events. There are classical concerts, plays, and garden talks as well as family activities (children's tours, story time, discover sculpture booklets) throughout the season. This 400-acre park and museum has one of the world's largest displays of outdoor sculpture. The permanent collection contains more than 120 works by 90 contemporary artists, including Isamu Noguchi, Louise Nevelson, Alexander Calder, David Smith, and Mark di Suvero. The surrounding landscape is lovely, with a backdrop of Schunnemunk Mountain. Truly one of the impressive stops in the region.

HISTORIC HOMES

Brick House (845-457-4921); take Route 17K into Montgomery and follow signs. Open May through October, Saturday and Sunday 10–4:30. Admission fee. A treasure trove of Early American furniture and decorative arts owned by the same family since 1768. Now run by the county, the house—a red Georgian mansion constucted with bricks imported from England—is considered one of the finest private homes built between New York City and Albany in the 18th century. It was a meeting site for colonial officers during the Revolution, and many of the original furnishings are still intact. Pieces include a very rare 17th-century chest from Connecticut, fine crystal, Lafayette china (produced to honor the French hero), chairs that may have belonged to the Washingtons, and an Eli Terry shelf clock. Brick House is also the site of a large autumn antiques show.

David Crawford House Museum (845-561-2585), 189 Montgomery Street, Newburgh. Call for hours and holiday tour information. Admission fee. Maintained and run by the Historical Society of Newburgh Bay and the Highlands, Crawford House was built in 1830 and modeled after a grand English country house. There are changing exhibits in the gallery and an annual celebration of landscape architect Andrew Jackson Downing's birthday. Visitors will enjoy the spectacular river views and the collection of pint-sized Hudson River sloop and ship models.

Hill-Hold and Brick House (845-291-2404), Route 416, Campbell Hall. Open May through October, Wednesday through Sunday 10–4:30. Admission fee. Once a section of a 30,000-acre estate, the land Hill-Hold stands on was presented to William Bull, an English stonemason, as a wedding present in the early 18th century. His son, Thomas Bull, built the home. Fortunately for lovers of 18th-century architecture, later family members donated the house and most of its furnishings to the county. The large Georgian mansion is graced by elegant wood- and stonework, with barrel-backed cupboards, paneling, and deep-silled windows. Rooms are furnished with many original Chippendale, Queen

Anne, and Empire pieces. Two kitchens are still extant in the house: one in the basement and a newer one, added in 1800, in a separate stone wing. Like most manor houses of the era, Hill-Hold was also the center of a thriving farm. Surrounding the farmhouse are the original outbuildings, including the granary, barn, summer kitchen, wagon house, smokehouse, and, of course, the privy. On the working farm sheep, cows, chickens, and geese are tended. Children will enjoy the farm animals, and flower lovers should spend some time in the summer gardens. Also on the site is the Goosetown school, a one-room schoolhouse still used for educational programs on daily life in the 19th century.

HISTORIC SITES

Balmville Tree, Balmville, just past Route 9W in Newburgh. Make a right turn onto Chestnut Lane and a left turn at the end of the street. The tree is in the middle of the road—an odd treat, but worth a visit. It has been standing since 1699 and has a trunk more than 25 feet in circumference.

Clove Furnace (845-351-4696), Route 17, Arden, south of Harriman. Admission fee. Open year-round Monday through Friday 8–noon and 1–5, weekends by appointment. Although not a very active site, this is an unusual one—a small museum devoted to the history of iron making in rural New York. The restored hot-blast furnace dates from 1854 and was used to produce artillery pieces during the Civil War. Exhibits outline the story of iron making and mining, and there are displays related to Orange County history. An enlightening stop for those interested in the commercial development of what was once a major industry in America.

Constitution Island and the Warner House (845-446-8676). Take Route 9W to West Point, enter the U.S. Military Academy gate, and take the first right past the Hotel Thayer. The dock and a large parking lot are at the end of the street. Tours are offered mid-June through late September, Wednesday and Thursday at 1 and 2 only. Call for reservations—only 40 people per tour. Admission fee. To visit a Hudson River island, take the boat from West Point to Constitution Island. There you will find a 17-room Victorian mansion, home to the Warner family from 1836 to 1915. The daughters, Anna and Susan, grew up on the island and were best known for their writing; Anna penned many hymns, including "Jesus Loves Me," and Susan's *Wide, Wide World* was a best-seller. After their father lost his fortune, the sisters stayed on in their home, living frugally and teaching Sunday school courses to West Point cadets, who never forgot the two spinsters. Their home is now a museum filled with their original possessions. Also on the island are the remains of **Fort Constitution,** a Revolutionary War–era fort, and the **Anna B. Warner Memorial Garden,** which is particularly lovely in late June. The surrounding Hudson is glorious anytime. If you visit the West Point cemetery, look for the sisters' graves; they were buried not far from their beloved home.

Knox Headquarters (845-561-5498), Forge Hill Road, Route 94, Vails Gate. Open Memorial Day through Labor Day, Saturday 10–5, Sunday 1–5; grounds open daily. Free. For several periods during the Revolution, the Ellison family's stone house served as headquarters for the colonial officers in the area. Gens. Henry Knox, Horatio Gates, and Nathanael Greene were only a few of the men who met in the house and planned campaigns in the gracious rooms. Today it is furnished with military camp beds and folding desks such as those that displaced the Ellisons' fine 18th-century furniture. There is also a small plant sanctuary on the grounds, dedicated to the memory of America's first woman botanist.

New Windsor Cantonment (845-561-1765), Temple Hill Road, off Routes 32 and 300, Vails Gate. Open April through October, Wednesday through Saturday 10–5, Sunday 1–5. Free. Washington's troops waited out the last months of the Revolutionary War here in anticipation of an announced cessation of hostilities. More than 10,000 soldiers, officers, cooks, and blacksmiths, along with their wives and other camp followers, constructed the snug log cabins, outbuildings, and a meeting hall, and here Washington quelled a mutiny of his troops, who resented Congress's slowness with wages and pensions. After the war, the buildings were auctioned off for the lumber and the land remained unused until the state acquired 70 acres and began restoration of the site.

A visit to the cantonment today provides a look into the everyday life of Revolutionary soldiers. At the orientation center a slide show is given on the history of the area during the war, and displays depict the difficulties faced by both the troops and their leaders. One fascinating display is of an original Badge of Military Merit, now known as the Purple Heart, which Washington presented to several soldiers (a separate hall of fame for recipients of the Purple Heart is open to the public). A walkway leads from the orientation center to the rebuilt parade grounds and buildings. Costumed guides go about their business, blacksmithing, drilling, cooking, and even entertaining (a fife player may be on hand). Although many of the buildings have been reconstructed from sketches that remain from the era, one was carted away and became an addition to a local house. There it remained for a century and a half, until its importance was realized and it was returned to the site. Just across the road, on the west side of Route 300, there is a small museum and re-created campground that illustrate the lives of the enlisted men during the war.

United States Military Academy (Visitors Center 845-938-2638), located near Route 9W, just north of Bear Mountain State Park; follow the signs. The Visitors Center is open 9–4:45 daily, except Thanksgiving, Christmas, and New Year's Day. The post is open year-round except major holidays; the museum opens daily at 10:30 except Christmas and New Year's. Admission is free, but there is a charge for a bus tour of the post.

JOSEPH PUGLISI

The cadet chapel at West Point has the largest church organ in the world.

Situated on the bluffs overlooking the Hudson River, this is where the nation's army officers have been trained since 1802; where Benedict Arnold attempted to bring the British to power; where such distinguished cadets as Robert E. Lee, Ulysses S. Grant, and Douglas MacArthur once marched; and where undistinguished cadets like James Whistler and Edgar Allan Poe discovered other talents. Tradition is important at West Point, and tradition is what you will find here, from the Long Gray Line of cadets to the quiet cemetery and imposing stone barracks.

It is very difficult to see all of West Point in one visit—there are statues, museums, chapels, and points of interest everywhere you turn. But even if you can't stay overnight, use your time well and make your first stop the Visitors Center on Main Street near the Thayer Gate entrance. Maps, schedules of events, and a display and movie about the cadets' lives at the Point are available at the center, where you can also pick up the USMA bus tour, which leaves every 20 minutes and lasts nearly an hour. (The USMA grounds are open to visitors, although some areas may be off-limits at various times.)

The second stop on your tour should be the **West Point Museum** (845-938-2203), which is in Olmstead Hall, right next to the Visitors Center. This is the oldest military museum in the country, and its holdings are among the largest in the world. Dioramas, permanent and changing exhibits, and thousands of artifacts are found throughout vast galleries, each with its own theme: the history of war, American warfare, weapons, the history of West Point. Visitors may see anything from a Stone Age hunting ax to the equipment used in Vietnam. Because the museum has so many collections, displays are changed frequently. Outside on the post itself, Trophy Point recalls the dead of the Civil War; there is also a 150-ton chain that was used to close off the Hudson River to British ships during the American Revolution. Although the attempt was unsuccessful, the chain represents the ingenuity that made America the victor. To the rear of the memorial is the Plain, the drilling area once used by Baron von Steuben to train and parade the troops. It is still used on Saturday for full-dress parades by the cadets.

The **Cadet Chapel** is open to the public and contains stained-glass windows, the largest church organ in the world, and an overpowering sense of the men and women who have worshiped there. Another restored section of the Point is Fort Putnam, which was used as a fortification in the Revolutionary War and offers exhibits on the lives of Revolutionary soldiers and a show about the battles fought in the area. It also offers a panoramic view of the surrounding mountains.

West Point is famous for its football games, played at Michie Stadium; tickets almost always have to be purchased in advance. Concerts are given throughout the summer at various sites on the post; most are free and include the West Point Military Band. The concerts alone are well worth the trip. **Eisenhower Hall Theatre** has shows ranging from classic country, to musicals, to plain classics; call 845-938-4159 for schedules and order information.

Washington's Headquarters (845-949-1236), 84 Liberty Street, Newburgh. Take Route 17 from the NYS Thruway to downtown Newburgh; watch for signs. Open Wednesday through Sunday 10–4; call for the schedule of special celebrations. Free. If Jonathan Hasbrouck's stone mansion set on a bluff overlooking the Hudson River could speak, it would say that Martha and George slept here, as did several aides-de-camp and personal servants. In fact, the end of the American Revolution was announced on the grounds. Construction began in 1750 but was not finished until 1782, when Washington's troops added a gunpowder laboratory, a barracks, a privy, and a larger kitchen. Washington remained here for nearly 1½ years, waiting for the British to leave New York under

JOSEPH PUGLISI

Washington's Headquarters in Newburgh, the first National Historic Site in the U.S.

the terms of surrender. The house and grounds were acquired by the government in 1848 and became the first National Historic Site.

Visitors can see firsthand how Revolutionary armies lived and worked. The orientation center displays clothing, equipment, and memorabilia from the War of Independence, including a few of the first president's personal items. There are uniforms, field shovels, decorations, and even links from the chain that was stretched across the Hudson to deter the British. (For vision-impaired and blind visitors, a Braille tour is available.) The story of the Revolution truly comes alive inside Hasbrouck House, where Washington is seen as a man who endured problems, boredom, and loss of the privacy that was so dear to him. (The house was owned by Tryntje Hasbrouck, a widow, who received notice of her eviction with a "sullen silence," or so history records.) Visitors are guided through the eight rooms in which Washington and his staff lived and worked. The dining room where George and Martha ate their meals still contains the original Dutch jambless fireplace, open on three sides. The plain bedrooms and offices are sparsely furnished, and a field bed with its tentlike covering speaks clearly of the winter cold, while bedrolls show that not everyone was fortunate enough to have a room. The grounds are well kept and offer wide views up and down the Hudson. Special events are held throughout the year and include kite-flying days, Martha Washington's birthday celebration, and military musters.

SCENIC DRIVES

The term *scenic drive* in Orange County is almost redundant; there are so many well-maintained roads where the pace is unhurried and the views are lovely that any drive around Orange is certain to please. Even the Thruway softens up a bit as it moves through the Harriman area— drivers can see deer at twilight and apple blossoms in spring. Route 9W is an attractive road, but the section known as Old Storm King Highway, between West Point and Cornwall, is spectacular. For a lovely country drive past lakes and trees, start at Harriman and take Route 6 east across Bear Mountain State Park to the Bear Mountain Bridge; from there 9W north offers vibrant Hudson River views on its way through West Point, Cornwall, and into Newburgh. Once in Newburgh, look for Route 32 around Cronomer Hill Park, a breathtaking sight in summer and fall. Another noted scenic highway in Orange County is Hawk's Nest Drive, Route 92, near Sparrow Bush. The road runs along the Delaware River for a short distance, but you can then follow Route 209 north to the Delaware and Hudson Canal Park (see *Green Space*). A different type of view is found along Route 17A, which cuts through the rich Black Dirt farming area around Pine Island.

WINERIES

Several wineries in Orange County are open to visitors, but it is suggested that you call for their operating hours, since these vary widely throughout the year.

Applewood Winery (845-988-9292), 82 Four Corners Road, Warwick. This small operation produces an unusual apple wine, along with a hard cider and several other apple-based beverages. Open Friday through Sunday 12– 5. The winery is a nice place to stop in the autumn, when old-fashioned, Dutch-style doughnuts are served.

Brotherhood Winery (845-496-9101), Route 94, Washingtonville, is America's oldest winery and offers visitors a tour of the wine production facility and the cellars. There is a fee, though a free tasting is included. Visitors can stroll the grounds and enjoy the special events, including concerts and shows in summer.

Baldwin Vineyards (845-744-2226), 110 Hardenburgh Estate Road, Pine Bush, has tours and tastings as well as a gourmet café.

Brimstone Hill Vineyard (845-744-2231), 61 Brimstone Hill Road, Pine Bush, offers a nice selection of wines.

Demarest Hill Winery (845-986-4723), Grand Street, 81 Pine Island Turnpike, Warwick, is open year-round (but closed holidays). The wine here is made in the Italian tradition; offerings include 18 different products.

Warwick Valley Winery (845-258-4858), 114 Little York Road, Warwick, has old-fashioned wines and ciders made from pears (once called perry), apples, and even raspberries. There is also a vineyard, and future plans call for wines made from grapes as well.

The Brotherhood Winery's cellars

TO DO

BOAT CRUISES

One of the best ways to see the Hudson is from the river itself. **Hudson Highlands Cruises** (845-534-SAIL [7245]) offers daily cruises from Haverstraw Marina and West Point. Tours run daily May through October.

Pride of the Hudson (845-782-0685), Hudson River Adventures, RD 3, Box 809, Monroe 10950. Call in advance for a schedule of cruises, which run from May through October on weekends only. All cruises depart from Newburgh Landing. From the NYS Thruway take exit 17 and follow 17K east, which becomes Broadway; at the end of Broadway turn left. Make the first right onto Second Street. Newburgh Landing is on the opposite side of the train trestle. **Bannerman's Castle,** which rises from the north side of Pollepel Island like a medieval fantasy, is one of the most intriguing sights on the Hudson River. Now travelers can discover the mystery and explore the history of the castle with a 40-minute lecture about the structure as the *Pride of the Hudson* hovers close to the island. For safety's sake, no one is allowed to disembark. However, the short video takes you on a fascinating tour of this treasure of the Hudson.

CANOEING

The Delaware River may not have the same cachet as the Colorado, but it can offer a beautiful day of canoeing. Most canoe rentals happen in the western part of the county; the trips may range from drifting idylls to challenging white water in spring. **Silver Canoe Rentals** (845-856-7055), 37 South Maple Avenue, Port Jervis; **Wild and Scenic River Tours and Rentals** (845-557-8783 or 1-800-836-0366), Barryville; and **Kittatinny Canoes** (1-800-FLOAT-KC), Barryville, all rent canoes and equipment, and transportation can be provided as well. Some places offer tubing and kayaking with guide services. For safety's sake, call and ask about river conditions before you go. (Because the Orange and Sullivan regions overlap in relation to the Delaware River, check out the listings in "Sullivan County" as well.)

FARM STANDS AND PICK-YOUR-OWN FARMS

Because so much of Orange County is agricultural (in the Black Dirt area alone, more than 10,000 acres are under cultivation), you will find dozens of farm stands here. Some specialize in one particular fruit or vegetable, others offer a wide variety, but everything is as fresh as it gets. And don't forget to plan a trip to the Orange County Onion Harvest Festival (see *Special Events*).

The Pine Island area offers several top-drawer farm stands and pick-your-own farms. **Scheuermann Farms** (845-258-4221), Little York Road, off County Road 1, open May through December, and **Pine Island Farm Fresh Produce** (845-258-4071), Pine Island Turnpike, open year-round, both stock lots of local produce; **Kamarad Orchard** (845-258-4471), Newport Bridge Road, open September through November, lets you pick apples.

Applewood Orchards (845-986-1684), Four Corners, Warwick, open September and October, has a roadside stand with vegetables but specializes in several varieties of pick-your-own apples. It also has wagon rides in-season, puppet shows, an animal petting area, and a nature walk. A great place to take the kids.

Ace Farms (845-873-1381), Highland Mills, 1.5 miles west of Route 32. Open year-round. Ace has a wide selection of fruits and vegetables (some pick-your-own) and, in autumn, hayrides and pumpkins. **Hodgson Farms** (845-778-1432), Goodwill Road, Montgomery, open May through Christmas, offers farm and greenhouse tours, along with pick-your-own berries, pumpkins, and flowers. **Overlook Farm Market** (845-562-5780), Route 9W, Newburgh, carries local apples, peaches, and nectarines in-season. **Sudol Farms** (845-258-4221), Pine Island Turnpike, Pine Island, has onions, potatoes, corn, squash, and much more Orange County produce.

For a different type of farm, visit **Swissette Herb Farm** (845-496-7841), 282 Clove Road, Salisbury Mills, which sells herbs and herb plants, dried spices, herbal and medicinal teas, and other herb-based products. Located off Route 94 in Vails Gate, the farm is open May through October, Tuesday through Sunday 1–5 or by appointment. **Krisco Farm** (845-355-4601), Purgatory Road (off the Sarah Wells Trail), Campbell Hall, offers unusual dairy delights: milk and yogurt. Christmas trees may be cut at **Fox Ridge Christmas Tree Farm** (845-986-3771), Fox Hill Road, Warwick, or at **Summit Hill Farm** (845-297-8191) on Route 17A, 1 mile north of Florida.

Farmer's markets also bloom in Orange. The selection is often unique, and always special. The **Goshen Farmers Market** (845-294-7741) is held off Main Street in the main parking lot every Friday 10–7, May through November. The **Warwick Farmers Market** (845-986-2720) is held Sunday 10–3, July through October, at the South Street parking lot. The **Middletown Farmers Market** (845-343-8075) sets up Saturday 8–noon, late June through October, at the municipal lot on James and Depot Streets.

HIKING

Trails range from easy to advanced and offer views of river, woodlands, and meadows. The **Appalachian Trail** weaves through the southwest section of the county; call the Palisades Interstate Parks Commission (845-786-2701) for maps and specific trail information.

Black Rock Forest, Route 9W, north of West Point, has marked and unmarked trails that vary in length; hiking skill is required.

Two other parks have trails of varying difficulty: **Schunnemunk,** Route 32 in Highland Mills, has six marked trails, the longest of which is 8 miles; and **Winding Hills Park,** Route 17K, Montgomery, has trails, a picnic area, and a nature study area.

Harriman State Park, Harriman exit, NYS Thruway, has hiking trails, swimming, and a variety of other outdoor activities.

ICE SKATING

Ice Time Sports Complex (845-567-0500), 21 Lakeside Road (Exit 6 off Interstate 84 at Route 17K), Newburgh 12550. There are two ice skating rinks here offering several public sessions Friday through Sunday and midday during the week. A great place for family fun. Lessons and skate rentals are available. There are lockers, a snack bar, and a pro shop, as well as a spacious seating area for spectators.

SKIING

Thomas Bull Memorial Park Area (845-457-3111), Route 416, south of Montgomery. You can enjoy the small hill, with a vertical drop of 131 feet, complete with lift and snowmaking, or take a cross-country tour, skate across a lake, or slide down a sledding hill.

Mount Peter Ski Area (845-986-4992), on Old Mount Peter Road, Warwick, has a vertical drop of 400 feet, two chairlifts, a snowboard area, and snowmaking capabilities. It is open daily, but call for hours.

Sterling Forest (1-800-843-4414), on Route 17A West in Tuxedo, is open daily and some evenings. Sterling Forest has racing, four double chairlifts, and snowmaking.

Cross-country enthusiasts will want to call the **Ring Homestead Camp** (845-361-3842) in Middletown for information on lessons and other adventure activities.

GREEN SPACE

Delaware and Hudson Canal Park (845-754-8870), just off Route 209 on Hoag Road, about 10 miles south of Wurtsboro in Cuddebackville; watch carefully for signs. The park is open year-round, with special events scheduled in the warmer months. The museum is open March through December, Thursday through Sunday noon–4, and by appointment. Admission fee. This 300-acre park, a registered National Historic Landmark, recalls an era when coal, lumber, and other goods were moved from Pennsylvania to New York by a combination of water, mules, and backbreaking labor. Huge barges were often run as family businesses, with the crew consisting of parents and children. And there wasn't much room for profit: The barges moved at a leisurely 3 miles per hour. The park sponsors seasonal events that evoke life in old-time New York State. Demonstrations have included ice cutting, story evenings, nature walks, and even a silent-film festival (the park was used by producer D. W. Griffith). The museum has exhibits about the canal and its people and is located in a restored blacksmith's house near the aqueduct; other buildings include a lockkeeper's house, a canal store, and a full-sized replica of a canal barge. Tours of the towpath are offered Sunday afternoons; call for a schedule.

Also see **Storm King Art Center** under *To See*.

LODGING

Caldwell House B&B (845-496-2954), 25 Orrs Mills Road, Salisbury Mills 12577. ($$$) If you want a truly deluxe B&B experience, try this establishment, a renovated home that dates back to 1803. There are four rooms, all with private bath, TV, and VCR; one has a Jacuzzi. All rooms are decorated with antiques; the four-poster beds have handmade linens.

Cromwell Manor Inn (845-534-7136), Angola Road, Cornwall 12518. ($$$) This recently renovated inn is a historic country estate dating back to 1820. It is situated on 7 acres of woodland and gardens near West Point and Stewart Airport. The 14 rooms and suites (all with private bath) are beautifully decorated with period antiques. Many rooms have a working fireplace and Jacuzzi, and all are air-conditioned. A full breakfast is served in the country dining room or on the veranda. Step back in time without sacrificing modern amenities. This inn is only a 10-minute drive from West Point and a few miles from Storm King Art Center (see *To See*). The lovely village of Cornwall, with its charming shops and variety of restaurants, is down the road. Jones Farm & Country Store (see *Selective Shopping*) is a neighbor of the inn. Open year-round.

Anthony Dobbins Stagecoach Inn (845-294-5526), 268 Main Street, Goshen 10924. ($$) A former stagecoach stop, this inn is located in the middle of a country town, a few minutes' walk from shopping, dining, and the racetrack and museum. Four rooms, all with private bath; rates include a full breakfast. Open year-round.

Eddy Farm Resort (845-858-4300 or 1-800-336-5050), Routes 42 and 97, Sparrow Bush 12780. ($$) Open May through October. Located on the banks of the Delaware River, this hotel has been taking care of guests for more than a century. When craftsmen took their logs down to Pennsylvania, they stopped at Eddy Farm; after the Civil War, families would visit from the city. This is a full-service resort with an outdoor pool, two golf courses, a dance floor, and a restaurant (meals can be included, and a B&B plan is an option). Both private and shared bath arrangements are available. The hotel will arrange rafting trips on the river and offers entertainment throughout the season, including an Irish cabaret.

The Glenwood House Bed and Breakfast (845-258-5066), 49 Glenwood Road, Pine Island 10969. ($$) Enjoy accommodations in an elegant Victorian farmhouse located only 10 minutes from the village of Warwick in a beautiful, rural area of Orange County renowned for onion growing. Both private and shared bath arrangements are available. Open year-round.

Heritage Farm (845-778-3420), 163 Berea Road, Walden 12586. ($$) This bed & breakfast is located on a working horse farm. The 18th-century Connecticut saltbox home is situated on 21 acres, an ideal place to stay for those who ride horses and want to do so. But all horse lovers will be delighted by a stay at this farm. There are three rooms—one with private bath, and two that share a bath. A full country breakfast is served.

Hotel Thayer (845-446-4731), U.S. Military Academy, West Point 10996. ($$$) The Hotel Thayer reflects a long-ago period of grandeur, with many guest rooms overlooking one of the most scenic parts of the Hudson River—the Hudson Highlands. There are 148 newly renovated rooms here. Although not included in the room rate, the dining room serves breakfast on the terrace, which offers an exquisite panoramic view of the Hudson Valley. The hotel is within minutes of the military academy's points of interest. Open year-round; reservations are required, especially on special-events weekends at the academy.

Mead Tooker House B&B (845-457-5770), 136 Clinton Street, Montgomery 12549. ($$) This elegant guest house is located in the historic section of town. The house itself has an interesting facade that will delight architecture buffs. The five guest rooms are decorated with antique French furniture, and a few rooms have a fireplace. All have private bath. Breakfast is created according to your taste. Three restaurants are within walking distance of the B&B. No smoking. Open year-round.

Peach Grove Inn (845-986-7411), 205 Route 17A, Warwick 10990. ($$) This restored 1850 Greek Revival home overlooks a 200-acre farm. There are four large rooms, all with private bath. The full breakfast features delicious home-baked breads and cakes.

Point of View Bed & Breakfast (845-294-6259), Ridge Road, RR #2, Box 766H, Campbell Hall 10916. ($$) Adjacent to one of Orange County's most beautiful horse farms, this establishment features a cozy, informal ambience coupled with spacious modern rooms, all with private bath, telephone, and cable TV. The owners, Elaine and Bill, have lived in Orange County for over 20 years and welcome both recreational and business travelers. Open year-round.

Stonegate B&B (845-928-2858), Route 32, Central Valley 10917. ($$) This turn-of-the-19th-century country estate has four elegantly appointed rooms, all with fireplace. Two rooms share one bath. Guests will enjoy a hearty gourmet breakfast and afternoon tea.

Storm King Lodge (845-534-9421), 100 Pleasant Hill Road, Mountainville. 10953. ($$) This comfortable country lodge—the converted carriage house of a former estate—has views of Storm King Mountain, and it's only minutes away from Storm King Art Center (see *To See*) and close to West Point. The four guest rooms all have private bath; two have a fireplace. The cozy ambience reflects the warmth of the family that operates the lodge. They have been in the area for years. Open year-round on weekends, every day in July and August.

Sugar Loaf Village B&B (845-469-2717), Pine Hill Road, Sugar Loaf 10981. ($$) This renovated house, over 100 years old, features two antiques-filled guest rooms with Jacuzzi baths. A nice mix of the old and new, and a great place to relax after shopping in Sugar Loaf.

WHERE TO EAT

DINING OUT

Bull's Head Inn (845-496-6758), Sarah Wells Trail, Campbell Hall. ($$) Open for dinner Tuesday through Thursday 5–9; Friday and Saturday 5–10, Sunday 3–8. Enjoy fine dining in a colonial atmosphere with many unusual American specialties. If you love garlic, make sure to order the baked garlic appetizer. Popular entrée selections include shrimp with four cheeses, filet mignon with peppercorn sauce, and pork tenderloin with fresh fruits.

Canterbury Brook Inn (845-534-9658), 331 Main Street, Cornwall. ($$) Open Wednesday through Sunday for dinner at 5. Hans and Kim Baumann offer up a touch of Switzerland in Cornwall. The fine Continental cuisine may be enjoyed while overlooking Canterbury Brook or dining fireside in the cooler months. Specialties of the house include roast duckling, veal langoustine, classic Wiener schnitzel, pasta with *fruits de mer,* New York sirloin steak, filet mignon, and an array of fresh

Storm King Highway

fish specials. The desserts are truly spectacular, and cappuccino and espresso are available.

Catherine's (845-294-8707), 153 West Main Street, Goshen. ($$) Open for lunch Monday through Friday 11:30–2:30; dinner Monday through Saturday 5:30–9. Contemporary American cuisine here features a variety of pasta and seafood specialties served in a comfortable country setting. The restaurant is housed in a historic building that dates back to 1869.

C. D. Driscoll's (845-566-1300), 1100 Union Avenue, Newburgh. ($$) Open daily for lunch and dinner 11–11. This establishment offers live entertainment Thursday through Saturday evening and is popular with jazz aficionados. The cuisine is American, although the spicy Mexican standards are very enjoyable. Not recommended for children on entertainment nights.

Château Hathorn (845-986-6099), 33 Hathorn Road, Warwick. ($$) Open for dinner Wednesday through Saturday 5–10, Sunday 3–8. Enjoy Continental cuisine with a French touch in a restored mansion dating back to the 1700s. The menu changes seasonally, but the rack of lamb and châteaubriand are specialties of the house. For dessert, try the coupe Denmark—melted Toblerone chocolate served over homemade vanilla ice cream and topped with fresh whipped cream.

Chianti (845-561-3103), 362 Broadway, Newburgh. ($$) Open for lunch Monday through Saturday 11–2:30; dinner Monday through Saturday

4:30–9:30. Dinner served Sunday 1–9. Every Wednesday evening there is live music. Northern Italian and Continental cuisines are the specialties here. The pasta is homemade, and there is an excellent wine list.

Cornucopia (845-856-5361), Route 209, Port Jervis. ($$) Open for lunch Tuesday through Friday noon–2; dinner Tuesday through Saturday 5–9, Sunday 1–7. Closed Monday. Reasonably priced Continental cuisine is served in a casual atmosphere. The specialties are sauerbraten and Wiener schnitzel; excellent salad bar.

88 Charles Street (845-457-9850), 88 Charles Street, Montgomery. ($$) Open for lunch Monday through Friday 11:30–4; dinner 5–10, Saturday 5–11, Sunday 4–10. The bar is open from 4 PM. The outstanding northern Italian cuisine here features veal, chicken, pasta, seafood, and steaks. Large portions, reasonable prices, romantic atmosphere.

Elegant Peasant (845-355-4455), Route 284, Slate Hill. ($$) Open Thursday through Saturday for dinner from 5. The Victorian building that houses this restaurant is over 150 years old. The menu ranges from rack of lamb and roast duckling to steak *au poivre* and grilled salmon, all prepared to order by the chef-owner. A cozy, romantic spot; vegetarian and other special diet requirements are easily accommodated.

✍ **Flo-Jean Restaurant** (845-856-6600), Routes 6 and 209, Port Jervis. ($$) Open for lunch and dinner Wednesday through Sunday noon–10. Situated on the banks of the Delaware River, this establishment has been in business since 1929. The building was formerly used to collect tolls for the bridge. On the upper level the main dining room offers scenic views of the river, while the intimate **Toll House** lounge on the lower level is casual. The Continental cuisine is of good quality; children are welcome.

✍ **Gasho of Japan** (845-928-2277), Route 32, Central Valley. ($$) Open daily for lunch at noon, dinner at 5:30. This authentic, graceful, 400-year-old farmhouse was dismantled in Japan, shipped to its present site, and reassembled. Gasho features hibachi-style fare: As you sit at heated steel-topped tables, Tokyo-trained chefs dazzle both eye and palate, preparing filet mignon with hibachi snowcrab, prime beef, and lobster tail before your very eyes. Shrimp, scallops, and eel are other specialties, and all dinners include soup, salad, vegetables, rice, and tea. After dinner, take a stroll through the Japanese gardens. Children welcome.

Il Cenacolo (845-564-4494), Route 52, Newburgh. ($$$) Open for lunch Wednesday through Monday noon–2:30; dinner Thursday at 5, Friday and Saturday at 6, Sunday at 4. Fine food from northern Italy is the byword at this restaurant, based on an Italian supper room. Select from buffalo milk mozzarella with roasted peppers, spinach gnocchi with venison sauce, tuna steak in garlic and olive oil, and many types of pasta. Save room for the homemade desserts and the excellent espresso. Not recommended for children; reservations required.

John's Harvest Inn (845-343-6630), 629 North Street, Middletown. ($$) Open for dinner Wednesday through Saturday from 5:30, Sunday 3–8.

The Continental cuisine here is very good, and the portions are hearty. The fresh seafood and veal dishes are specialties of the house.

The Jolly Onion Inn (845-258-4277), Pine Island Turnpike. ($$) Open daily, except Monday and Tuesday, for dinner at 5; open Sunday at noon. A local tradition serving Continental cuisine, this inn is located right next to a large farm stand in the scenic farm region of Orange. There is an extensive doll collection on display.

Lake View House (845-566-7100), 205 Lakeside Road, Newburgh. ($$) Open for dinner daily, except Tuesday; lunch served weekdays, except Tuesday, 11:30–2:30. Watch the sun set over Orange Lake while dining at a restaurant in operation since 1899. The chef-owner specializes in traditional American fare. Hearty soups, salads, and sandwiches are served for lunch.

La Masquerade (845-294-6888), Route 17M, Goshen. ($$$) Open daily, except Monday, for lunch at 11:30; dinner at 5. The French and Continental cuisines here are first-rate, and the restaurant is housed in a restored, mid-19th-century building. Not recommended for children. Reservations are required on weekends and holidays.

Monserrat at North Plank Road Tavern (845-565-6885), 18 North Plank Road, Newburgh. ($$) Open Monday through Saturday 11:30–10:30. Monserrat Margalef was once chef to the president of Mexico and to Arnold Schwarzenegger. She opened her own restaurant in the summer of 1997 featuring international cuisine highlighting Mexican, Italian, and French cooking. Enjoy burritos, pasta, or crêpes, depending on your mood, all available at the same restaurant.

☙ **Painter's Tavern** (845-534-2109), Village Square, Route 218, Cornwall-on-Hudson. ($$) Open daily for lunch and dinner 11:30–10. Perfect for either meal. There are nightly dinner specials, along with creative variations on burgers, sandwiches, and salads. The sun-dried tomatoes with cream pasta sauce is an excellent selection, and there are dozens of imported and domestic beers bottled and on tap. Children are welcome.

River House Restaurant (845-561-5255), Park Place, Newburgh. ($$) Open for lunch daily 11:30–4; dinner 5–10. Closed Monday and Tuesday from October through March. Arrive by boat if you like at this Hudson River establishment; you can dock in one of the slips owned by the restaurant. Relax and enjoy all kinds of fresh seafood (crab legs, shrimp scampi, lobster) in a casual atmosphere.

☙ **Sugar Loaf Inn** (845-469-2552), King's Highway, Sugar Loaf. ($$) Open for lunch Tuesday through Saturday 11:30–3; dinner Tuesday through Sunday 5–9; Sunday brunch 11–3. Country dining in a Victorian setting amid plants and flowers. A nice place for lunch or drinks; the home-baked breads and desserts are especially good. The emphasis is on freshness, and the entrées are both classic and unusual. Summer diners may enjoy the garden tables. Children welcome.

Sweet Basil Restaurant (845-783-6928), Route 17M, Harriman. ($$)

Open Tuesday through Friday for lunch 11:30–2:30; dinner 5–9 week-days, Saturday 5–11, and Sunday 4–9. Continental cuisine with an Ital-ian flair in a country bistro atmosphere. Specialties of the house are veal Luigi, honey-roasted fillet of salmon, and rack of lamb. Signature desserts include Grand Marnier cheesecake baked in a hollowed-out orange, and bananas Foster.

Ten Railroad Avenue (845-986-1509), 10 Railroad Avenue, Warwick. ($$) Open for lunch Monday through Friday 11:30–2:30; dinner Monday through Saturday 5–10. Spanish and Italian cuisines are served here in a casual atmosphere; fish, pasta, and chicken specials daily. The chef suggests the paella, if you enjoy that dish. Live music on Friday and Saturday evening.

✎ **Warwick Inn** (845-986-3666), 36 Oakland Avenue, Warwick. ($$) Open Wednesday through Saturday at 5 PM, Sunday at 1. This 170-year-old mansion has been owned and operated by the Wilson family for the past 25 years. Original moldings, fireplaces, and antiques add to the cozy atmosphere. Roast prime rib and fresh roast turkey are served Friday through Sunday. Seafood specialties include baked stuffed shrimp, swordfish, and boiled stuffed flounder. Children welcome. Reservations suggested.

Westbank Bistro (845-567-0444), 631 Route 17K, Montgomery. ($$) Open for dinner Tuesday through Thursday 5–9, Friday and Saturday until 10. The New American cuisine here is healthful, imaginative, and fresh. The chef-owner, a Culinary Institute graduate, serves interesting varia-tions on popular meat, chicken, and fish dishes.

White House Inn (845-294-9795), Route 17M, Goshen. ($$) Open for lunch Tuesday through Friday 11–3; dinner Tuesday through Saturday 4–11, Sunday 1–8. Italian and Continental cuisines are prepared to or-der here. Try the veal bellanotte and the homemade pastas. The tempt-ing desserts include raspberry cheesecake and Mississippi mud pie. The atmosphere is casual; the restaurant is housed in a restored Victorian mansion with a lovely fireplace.

Winding Hills Clubhouse Restaurant (845-457-3187), 1847 Route 17K, Montgomery. ($$) Open for lunch daily noon–2; dinner Tuesday through Thursday 5–9, Friday and Saturday 5–10; Sunday brunch 9:30–3, dinner 3–8. Enjoy international favorites, as well as steaks and sea-food, in a beautiful dining room with scenic views of the golf course.

✎ **Yobo Oriental Restaurant** (845-564-3848), Union Avenue, Newburgh. ($$) Open for lunch and dinner daily 11:30–11. Fine Pan-Asian cuisine—hibachi steaks, Korean *bulgogi*, Indonesian satés, and regional dishes of China—under one roof. The dim sum is excellent; the sushi is the region's best. A popular and interesting dining experience. Children welcome.

EATING OUT

✎ **The Barnsider Tavern** (845-469-9810), King's Highway, Sugar Loaf. ($$) Open daily, except Monday, from 11:30 AM. This tavern has a beautiful

JOSEPH PUGLISI

Commodore's Candy Shop

taproom with handwrought beams, country decor, and a glassed-in patio with a view of the Sugar Loaf Crafts Village (see *Selective Shopping*). A fire is always crackling on the hearth in winter, and the menu of burgers, quiche, and other fine café foods makes this a nice stop for lunch. Children welcome.

Commodore's (845-561-3960), 482 Broadway, Newburgh. ($) Open daily 10–6; closed Sunday during the summer. Located in an old-fashioned ice cream parlor, Commodore's has been in business and been run by the same family since 1935. They are famous for their handmade chocolates and candies. There are the usual delicious classics like marzipan and truffles, as well as Swedish fudge and almond bark. In late November call in advance to find out when they start handmade candy cane demonstrations, which are held on weekends noon–4.

Cosimo's on Union (845-567-1556), Union and Orr Streets, Newburgh. ($) Open daily 11:30–10 for lunch and dinner. The specialty here is the brick-oven-baked, personal-sized pizza. There are dozens of toppings. Also available is a large selection of pasta dishes. The restaurant is very close to Stewart Airport. If you are traveling with children, this is a good choice.

Daily Bean Cafe (845-457-1485), 11 Union Street, Montgomery. ($) Open Monday, Tuesday, and Thursday 9–6; Friday and Saturday until 7; Sunday 12–5. Closed Wednesday. Enjoy homemade soups and sandwiches with cappuccino or espresso in a relaxed atmosphere. Try the tarragon

Prima Pizza ships their brick-oven-cooked pizzas throughout the United States.

chicken salad or eggplant with sun-dried tomato and mozzarella sandwiches, favorites with local residents. There's music here on most weekends, and it's a great place to enjoy a freshly prepared dessert like chocolate mousse cake.

🖊 **Hawk's Nest** (845-856-9909), Route 97, Port Jervis. ($) Open daily at 11 AM; at 8 Saturday and Sunday in summer. A wonderful place for breakfast or lunch after canoeing on the Delaware River. The views are spectacular, and there are great pancakes, waffles, omelets, and ice cream; for lunch, chili and homemade soups are nice. The restaurant sits like a hawk's nest on the peak of the river gorge, 300 feet up, and on a clear day a stop here should not be missed.

🖊 **Hudson Street Café** (845-534-2335), 237 Hudson Street, Cornwall. ($) Open Tuesday through Sunday, 7 AM–3 PM. They serve hearty breakfasts and lunches here, as well as a special Sunday brunch featuring a variety of omeletes, eggs benedict, and waffles. The wraps, burgers, and sanwiches make this a popular lunch spot with local residents. If you take the scenic route (Route 218) to West Point (the road is closed during the winter months), you will pass the café.

🖊 **Prima Pizza** (845-534-7003 or 1-800-22-NY-PIE), 252 Main Street, Cornwall. ($) A family restaurant for over 35 years, this is a must for anyone passing through Cornwall or heading south on Route 9W. The detour is worth it. Owner Anthony Scalise regularly airmails brick-oven-cooked pizzas to places as far away as California; he was asked to send pizza to the troops in the Middle East during Operation Desert Storm. The finest blends of mozzarella cheese and fresh dough are made daily. All sauces and meatballs are cooked on the premises, and cholesterol-free oil is used with everything served here. Our favorite slice of life is the fresh basil and tomato. Sweep the Kitchen has everything on it, and we are looking forward to trying one on our next visit to Prima. There are calzones, subs, salads, and an array of pasta dishes for those who prefer other Italian specialties. Ask about shipping a pizza anywhere in the United States.

SELECTIVE SHOPPING

ANTIQUES AND AUCTIONS

The love of history found across Orange County extends to a love for antiques and collectibles, and there are many shops that cater to the connoisseur. Auctions are usually held on a regular basis, whether once a month or once a week. Estate sales may provide the antiquer and junker with everything from Persian rugs to eccentric collectibles. The best way to locate what's going on where is to check the classified listings in a local newspaper. Flea markets are another treat that springs up on warm weekends; look for markets that jumble together new and old, rather than just offering overstock and discontinued items. Most auctions and markets will not accept out-of-state checks; they will accept credit cards (sometimes), cash, and traveler's checks.

Old Red Barn Antiques and Auctions (845-754-7122), in Cuddebackville, has weekend auctions the first Saturday of the month. It also has a line of antiques and is open weekend afternoons.

Mark Vail Auction Services (845-744-2120), at Kellyl Avenue in Pine Bush, has antiques and estate auctions approximately twice a month. Call for dates. Also in Pine Bush is **Roberson's Auction Service** (845-744-9934) with Wednesday and Saturday auctions; call for dates. **Pine Bush Auction** (845-457-4404), 157 Ward Street, holds auctions twice a month on Tuesday.

New Windsor Auction Gallery (845-562-0638), Route 94, stocks fine paintings and sculpture; auction lovers will find what they want here.

COUNTRY STORE

Jones Farm & Country Store (845-534-4445), 190 Angola Road, Cornwall. Open every day year-round, weekdays 8–6, weekends until 5. Since 1914 this fifth-generation family farm has served the Hudson Valley with home-grown produce, fresh eggs, maple syrup, honey, preserves, coffees, and many gourmet items. Grandma Phoebe's kitchen features homemade baked goods, cream and butter fudge, and wonderful apple cider doughnuts. Children are always welcome to visit the animals and enjoy the observation beehive. The second floor of the store is an enormous gift shop with books, china, novelty items, and wonderful handcrafted goods. This store makes an interesting stop in Cornwall, a lovely village with a number of fine shops and restraurants.

CRAFTS

Sugar Loaf Crafts Village (845-469-9181). Take exit 16 off the NYS Thruway to Route 17 and go west for 8 miles to exit 127; follow the signs. Open 11–5 daily, except Monday, year-round (open Monday holidays). Once a bustling stagecoach and river stop, this area lost much of its trade when the railroads bypassed it in the mid–19th century. But in the last two decades Sugar Loaf has regained its spirit. Home to dozens of craftspeople who live and work in many of the buildings along King's Highway and Wood's Road, the village is a terrific place to look for a special gift or add to a collection. You'll find handcrafted stained glass, pottery, paintings, and jewelry. As befits an arts colony, there are fine crafts fairs and art shows throughout the year, as well as a fall festival and holiday caroling. The village is lovely, and it is an excellent place to spend an afternoon talking to the artists or watching them at work. Visitors will do lots of walking; there is parking at either end of the village in well-marked lots.

FACTORY OUTLETS

If you ever get tired of seeing the beauty of Orange County, there is shopping—and plenty of it. Factory outlets have come a long way from the dingy shops of the past, and a stop at **Woodbury Common** (845-928-4000), Route 32, Central Valley (open daily year-round, except major holidays), will prove this. There are more than 220 shops in this Colonial-style mall, selling everything from shoes, clothing, crystal, sweaters, and watches to toys, wallets, and stockings. The mall sponsors special events throughout the year, and there is a large food court.

✎ **Gillinder Glass** (845-856-5375), corner of Erie and Liberty Streets, Port Jervis. Hours vary, so call ahead for tour times and for group information. Open year-round; weekends seasonal. This site offers visitors a rare chance to watch glass being heated, molded, shaped, and cooled into fine collectibles. The factory has a viewing area, and the furnaces glow as the craftspeople use the same techniques employed a century ago. After a tour, stop by the **Tri-States Monument** (at the junction of the Neversink and Delaware Rivers, Laurel Grove Cemetery). Just under the I-84 bridge is a rock on which you can stand in three states (New York, Pennsylvania, and New Jersey) at once; it also notes the boundary between New York and New Jersey.

SPECIAL EVENTS

✎ *July–September:* **New York Renaissance Faire** (845-351-5171, after June 1), Route 17A, Sterling Forest, Tuxedo; watch for signs. Open late July through mid-September, weekends only. Call for exact dates and hours.

The joust at the New York Renaissance Faire in Tuxedo

Admission fee. Knights and ladies, sorcerers and their apprentices, fools and varlets, bumpkins and wantons all gather on the glorious grounds of Sterling Forest to re-create the lusty days of a merry English fair. The festival runs for eight consecutive weekends and presents a colorful, noisy look at a misty period of time somewhere between King Arthur and Shakespeare. Falconers show off the skills of their birds, opera and Shakespeare are presented at the Globe Theatre, Maid Marian flirts with Robin Hood, ladies dance beneath a maypole, and the extensive rose gardens are open for strolling. Craftspeople display and sell their wares (many belong to the Society for Anachronisms and stock things like chain-mail shirts), and the aromas of foods such as "steak on a stake," mead, and cheese pie flavor the air. There are jugglers, knife throwers, mud fights, and a living chess game in which the "pieces" wander the gardens to their squares. The actors play their roles throughout the entire festival, so authenticity combines with the personal touch. Kids adore the noise and action, and there is enough to see and do for every taste.

July–August: **Orange County Fair** (845-343-4826), Wisner Avenue fairgrounds, Middletown. Dates are usually mid-July to early August; gates open at noon. Admission fee. One of the oldest county fairs in New York State, this one started as an agricultural display between 1818 and 1825. Local interest did not really begin to build until 1841, however, when the New York State Agricultural Society entered the picture. From then on the fair was a hit. The 1841 extravaganza featured horses, cows, pigs, farm exhibits, and races; a visit to the fair today will turn up top-name entertainment, scores of food booths, thrill-a-minute rides, and some rather unique events, such as pig racing, where swift-footed swine dash for the purse—a cookie. Visit the lumberjack exhibition for a display of woodsmen's skills and a log-rolling contest. Native American shows, stock car racing, and petting zoos are also on-site, along with the finest local produce and livestock and even an old-fashioned tent circus.

August: **Orange County Onion Harvest Festival** (1-877-ONION-99) is held in August each year. The event celebrates Polish settlers' contribution to the onion industry (and those of Irish, German, and Italian settlers as well) with song, dance, and plenty of onions (great food.)

III. Sullivan County

Only 90 miles northwest of New York City lies Sullivan County: 1,000 square miles of outdoor paradise. Along the Delaware River, which snakes along the border and down into Pennsylvania, the rugged, untamed country is home to bald eagles. To the north, visitors will discover the charm of silvery lakes, lush forests, and narrow valleys where tiny villages nestle beside bubbling streams. Sullivan also offers some of the world's best trout fishing, and on opening day of the season—rain or snow—rods and flies are taken from basements and garages across the county in pursuit of the annual dream of catching "the big one." Only a small percentage of the county is considered agricultural, but there are dairy farms, pick-your-own farms and orchards, and organic farms. A drive through Sullivan County is a reminder that this area was the frontier not too long ago, a place where bears, bobcats, and the mysterious panther haunted the uneasy sleep of woodsmen and pioneers.

GUIDANCE

Sullivan County Visitors Association (845-794-3000, ext. 5010, or 1-800-882-CATS), County Government Center, Monticello 12701; www.scva.net.

GETTING THERE

Sullivan County is accessible from Route 17 (new Route 86) and from Route 209.

MEDICAL EMERGENCY

Community General Hospital (845-794-3300), Harris.
Grover-**Herman Hospital** (845-887-5530), Callicoon.

TO SEE

Canal Towne Emporium (845-888-2100), located at the intersection of Sullivan and Hudson Streets in Wurtsboro. Open daily 10–5 year-round. Free. Originally opened in 1845 as a dry goods establishment near the Hudson and Delaware Canal and now restored to its turn-of-the-20th-century charm, this country store has received awards for historic preservation. The fixtures, furnishings, and equipment are all antiques, and include the first electric coffee mill ever used in the store, advertising

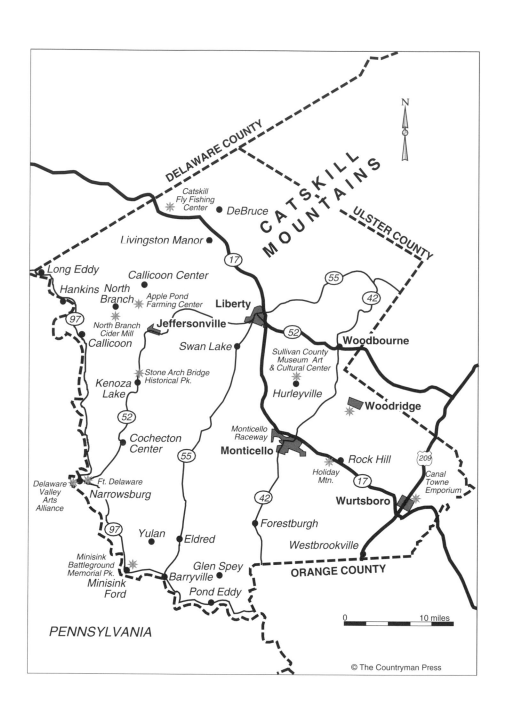

prints, tins, and jars. Today the emporium sells fine furniture, handcrafted items, and decorative accessories as well as books. Try the penny candy or the pickles! There is a restaurant next door.

Catskill Fly Fishing Center (845-439-4810), Main Street (Old Route 17), Livingston Manor. Open daily late March through October, 10–4; November through March, Monday through Friday 10–1. Admission fee. Dry-fly fishing enthusiasts will certainly find a lot to do in Sullivan County, where they'll discover some of the best trout streams in the nation. Visitors should not miss this museum, located on 35 acres along Willowemoc Creek. The center offers a changing exhibit of fly-fishing equipment (such as rods, reels, and flies), memorabilia, a library, and a hall of fame; it also presents the story of Lee Wulff, a streamside legend who brought elegance and science to the fly-fishing art. Special appearances by well-known anglers and craftspeople take place during the season, and there are special events, including workshops, seminars, and just-plain-fun get-togethers.

North Branch Cider Mill (845-482-4823), Main Street, North Branch. Open daily mid-April through Christmas, 10–5:30. Free. This mill still uses a turn-of-the-19th-century cider press and is the only mill licensed in the state of New York to produce hard cider (which helped produce many Catskills tall tales). It is a great place to watch apples moving from ruddy fruit to golden liquid: they are crushed, placed in a "bed," and pressed. In times past even the leftovers, called pomace, were spread on the fields as fertilizer to ensure a continued crop of apples. A well-stocked roadside stand sells apples and pumpkins in fall and offers Christmas trees in November and December. Inside, the cider press thumps away, and the Mill Store is chock-full of locally made cheeses, baked goods, apple cider, and candy.

HISTORIC SITES

Apple Pond Farming Center (845-482-4764), Hahn Road, Callicoon Center (call ahead for detailed directions). Open year-round. Admission fee. Today most farms are run with advanced technology as older agricultural methods and theories are slowly being lost in an avalanche of computer information. But there are still many farmers who cherish the old ways and believe that if the land is worked well, it will yield a bountiful harvest. At the Apple Pond Farming Center, an educational center and working farm, visitors can judge for themselves the merits of organic farming practices and horse-drawn equipment. The farm is located on a rocky hillside with enchanting views of meadows, mountains, and valleys. Visitors can enjoy one of several different tours, which may include wagon rides, a sheepherding demonstration, beekeeping, haying, and logging. Sleigh rides can be arranged in winter. The farm is stocked with sheep, draft horses, goats, cows, and several incredible Border collies, whose obvious dedication to the task of sheepherding is alone worth the trip. Special activities like outdoor lamb roasts, riding lessons, spinning demonstrations, foliage drives, and draft-horse work-shops are held throughout the year, but all activities require reservations. A gift shop offers products made with farm produce. Don't expect a neat little restoration, and do expect to get a little mud on your shoes.

✎ **Fort Delaware Museum of Colonial History** (845-252-6660), Route 97, Narrowsburg. Open Memorial Day weekend, weekends in June, and daily from late June until Labor Day, 10–5. Admission fee. Much attention is paid to the people who settled the main cities of New York, but those who decided to take on the wilderness are often forgotten. At the Fort Delaware Museum the daily life of the backwoods settler is explored through exhibits, crafts demonstrations, and tours. The fort is a recon-struction of the original frontier settlement of Cushetunk on the Dela-ware River, with its stockades and stout log homes, which offered the only protection from Native Americans and, later, English troops. The fort consists of a small settlement entirely surrounded by high log walls, or stockades. During the tour visitors see the blockhouses (where arms and ammunition were stored), settlers' cabins, a meetinghouse, a blacksmith shop, a candle shed, a loom shed, and more. Outside the fort walls, you'll find a small garden planted with crops typical of the era and the stocks, which were used to punish minor infractions of the law. Costumed guides and staff members demonstrate skills and crafts from the period, includ-ing candle making, blacksmithing, and even weaponry. Special events are scheduled throughout the season, so your visit may include a show by Revolutionary soldiers, weavers, or cooks.

Minisink Battleground Park, Route 168, Minisink Ford. Open May through October, dawn to dusk. Free. One of the unusual and forgot-ten Revolutionary War battlegrounds in the region, this site offers visi-tors a chance to walk along trails that tell stories of both nature and combat. In July 1779 the area's most important historic battle took place when a group of American rebels were defeated by Mohawks in a mas-sacre that took almost 50 lives. In an eerie postscript, the bones of the dead were not gathered and buried until more than 40 years after the battle, because the area was wilderness and not many people visited it.

Today the 56-acre park has three walking trails from which to ex-plore its history and the surrounding natural setting. The blazed trails have descriptive markers that tell the story of the area, and written trail guides can be picked up at the interpretive center. The Battleground Trail depicts the tactics and strategy of a woodland skirmish, and in-cludes stops at Sentinel Rock, where the lone American defender was killed; Hospital Rock, where a rebel doctor lost his life while tending to his wounded charges; and Indian Rock, which legend says was set up to commemorate the dead. The Woodland Trail meanders through wet-land, understory, second growth, and ferns. The map points out the trail's flora and describes some of the animal life you may encounter, such as foxes, wood frogs, raccoons, and maybe even a bald eagle. On

JOSEPH PUGLISI

Roebling's Suspension Bridge on the Delaware River was built by the designer of the Brooklyn Bridge.

the Old Quarry/Rockshelter Trail discover the logging, quarrying, and Native American histories of this section through trail markers. You may also want to plan a visit to the battleground in time for the small memorial service held each July 22 to honor those who fell here.

Roebling's Suspension Bridge. Look for the historic marker opposite the entrance to the Minisink Battleground. Built by the designer of the Brooklyn Bridge, this crossing on the Delaware River is the oldest of its kind still standing. The aqueduct was constructed because canal boats and logging rafts kept crashing into one another on the river; the aqueduct would actually carry the canal boats over the river itself. The aqueduct was turned into a bridge crossing in the late 19th century, and today it still carries traffic across to Pennsylvania.

SCENIC DRIVES

With more than 1,000 square miles of countryside, just about any drive through Sullivan County will take you past exquisite views that change with the seasons: The earliest blush of spring may be enjoyed by driving along any back road or even on the Quickway (Route 17); summer is lush and lazy anywhere you turn; fall splashes the meadows and forests with color; and winter here can be lovely, if chilly. Sullivan County offers detailed theme driving tours; call 1-800-882-CATS for a copy of the guide.

If you want to travel the southernmost section of Sullivan County and see some spectacular river and mountain scenery, start your tour in **Monticello.** From there head south on Route 42 to Sackett Lake Road (you will go through a town called Squirrel Corners), and keep going south to Forestburgh Road, where you will make a right. This is the reservoir area of Mongaup Falls, a good spot to sight bald eagles. At Route 97 head west along the snaking river drive known as Hawk's Nest, with its views of New York and Pennsylvania; you will pass Minisink Battleground Park and Roebling's Suspension Bridge (see *Historic Sites*). At Narrowsburg, home of the Fort Delaware Museum (see *Historic Sites*), head north on Route 52 to Liberty, where you can pick up Route 17 back to Monticello.

A second drive, which will take you past some of the few remaining covered bridges in the county, begins at **Livingston Manor** (exit 96 off Route 17). Turn onto Old Route 17 from the Vantran covered bridge, built in 1860 and one of the few existing bridges constructed in the lattice-truss and queen-post styles. Go back to Livingston Manor and follow the signs east from town along DeBruce Road to Willowemoc, which has a covered bridge that was built in 1860 in Livingston Manor, then cut in half and moved to its present site in 1913. From Willowemoc take Pole Road to West Branch Road, which leads into Claryville. The Halls Mills covered bridge, built in 1912, is on Claryville Road over the Neversink River. Head south from Claryville to Route 55, then west back to Liberty.

Another sight worth making time to see is **Tomasco Falls,** often called the Niagara of Sullivan County. These spectacular waterworks are enjoyable on a hot summer's day. They're located off Route 209 in Mountaindale, and there are daily tours May through October. Call 845-434-6065 for more information.

Other roads that offer outstanding views include Route 209 and Routes 55 and 55A. Route 17, also called the Quickway, is the main north–south road through Sullivan County and provides access to most of the region's scenic areas.

TO DO

CANOEING AND RAFTING

Canoeists and rafters enjoy the Delaware's rapids and eddies from spring to fall. Both the Upper Delaware (from Hancock to Port Jervis) and the main section of the river (from Port Jervis to the Chesapeake) are used for canoeing and rafting, although there are sections that are particularly good for novices and the less adventurous. As with any other water sport, a few guidelines and suggestions will make your trip comfortable and safe; most rental agencies require that you know how to swim and that flotation gear be worn by anyone in a canoe or raft—it may look harmless, but the Delaware can reach depths of 15 feet! For your own comfort, take along sunscreen, lightweight sneakers, extra clothing, snacks, and a hat. If you go very early in the season, the water may be higher and colder than if you go in late July or August. The companies listed below rent equipment and canoes, and some offer a return trip to your starting point. Although you don't need to make a reservation, on busy summer and holiday weekends it may pay to call before you go. Rates are often lower midweek. The river is now managed by the National Park Service; for information, call 717-729-7134, 717-685-4871, or 845-252-3947.

Cedar Rapids Kayak and Canoe Outfitters (845-557-6158), Barryville, has double and single kayaks, canoes, rafts, and tubes for rent; there also is a riverside restaurant where you can watch the fun.

Kittatinny Canoes (1-800-FLOAT-KC), Route 97, north of Barryville, is one of the oldest (58 years) operating canoe rental companies, and it has rafts, tubes, canoes, and kayaks. It also offers camping and special discounts.

Landers River Trips (1-800-252-3925), Narrowsburg, has campgrounds and a motel for guests, in addition to full river equipment (canoe, tubes, kayaks).

Upper Delaware Campgrounds (845-887-5344), Callicoon, has complete float and package trips for river rats.

Wild and Scenic River Tours and Rentals (845-557-8783 or 1-800-836-0366), Barryville, has adventure vacations for all ages and skill levels, along with canoe, raft, tube, and kayak rentals. Fishing trips are also available.

The following companies also rent canoes and tubes: **Jerry's Three River Canoe Corporation** (845-557-6078), Pond Eddy; **Silver Canoe Rentals** (845-856-7055 or 1-800-856-7055), Pond Eddy; **Whitewater Willie's Raft and Canoe Rentals** (845-856-2229 or 1-800-233-7238), Pond Eddy; **Catskill Mountain Canoe and Jon Boat Rentals** (845-887-4995), Hankins; **Indian Head Canoes** (845-557-8777 or 1-800-874-BOAT).

FARM STANDS AND PICK-YOUR-OWN FARMS

Nothing tastes like fruits and vegetables that still have the blush of the sun and the mist of the morning on them. Harvesting begins in Sullivan County in late spring with asparagus and berries and ends in late fall with pumpkins and apples, although some stands stock local eggs, maple syrup, and honey year-round. Hours vary with the season and harvest, and not all stands are open daily, so it is suggested that you call before you take a special trip. There are also lots of small, family-run farm stands that carry only one or two items and are open for only a few weeks a year; keep an eye out for these, too. They often have unusual selections or heirloom varieties. Whether you pick the produce yourself or buy from a roadside stand, the selection and quality in Sullivan County are excellent. Many area farmers attend the **Sullivan County Area Farmers' Market** (845-292-5250 for information), Darbee Lane, Liberty. It's held Friday 3–7 PM from June through October.

Apple Pond Farming Center (845-482-4764), Hahn Road, Callicoon Center, is an organic farm that sells a variety of fruits and vegetables at its roadside stand. Since it's off the beaten track, you may want to combine a tour of the farm (see *To See—Historic Sites*) with a visit to the farm stand.

Diehl Farm (845-887-4935), Gabel Road, Callicoon, is a well-stocked stand with a full range of local crops, from apples to eggs and dairy products.

Fisher Farm (845-292-5777), Aden Road, Liberty, has only pick-your-own pumpkins and squash in fall.

Gorzynski Organic Farm (845-252-7570), Route 52, Cochecton Center, raises vegetables, apples, berries, cherries, and more using organic methods.

Maas Farm Stand (845-985-2686), Route 55, Grahamsville, has lots of pick-your-own peppers, eggplant, and squash, among many other crops.

River Brook Farm (845-932-7952), Route 97 and C. Meyer Road, Cochecton, will provide heirloom potatoes along with beans, carrots, garlic, and lots of other greenery.

Silver Heights Farm (845-482-3572), 275 Eggler Road, Jeffersonville, has an unusual specialty: heirloom tomatoes and roses.

Herbs are the specialty at the **Catskill Morning Farm** (845-482-3984), Youngsville, and vegetables and flowers are colorful crops; call for hours before you go. Eggs are extra special at **Egg University, Kaplan's Farm** (845-434-4519), Glen Wild Road, Woodridge.

Sullivan County hosts a **Down on the Farm Day** each summer, when self-guided driving tours of several local farms are offered to visitors. Call 845-794-3000, ext. 5010, for the schedule. Some farms also offer visitors the chance to select and cut their own Christmas trees; you can bring your own saw or rent one for the day. Dress warmly, bring rope to tie the tree to the car, and have a nice holiday! But remember, call ahead for directions, hours, and prices: **Ted Nied Christmas Trees** (845-482-5341), Jeffersonville; **Pine Farm Christmas Trees** (845-482-4149), Livingston Manor; **Trees of the Woods** (845-482-4528), Callicoon Center; **Fred Weber Tree Farm** (845-557-8440), Yulan.

FISHING

Sullivan County is an angler's paradise. The famed Willowemoc and Beaverkill streams produce prizewinning trout each year, in addition to being recognized as the cradle of American fly-fishing. The Delaware River offers its rich bounty to the patient angler, as do Mongaup Creek and Russell Brook. Then there are the icy lakes of the county, with such entrancing names as Kiamesha, Kenoza, Swan, and Waneta. There are hundreds of fine fishing areas in Sullivan County and too little space to do them all justice. The following general information, however, will assist you in finding the perfect spot to enjoy a rocky stream, a sunny sky, and, just maybe, a record catch!

The county's streams and rivers are famed for their brook, brown, and rainbow trout, but bass, pickerel, walleye, and shad are also plenti-

Fly-fishing in Sullivan County

ful. All streams on state land are open to the public; other streams often have public fishing rights through state easements, which are indicated by signs. New York State requires fishing licenses for people over 16, as well as special reservoir permits (call the New York City Board of Water Supply for application information). There are strict fishing seasons for certain species, and you could be in for a heavy fine if you disobey the law. The brochure you receive when you get your license should answer all your questions. Lake fishing is also popular in Sullivan, but there are separate use fees charged and some lakes are privately owned by hotels or resorts, so check on the site before you fish.

The Beaverkill is one of the best-known trout streams in the world and may be reached from Roscoe, Livingston Manor, Lew Beach, Beaverkill, and Rockland. Fly-fishing tackle may be purchased in Roscoe at **The Beaverkill Angler** (607-498-5194), Stewart Avenue. Or call **White Cloud's Beaverkill Fly Fishing School** (607-498-4611) in Roscoe: This private school offers students a chance to learn casting, fly-tying, and moving-water fishing techniques. Although there are three lessons, you can schedule them to meet your needs.

Willowemoc Creek is found between Roscoe and Livingston Manor along Old Route 17; Mongaup Creek runs from Livingston Manor to Mongaup Pond; the Neversink River is at Claryville on County Routes 19 and 15; and you can pick up the Delaware River at East Branch on Route 17.

Among the lakes are Kenoza Lake (Route 52, Kenoza Lake Vil-

Soaring excursions may be arranged from Wurtsboro Airport.

lage); Swinging Bridge Lake (Route 17B, Mongaup Valley); Swan Lake (Route 55, between Liberty and Kauneonga Lake); White Lake (junction of Routes 17B and 55); Waneta Lake (County Route 151 in Deckertown); Cable Lake (Route 17 northwest of Roscoe, end of Russell Brook); and Kiamesha Lake (Route 42, Kiamesha).

The **Eldred Preserve** (845-557-8316 or 1-800-557-FISH), Route 55 between Barryville and White Lake, has some restrictions on fishing for nonguests, so call ahead. It allows trout fishing (no license required) and bass fishing on its lakes by boat rental reservation only.

GLIDING AND SOARING

Wurtsboro Airport (845-888-2791), Route 209, Wurtsboro. Open daily, weather permitting. Established in 1927, this airport is home to the oldest soaring site in the United States. Soaring is done in sailplanes—motorless craft that are towed into the air and released. The pilot then sails the plane on the air currents before coming in for a landing. A 20-minute demonstration flight with a certified pilot can be arranged; if you enjoy the sport, flight instruction is available.

GOLF

The beauty of Sullivan County's farm country carries over to its golf courses. Many resorts have outstanding courses open to the public, but you should call to check on schedules.

Grossinger's Country Club (845-292-9000), Grossinger's, has 27 holes of golf, a driving range and putting greens, and full facilities.

Island Glen Golf Course (845-583-1010), Route 17B, Bethel, has nine
holes, a practice green, and a clubhouse.

Tennanah Lake Golf (607-498-5502), Roscoe-Hankins Road, Roscoe, is
open May through October and has package rates for guests who want
to enjoy a lovely 18-hole course.

Villa Roma Country Club (845-887-4880), Callicoon, has an 18-hole
course, a putting green, and full facilities.

Public courses include **Sullivan County Golf and Country Club** (845-
292-9584), Route 52, Liberty; **Tarry Brae** (845-434-2620), South
Fallsburg; and the **Lochmor Golf Course** (845-434-9079), Loch
Sheldrake.

HARNESS RACING

Monticello Raceway (845-794-4100). Take Route 17 to exit 104; follow
signs. Open year-round, but days and hours vary, so call. Admission fee.
Recognized as one of the world's fastest $\frac{1}{2}$-mile harness tracks,
Monticello Raceway is home to many famous pacers and trotters. Because it is not as large as other harness tracks, Monticello has smaller
crowds and plenty of parking. But the action at Monticello is just as
heart pounding, the crowds just as enthusiastic. The grandstand is glass
enclosed and the racing goes on rain or shine. There is exotic and pari-
mutuel wagering, and the paddock is indoors. On special-events days,
meet the drivers and their horses or enjoy a meal while watching the
races from your table.

WINTER SPORTS

CROSS-COUNTRY SKIING

There are so many places to cross-country ski in Sullivan County that
you would have to spend several winters here in order to try all the
trails. Many local parks allow skiing for free, but often the trails are not
groomed and there are no nearby rentals. At the large resorts some
trails are open for a fee to day visitors, but if you are uncertain of a
hotel's policy, it is recommended that you call ahead; policies may also
change from year to year.

Try the 160-acre **Town of Thompson Park** (845-796-3161), Old
Liberty Road, 1.5 miles past the Monticello Post Office; 110-acre **Hanofee
(Liberty) Park** (845-292-7690), on Infirmary Road, off Route 52 east, in
Liberty, where you will find rentals, a trail fee, and a heated hut on
weekends; and 260-acre **Walnut Mountain (Pearson) Park** (845-292-
7690), Liberty, with rentals and a heated weekend trail hut.

Ski resorts open to the public include **The Inn at Lake Joseph**
(845-791-9506), Forestburgh, for cross-country skiing; **Kutsher's
Country Club** (845-794-6000), Monticello, for downhill and cross-
country skiing; **Mountain View Inn on Shandelee** (845-439-5070),
913 Shandelee Road, Livingston Manor, with cross-country trails; and

Villa Roma Country Club (845-887-4880), Callicoon, for downhill and cross-country skiing, with night skiing and 100 percent snowmaking.

DOWNHILL SKIING

While downhill skiing in Sullivan does not revolve around huge resorts like Hunter or Gore, it does have a few centers that offer lots of fun for all ages. (See also *Cross-Country Skiing*.)

Holiday Mountain Ski Area (845-796-3161), Route 17, exit 107 at Bridgeville, has both day and night skiing, 15 slopes, 90 percent snowmaking, and a vertical drop of 400 feet. The longest run is 3,500 feet, and both beginners and advanced skiers enjoy the slopes; cross-country skiing is allowed and snowboarding may be enjoyed. A ski shop, snack stand, and trailer parking are all available, although a call ahead is recommended if you plan to stay the night.

ICE FISHING

Those who enjoy the bracing thrills of ice fishing will want to check with the Sullivan County Visitors Association (845-794-3000, ext. 5010) to find out when the **King of the Ice Contest** is scheduled and which ponds are open for ice fishing. There is also a winter **Ice Tee Open** (golf on ice!).

GREEN SPACE

Eagle Institute (845-557-6162), Barryville. Call for information. This organization is a strong advocate and educational center for information about the bald eagle, which is found throughout Sullivan County. (Benjamin Franklin disliked this bird, by the way; he wanted the wild turkey as the national symbol. You can see many wild turkeys in Sullivan County fields.) At least 100 eagles stop in Sullivan during their winter migration; some have even made the county their year-round home. The Eagle Institute leads eagle-watching tours and interpretive programs that teach the ways and wherefores of these mighty birds. Eagle-watches are held January through March, and are a great way to learn about the natural world in the off-season.

The Potager (845-888-4086), 180 Sullivan Street, Wurtsboro. Open daily, except Tuesday, 10–4; Friday and Saturday 10–8:30. Free. Located in a century-old church, The Potager has display and viewing gardens open to the public, plus a wonderful gift area with baskets, plants, and treats for the gardener. The daffodil festival brings spring fever to all, and the fall festival is colorful and rustic. Enjoy a stop at the garden café.

Stone Arch Bridge Historical Park, Route 52, Kenoza Lake. Open year-round. Free. This three-arched stone bridge, which spans Callicoon Creek, is the only remaining one of its kind in this country. Built in 1872 by two German stonemasons, the bridge was constructed from hand-cut local stone and is supported without an outer framework. Replacing an earlier wooden span that finally collapsed from the constant weight of

The Stone Arch Bridge in Kenoza Lake is the only one remaining of its kind in the U.S.

wagonloads of lumber, the Stone Arch Bridge gained fame not only for its graceful design and unusual construction but also for a bizarre murder that took place on or near it in 1892. A local farmer, believing that his brother-in-law had put a hex on him, convinced his son that only the brother-in-law's death could lift the curse. So the young man carried out the murder and dumped the body into the river. The case drew enormous publicity because of the witchcraft angle, and there have even been reports of a ghost appearing on the bridge. Today visitors fish from the banks, picnic on shore, or just walk through the 9-acre landscaped park and along the nature trails. Children will enjoy the small play area.

Woodstock Festival Site (845-295-2448), Hurd Road, Bethel. This is where it happened: the days of peace, mud, and rock 'n' roll. There is a small monument to the 1969 festival here; plenty of people stop and share stories.

LODGING

Sullivan County is probably best known for the Catskills resorts that have flourished there for nearly a century. While some of the hotels, like Kutcher's, still welcome guests, others have shut their doors forever. But the region offers a very wide variety of bungalow colonies, resort hotels, and inns, which range from inexpensive to luxury. Be certain to call before you go; the resorts can be booked well in advance of the summer months and winter holidays.

All Breeze Guest House (845-557-6485), 1101 Haring Road, Barryville

12719. ($) This bed & breakfast will also serve dinner with advance notice, and it offers a nice getaway for families with children. There are ponds to swim in and fields and woods to walk and explore. The guest house is close to several of the rafting outfitters. There are four rooms, and all have private bath. Open April through December.

Beaverkill Valley Inn (845-439-4844), Beaverkill Road, Lew Beach 12753. ($$$) This National Historic Site, built in 1893 and restored in recent years by Laurance Rockefeller, offers a perfect retreat for those who love the outdoors. Located within the Catskill Forest Preserve, near hiking trails and some of the best fishing anywhere, the inn also has tennis courts and an indoor pool. During the summer you can bike, hike, and fish; in winter, cross-country ski. There are a total of 20 rooms, and all have private bath. Open year-round.

Bradstan Country Hotel (845-583-4114), Route 17B, White Lake 12786. ($$) This unique bed & breakfast features a cottage and five comfortable suites with private bath overlooking beautiful White Lake. Also on the premises is a cabaret with live entertainment and a full bar. A gourmet breakfast is served, and special diets can be accommodated. Open year-round.

Dai Bosatsu Zendo (845-439-4566), Beecher Lake, Lew Beach 12753. ($$) This Buddhist monastery on 1,400 wooded acres overlooking Beecher Lake—which, at 2,700 feet above sea level, is the highest in the Catskills—is open to visitors. Harriet Beecher Stowe lived here for a time and is said to have written parts of *Uncle Tom's Cabin* here. There are no phones, televisions, or recreational facilities, but the rooms in the guest house are carpeted and comfortable; some have a fireplace. The cost is exceedingly reasonable and includes three vegetarian meals daily. There are eight rooms, one with private bath; four share two baths, and three share one bath. This unique inn has been discovered as a relaxing getaway for stressed city dwellers. Not recommended for children. Open April through October; you must make reservations.

DeBruce Country Inn (845-439-3900), DeBruce Road, off Route 17 (exit 96), DeBruce 12758. ($$) This inn, which dates from the turn of the 19th century, is located within the Catskill Forest Preserve and on the banks of Willowemoc Creek. A restaurant serves three home-cooked meals a day, with Pilgrim pumpkin soup, stuffed trout, quail, and veal as some of the specialties. The **Dry Fly** piano lounge is the perfect place to unwind at the end of the day. Three suites have private bath; 15 rooms have private bath; daily rates include breakfast and dinner. Hotspring spa, sauna, exercise room, outdoor pool. Open year-round.

Gable Farm (845-252-7434), 90 Gables Road, Narrowsburg 12764. ($) Located on 106 acres of quiet meadows and woods that belong to a working farm, near where the original Woodstock concert took place, this picturesque establishment offers cross-country skiing in winter and an in-ground pool in summer. Two of the four guest rooms have private bath;

two share a bath. There are goats and sheep here, and visitors are allowed to bring pets. Open year-round.

Griffen House (845-482-3371), 178 Maple Avenue, Jeffersonville 12748. ($$) This award-winning Victorian mansion, tucked away on a 2-acre estate in the village, once hosted FDR. All guest rooms have private bath. There is a gourmet restaurant and gift shop on the premises. Open year-round.

The Guest House (845-439-4000), 223 DeBruce Road, Livingston Manor 12758. ($$$) This luxurious retreat is the perfect romantic getaway for those who want to rekindle a relationship. There are four rooms with private bath in the main house and three other rooms in cottages on the premises; one has a whirlpool bath surrounded by palm trees. A fully equipped fitness room is available, and guests can book tennis lessons or a massage. Breakfast is served any time in the morning—or early afternoon. Located on Willowemoc Creek, with private fly-fishing. Open year-round.

✍ **The Inn at Lake Joseph** (845-791-9506), County Road 108, off Route 42, Forestburgh 12777; www.lakejoseph.com. ($$$) A 19th-century Victorian mountain retreat nestled in the Catskills and surrounded by acres of forest, this inn was built by a prosperous businessman who then sold the house to the Roman Catholic Church, which used it as a retreat for Cardinals Hayes and Spellman. A private spring-fed lake offers swimming, boating, and fishing. There are two tennis courts as well. This is a secluded spot where every detail is attended to, making it one of the county's best inns. The dining room is open to the public by reservation only. The mansion has six fireplaces, and each guest room has a canopied bed, Persian rugs, lacy linens, and fine antiques. Fifteen rooms with private bath. The carriage house is perfect for families, with its own library, TV, and stereo. Outdoor pool. Open year-round.

✍ **Kutsher's Country Club** (845-794-6000 or 1-800-431-1273), Kutsher Road, off Route 42, Monticello 12701. ($$$) Since 1907 the Kutsher family has been running this resort. Although it's large (more than 400 rooms), an informal, homey atmosphere prevails. There is an 18-hole golf course on the grounds, and the indoor ice rink is open all year. The lake offers boating and fishing. Guests will enjoy indoor and outdoor pools, a health club, racquetball, tennis, and a full children's program. Rates include three meals a day. Open year-round.

Magical Land of Oz (845-439-3418), Box 455, Shandelee Road, Livingston Manor 12758. ($) This elegant century-old farmhouse is as eclectic as its name is unusual. You can enjoy a hot tub on the terrace, the exercise room, or nearby lake swimming. There is even a petting zoo on the premises, and lovely gardens in-season. Five rooms share three bathrooms. Open year-round.

✍ **Mountainview Inn on Shandelee** (845-439-5070), Shandelee Road, Livingston Manor 12758. ($$) A 77-year-old building with a taproom and restaurant houses this family-owned and -operated inn. Guest rooms—each one is different—are furnished with period pieces, and some have canopied beds. The full breakfast includes homemade breads, jams, juice, and coffee. A lake is nearby for swimming, fishing, and boating, and there are cross-country ski trails. Eight rooms, each with private bath. Children welcome. No pets. Open year-round.

New Age Health Spa (845-985-7601 or 1-800-682-4348), Route 55, Neversink 12765. ($$) This is a quiet, casual, reasonably priced retreat that focuses on weight loss, de-stressing, and regenerating vitality. The approach is a combination of exercise and nutrition, helping guests develop permanent changes in their daily regimen and habits they can take home with them. In addition to massages, mud baths, facials, and aromatherapy, classes are available throughout the day in stretching, body conditioning, yoga, and tai chi. The indoor pool and Jacuzzi are first-rate, and you'll find a sauna and steam room. A daily hike is organized for guests; the spa is located on the edge of a state forest and there are many scenic trails to explore. The spa pampers guests with gourmet, healthful meals that are both low fat and delicious. This is a great place to stay for those on special diets, since the menu features fresh fruits, vegetables, and juices. Most of the herbs are grown in greenhouses on the premises during warm-weather months. The dining room is open to the public. Great value for the money; special two-for-one packages during the off-season. Open year-round.

Sivananda Ashram Yoga Ranch (845-434-9242), P.O. Box 195, Budd Road, Woodbourne 12788. ($) There are 36 rooms, all with private bath, on this 78-acre retreat. A yoga vacation includes twice-daily classes and vegetarian meals. There are classes in meditation, guest lectures and workshops, cultural programs, and family yoga. Sauna and exercise rooms.

✍ **Villa Roma** (845-887-4880), Villa Roma Road, Callicoon 12723. ($$$) More than 215 air-conditioned rooms make this full-service resort a large one, but it has everything: fishing, swimming, golf, horse-drawn sleigh rides, and a decidedly Italian accent. All room rates, of course, include great food, and there's even a weekly Caesar's Night feast. Special events include children's programs, auctions, and rafting expeditions.

WHERE TO EAT

DINING OUT

✍ **Bernie's Holiday Restaurant** (845-796-3333), Route 17, Rock Hill. ($$) Open for dinner daily at 5; closed Monday from September through May. The largest restaurant in Sullivan County and also one of the best. Try visiting on Gourmet Friday for a truly sumptuous meal. The specialties here are Chinese and American cuisines, and the Cajun dishes are first-rate. Children welcome.

⚘ **Christopher's Seafood House** (845-436-8749), 219 Main Street, Hurleyville. ($$) Open Wednesday through Sunday for lunch from 11–2; dinner, 2–10. From Memorial Day weekend through Labor Day weekend, open every day. The Continental cuisine includes all of the Italian specialties. The chef's favorites are the seafood cannelloni, sauteed soft shell crabs (in season), prime rib, and zuppa de pesce. The kids will enjoy the spare ribs.

Dead End Cafe (845-292-0202), Route 17, Parksville. ($$) Open daily (except Monday and Tuesday) at 5 for dinner; open every night in summer. All kinds of Italian fare are served here, with unusual seafood specials nightly. There is a live music charge, and excellent espresso and cappuccino.

⚘ **Eldred Preserve** (845-557-8316), Route 55, Eldred. ($$) Open for dinner Monday through Saturday 5–9, Sunday 1–8. The dining rooms here overlook three stream-fed ponds stocked with rainbow, brown, brook, and golden trout, as well as 2,000 acres of unspoiled forest. Needless to say, the specialty is trout from the preserve's ponds. The fish is served many ways, including smoked, and all baking is done on the premises. There is also a 21-room motel, and two private lakes are open for boating and fishing (see *To Do—Fishing*). Guests can enjoy the tennis courts and outdoor pool in warm weather, or ice fishing in winter. Children welcome.

Gaetano's (845-796-4901), Route 17B, Mongaup Valley. ($$) Open Wednesday through Sunday for dinner 5–9. Enjoy fine northern Italian cuisine in this delightful restaurant, located only 4 miles from the Monticello Raceway. Reservations requested.

⚘ **House of Lyons** (845-794-0244), Jefferson Street, Monticello. ($$) Open Tuesday through Friday noon–3; Tuesday through Sunday 5–9:30. The specialties here are fresh seafood and prime rib, but the menu is huge and offers a range of Continental cuisine. There are chicken wings and burgers for children, who are welcome.

⚘ **The Millbrook Inn** (845-856-7778), Route 97, Pond Eddy. ($$) Open for dinner Thursday through Saturday 5–9:30, Sunday noon–8. Fine country dining features a mix of American and European favorites. The emphasis here is on freshness, and the entrées are imaginative. A few of the specialties are tidewater shrimp, maple walnut chicken, and game pie. Children are welcome.

The 1906 Restaurant (845-887-1906), Main Street, Callicoon. ($$) Open daily for dinner 5–9; call for winter hours. Enjoy both traditional favorites and nouvelle cuisine specialties prepared by a Culinary Institute–trained chef. The Black Angus beef is popular, and so are the game dishes, which include venison, quail, and rabbit. All soups and desserts are made on the premises. Entertainment on weekends. Reservations suggested.

Old Homestead Steakhouse (845-794-8973), 472 Bridgeville Road, Monticello. ($$) Open daily 4:30–10. This is the place to go for surf and turf. The large 24-ounce sirloin steak is a specialty of the house. You can also try steamed or stuffed lobster, grilled salmon or swordfish, along with a large menu featuring an array of steak dishes.

Piccolo Paese (845-292-7210), 271 Route 52, Liberty. ($$) Open for lunch Monday through Friday noon–3; dinner served daily 4:30–10. This elegant yet moderately priced northern Italian restaurant features fresh homemade pasta, seafood, chicken, veal, and imaginative appetizers. The chef-owner creates terrific daily specials that we highly recommend.

Tre Alberi (845-557-6104), Route 97, Barryville. ($$) Open for dinner daily, except Monday, 5–10; reservations suggested. This restaurant serves the best northern Italian cuisine in Sullivan County. There are different pasta, fish, and poultry specials each day, and all are prepared to order. The desserts are made on the premises, and the chef-owner oversees their preparation. A worthwhile stop for those who appreciate fine dining.

EATING OUT

Frankie & Johnnie's (845-434-8051), Main Street, Hurleyville. ($) Open daily year-round 11:30–10. This reasonable Italian American restaurant specializes in steak, seafood, pasta, and pizza. It's a great spot for lunch or dinner if you're traveling with children.

Pete's Pub (845-932-8110), Route 52, Lake Huntington. ($) Open daily (except Tuesday) Monday through Friday 4–10, Saturday and Sunday noon–10. This family-style restaurant offers an array of old favorites like pot roast, beef stew, and lobster tails. On weekends there's a salad bar. The fare is simple and the portions are hearty. There are also steaks, pasta dishes, and burgers of all kinds.

ENTERTAINMENT

ARTS

Sullivan County has a long history of supporting the arts, and the cultural programs and shows that are offered throughout the region are some of the best in the state. The **Delaware Valley Arts Alliance** (845-252-7576) is headquartered in the Arlington Hotel in Narrowsburg, which is on the National Register of Historic Places. Its gallery is open year-round for exhibits and special events, so call for a schedule. **Catskill Art Society** (845-436-4227), Hurleyville, sponsors art, studio, and architectural tours, workshops, and more. Call for locations and schedules of events in the county.

The Sullivan County Museum Art and Cultural Center (845-434-8044) in Hurleyville is open year-round Wednesday through Sunday and displays local historical material as well as the work of local artists.

FILM

The Narrowsburg International Independent Film Festival (845-252-3909), P.O. Box 148, Narrowsburg 12764. Every August a weeklong film festival showcases new talents in the independent film world. There are screenings of feature films, shorts, and documentaries, as well as seminars and panel discussions on producing, directing, financing, and acting.

PERFORMING ARTS

A summer stock theater housed in a 128-year-old barn can only mean fun, and that's what you'll have when you attend a performance at the **Forestburgh Playhouse** (845-794-1194), RD 1, Box 250, Forestburgh 12777. Drama, comedies, and musicals are all on the bill, and there is a dinner theater and cabaret format in fall. Call for information and schedule.

Sullivan Performing Arts (845-436-9916), Sullivan Community College, Loch Sheldrake, has dance, theater, and musicals as part of its series, along with holiday offerings and family shows. **Delaware Valley Opera** (845-252-3910) is located at the Tusten Theater, Bridge Street, Narrowsburg, but performs at parks and art centers throughout the county; catch this company in summer.

SELECTIVE SHOPPING

ANTIQUES

The search for treasures in Sullivan County can take you to a dusty little shop on a side road or into full-fledged auction barns where the prices are steep and the sales are fast. Many antiques shops are open all year, but some serve only the vacation crowds; call before you go to avoid disappointment. There are dozens of shops throughout the county, and the following is only a sampling of the wide selection.

Ace Trading Company (845-434-4553), Main Street, Hurleyville, has a wide selection ranging from antiques to odds and ends.

The Antique Palace Emporium (845-292-2270), 300 Chestnut Street, Liberty, has more than two floors of restored furniture and original collectibles.

Callicoon Flea Market (845-887-5411), Main Street, Callicoon, has everything from furniture to collectible pottery, along with reproduction furniture and decorative items.

Fisherman's Wife (607-498-9955) Stewart Avenue, Roscoe. Open year-round Tuesday and Wednesday by chance. Fine selection of furniture; a great place to browse while someone else is casting his or her line.

Larry's Dog House Woodstock Memorabilia (845-583-5991), corner of Route 17B and Dr. Duggan Road. Open May through September, but will open at other times with a little notice. This is it: the Woodstock collector's vision of paradise. Quirky but grandly local.

Memories (845-292-4270), Route 17 (Quickway), between exits 98 and 97 (watch for signs), has a very large general line and has long been a popular stop with vacationers.

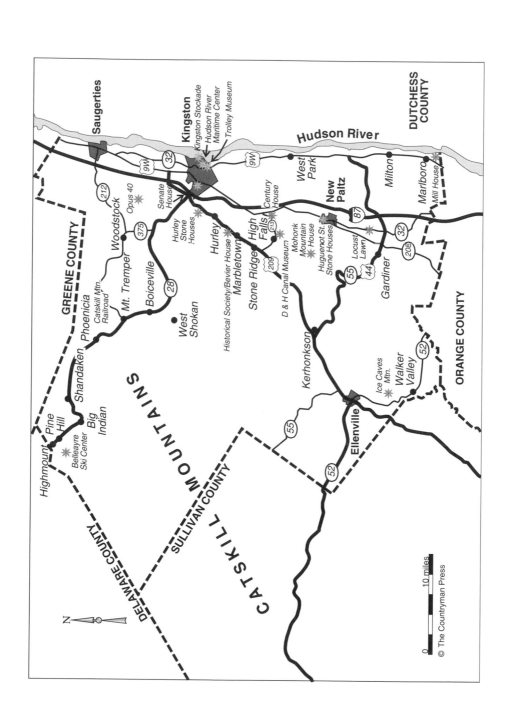

IV. Ulster County

Both the Dutch and the English settled in Ulster County, drawn by the lush farmlands along the Hudson. Snug, well-built homes were constructed of stone, brick, and wood; many still stand and are open to the public. Ulster County was not always blessed with peace and wealth, however; it was the scene of conflict during the American Revolution, when the city of Kingston was burned by the British and spies were hanged in outlying orchards. But the area rebuilt itself through the years, and today Ulster is a study in contrasts. Businesses have settled alongside farms, and artists' colonies thrive among boutiques. Dutch names of towns and lanes recall the past, while a thriving community of second-home owners and vacationers has brought different cultures to the region.

The outdoors offers excellent fishing, skiing, and hiking, and the mountains are said to be still haunted by the witches and goblins of centuries past. Ulster is mountainous, flat, river lined, and forested by turns; there's enough here to keep visitors busy for another century or so. The region is easy to travel, with several major roads and enough byways to please every traveler. Bring a camera when you visit, because the seasonal changes in Ulster are dramatic, spring giving way to summer overnight and winter making guest appearances as late as April!

GUIDANCE
Ulster County Tourism (845-340-3566 or 1-800-DIAL-UCO), 10 Westbrook Lane, Kingston 12401; www.co.ulster.ny.us.

GETTING THERE
Ulster County is accessible from New York State (NYS) Thruway exits 18, 19, and 20, and in the southern section of the county from Route 17.

MEDICAL EMERGENCY
Benedictine Hospital (845-338-2500), 105 Mary's Avenue, Kingston. Dial 911 anywhere in the county for emergency assistance.

VILLAGES

Hurley. Take Route 209 south to Hurley and follow signs. Every July for one day only the historic stone houses are open to the public. **Hurley Stone House Day** (call Ulster County Tourism for information) is held the second Saturday in July; admission is charged for the tour. The vil-

One of the many stone houses on Huguenot Street in New Paltz

lage of Hurley was established in 1651 by Dutch and Huguenot settlers, who built wooden homes along Esopus Creek. After a short war
with the Esopus Indians, which resulted in the burning of much of the
settlement, the homes were replaced with stone structures, 25 of which
are still standing. Hurley was a hotbed of activity during the Revolution, serving as the state capital when Kingston was burned, a resting
place for troops, and a meeting place for spies. Later, Hurley was a stop
on the Underground Railroad, the escape route for slaves fleeing to
Canada, as well the home of abolitionist Sojourner Truth.

Visitors can still walk around the town and see the largest group of
stone houses still in use in the country. Although the homes are open
only one day a year, Hurley is worth a walk, and many of the buildings
have historic markers that tell something of their history and lore. Along
Main Street look for the **Polly Crispell Cottage** (built in 1735), which
was once used as a blacksmith shop. This house was also equipped with
a "witch catcher"—a set of iron spikes set into the chimney, presumably
to discourage witches (and birds) from flying in.

The **Jan Van Deusen House** became the temporary seat of New
York's government in 1777, and a secret room was used to store important documents. The outer door is set off by the work of an early Hurley
blacksmith, and a date stone is visible. Stop in at the **Van Deusen Antiques Shop,** which is now located in the back of the house.

Also on Main Street: the **Dumond House,** which was used to confine a convicted British spy before he was hanged from an apple tree across the road; the **Parsonage,** built in 1790; and the **Elmendorf House** (once the Half Moon Tavern), built in the late 1600s. A burial ground can be found between the Crispell and Elmendorf buildings. If you drive west on Main Street, follow the Hurley Avenue Extension and you will see several more stone buildings.

A corn festival, held in mid-August, celebrates the local sweet corn industry. Held on the grounds of the Hurley Reformed Church, the festival offers lots of crafts and lots of corn. Fresh ears of corn by the thousands are dished up with butter. There is corn chowder, corn bread with honey, entertainment, and good fellowship.

Woodstock. The town of Woodstock has long attracted creative people. Home to farmers and quarrymen for two centuries, the hamlet saw new changes in the spring of 1902, when Ralph Radcliffe Whitehead, an Englishman schooled in the theories of John Ruskin, was searching for a place where an arts colony could be organized. With two friends as partners, Whitehead bought seven lush farms and formed a community called Byrdcliffe (a combination of his and his wife's names). Workshops for metalworkers, potters, and weavers were soon built, and over the years the colony has continued to attract artists and craftspeople. During the 1930s folksingers discovered Woodstock; later the town became a haven for beatniks, and then talents like Pete Seeger, Bob Dylan, Joan Baez, and Peter, Paul, and Mary discovered the inspiration Woodstock was famous for. In 1969 a concert actually held nearly 50 miles away on a farm in Bethel (Sullivan County) made Woodstock a legend in the world of rock music.

Today the sometimes eccentric but never dull town is still a gathering place for talent of all types. The surrounding mountains create a dramatic backdrop for local galleries and shops. Woodstock's main thoroughfare is Mill Hill Road, which eventually becomes Tinker Street (according to legend, a tinker's wagon sank into the spring mud here, and the horse's harness bells can still be heard on quiet days). Just about everything in town can be reached by an easy walk. For parking, try the lots on Rock City Road or Tannery Brook Road. There is also a municipal lot near the town offices; watch for signs.

Kids will love **Woodstock Wonderworks,** an amazing playground designed by the town's kids themselves and built, under the guidance of an award-winning company, by the parents, youngsters, and townspeople. And if you get tired, sit on the village green and watch the colorful parade of people go by.

ART GALLERIES

Anyone interested in the the arts should leave a couple of hours in the afternoon free to drive to the following galleries and points of interest.

In the uptown area, don't miss the **Coffey Gallery** (845-339-6109), 330 Wall Street, open Tuesday through Saturday, 11–5, which has a new exhibition of paintings or sculpture every month. **The Art Society of Kingston (A.S.K. Gallery)** (845-338-0331), 37 North Front Street, 2nd floor, features the work of local artists. Just next door, also on the 2nd floor, is **Up Front Art** (845-246-2166), 35B North Front Street, open Friday through Sunday from noon–5.

In the Rondout area of the city, make sure to stop at **Donskoj & Co.** (845-338-8473), 93 Broadway, open Friday and Saturday from 1–6. A few doors down the street is the **Deep Listening Space** (845-339-6858), 75 Broadway, open weekends 1–5 or by appointment on weekdays. The **Tenshi Gallery** (845-339-3853) at 27 Broadway is open Monday and Thursday, noon–5; Saturday and Sunday, 11–7. The **Watermark Cargo Gallery** (845-338-8623), 111 Abeel Street, has ongoing exhibits of African art and artifacts; hours are by appointment.

Don't miss **The Center for Photography at Woodstock** (845-679-6337), 59 Tinker Street, Woodstock, open Wednesday through Sunday noon–5, which offers a changing selection of photography exhibits throughout the year. Participants include some of the most innovative photographers in the world, both established and new. Past shows have focused on local scenes, the nude, videos, and other topics.

The Woodstock Guild (845-679-2079), 34 Tinker Street, Woodstock. Open year-round, Friday through Sunday noon–5. Featuring changing exhibits of local artists.

A few doors away is the **Woodstock Artists' Association** (845-679-2940), 28 Tinker Street, Woodstock. Open year-round, Thursday through Monday noon–5, it offers a variety of work by the town's artists.

The Woodstock Framing Gallery (845-679-6003), 31 Mill Hill Road, Woodstock, is open daily 11–5. The emphasis in this lovely gallery is on contemporary art, and the majority of exhibitors are Hudson Valley artists.

Elena Zang Gallery (845-679-5432), 3671 Route 212, Shady, open daily 11–5, is located 4 miles outside Woodstock. This on-site pottery features hand-made porcelain and stoneware along with contemporary painting and the sculpture of many internationally known artists. From July through September there is an outdoor sculpture show in a beautiful garden setting. Visitors may walk around the grounds and enjoy the stream that runs through the property. Children are welcome. Open year-round.

A little up the road on Route 212 on the right is Harmati Lane, which is where **Genesis Studio/Gallery** (845-679-4542) is located. This gallery, open Thursday through Monday noon–5, features exotic creations inspired by the Middle East. Paintings and prints of the Holy Land, silver miniatures, Yemenite and Bedouin silver jewelry, replicas of ancient pottery, and ceramic dolls may be found here. Marble, stone, and steel sculptures are displayed along a path that encircles the pond. Visitors can take this walk and enjoy art in the outdoors.

The **James Cox Gallery** (845-679-4265), 4666 Route 212, Willow, is a few miles farther along Route 212 heading away from Woodstock toward Mount Tremper. This gallery is open daily 10–5. Cox is a veteran art dealer who relocated to Woodstock from Manhattan in 1990, and his gallery has changing exhibits of painting and sculpture.

TO SEE

Catskill Corners Festival Marketplace (845-688-5300), Route 28, Mount Tremper. Open year-round daily (except Tuesday) 10–7. Admission fee. This is it: **Kaleidoworld,** home of the *Guinness Book of World Records*–certified world's largest kaleioscope. Visitors actually walk into the 60-foot-high, silo-shaped room, where they experience a color and sound show unlike any other. Then step into the shops, which feature the largest selection of kaleidoscopes in the country, in addition to books, furniture, and home, nature, and children's gifts. The site also has the second largest kaleidoscope in the world, along with a John Burroughs nature park, art galleries, and The Lodge, a fantasy of what everyone thinks a mountain resort should look like (see *Lodging*). A don't-miss for the family.

Delaware and Hudson Canal Museum (845-687-9311). Take Route 213 to High Falls and turn right onto Mohonk Road. Open May through October; hours vary. Admission fee. This museum is dedicated to the history and lore of the great Delaware and Hudson Canal. Built in the early 19th century, the canal was used to ship coal from the mines in Pennsylvania to the factories of New York; later, cement was shipped south to be used in bridges and skyscrapers. The canal's designer was also responsible for the Erie Canal, and the locks, basins, and dams were engineering wonders of their era. In the museum visitors find a miniature setup of the canal and its workings, and they can get a sense of what life was like on the canal boats used for the 6-day trips. While you are at the museum, take the self-guided tour of the locks (located across the road); along the tour you will see examples of stonework, snubbing posts, weirs, locks, and loading ships.

Empire State Railway Museum (845-688-7501, Ulster & Delaware Railroad Station, Phoenicia (watch for signs from Main Street). Open weekends Memorial Day through Columbus Day, 11–4. Donation. This small museum offers excellent exhibits about railroads and life in the Catskill Mountains. Past shows have included photographs and artifacts related to the building of the reservoirs, tourism history, and railroads in the Catkills. The volunteer guides all love trains and their history.

Fred J. Johnston Museum (845-339-0720), 63 Main Street, Kingston. Open May through October, Saturday and Sunday 1–4; admission fee. For the lover of American decorative history and fine antiques, a stop here is mandatory. This extraordinary collection was assembled by

Johnston, a dealer and friend of Henry du Pont, who compared Johnston's furniture and decorative items to those found in du Pont's own museum, Winterthur. The house was built around 1812 for a prominent local attorney, who counted Washington Irving and Martin Van Buren among his friends and guests. Visitors today will enjoy the fine 18th- and 19th-century examples of furniture, porcelain, and needlework that fill the house, including examples by local cabinetmakers and artists like John Vanderlyn.

Overlook Observatory (845-246-4294), West Saugerties Road between Saugerties and Woodstock. Hours by appointment; fee charged for classes. Both home and scientific workshop to astronomer Bob Berman, the observatory offers visitors a guided tour of the night sky, with all its mysteries, quirks, and wonders, and outstanding instruments for viewing the heavens. Bob is a knowledgeable and enthusiastic guide.

A. J. Snyder Estate (845-658-9900), Route 213, Rosendale (watch for signs). Tours from May through October, Saturday, Sunday, and Wednesday 1–4 and by appointment. Admission fee. This estate sits directly across from the Delaware and Hudson Canal. The house is open for tours, and the carriage house, with its fine collection of more than 20 antique sleighs and carriages—some dating from the 1820s—is a must-see. Phaetons, wagons, and cutters are all here and in beautiful condition. There are also the ruins of old cement kilns on the property, the canal slip, and the Widow Jane Mine. Special events include concerts and plays; call for a schedule.

Tibetan Buddhist Monastery (845-679-5906, ext. 19). At the Woodstock village green turn onto Rock City Road (which becomes Meads Mountain Road); follow it for 2.6 miles to the top of the mountain. Admission fee. Group tours are offered Tuesday through Friday; call ahead for reservations. Monastery tours for individuals leave the bookstore Saturday and Sunday 1:30–3. Karma Triyana Dharmachakra Monastery is situated high above Woodstock and is worth a trip any time of year. Founded in 1978, the monastery combines traditional Tibetan architecture and design with Western construction. The main shrine room is 2,400 square feet and features one of the largest statues of Buddha in North America, while smaller shrines are decorated with traditional art. Be sure to see the bookstore, with its wide assortment of Himalayan gifts and books.

Trolley Museum (845-331-3399), 89 East Strand, Kingston; follow Broadway south to its end, turn left, and watch for signs. Open Saturday and Sunday, Memorial Day through Columbus Day, noon–5; open also on Friday in July and August. Admission fee. For anyone who remembers the ring of a trolley bell or the rolling ride of a self-propelled car, this museum offers lots of nostalgia. Housed in an old trolley shed along the Rondout, the museum offers displays and short rides on restored trolley cars.

Widmark Honey Farm (845-255-6400), Route 44/55 in Gardiner. Hours and times vary; call for a schedule and a listing of special events.

Admission fee (credited to any purchase). The farm offers bears and honey, but here the bears have been raised practically as family pets, and they will entertain you with their wrestling, climbing, and active antics. A perfect outing for anyone with small children; adults will also enjoy the self-guided apiary tours and the honey tastings. There is a retail shop with local farm goods and, of course, many varieties of honey.

HISTORIC HOMES

Bevier House (845-338-5614), 6 miles south of Kingston on Route 209. Open June through September, Wednesday through Sunday 1–5. Admission fee. Built in the late 1680s, this stone house now serves as headquarters of the Ulster County Historical Society, and it is a treasure trove of odd collections and memorabilia. Once a single-story Dutch farmhouse, much of the present structure was added during the last three centuries. Throughout the house you will see fine Hudson Valley Dutch and Victorian furniture, in addition to the tool and kitchenware collections, ceramic pottery from an early factory in Poughkeepsie, portraits, and decorative accessories. The Bevier House is not a very formal museum, and it has a great old-fashioned feel to it.

Huguenot Street's Stone Houses (845-255-1660 or 255-1889), located on Stone House Street, off Route 32 in New Paltz. The street is open year-round; tours are offered late May through September, Wednesday through Sunday 9–4. Admission fee; Deyo Hall and Grimm Gallery are free. In 1677 a group of 12 Huguenot men purchased almost 40,000 acres of land from the Esopus Indians and began the settlement that was referred to as "die Pfalz," after an area in the Rhineland Palatinate. By 1692 the original log huts were being replaced by stone houses, several of which still stand today as a result of the efforts of the Huguenot Historical Society. A trip to New Paltz offers a unique chance to see what life was like three centuries ago in upper-middle-class homes. The walking tour begins with **Deyo Hall** and **Grimm Gallery,** which were, respectively, a glass factory and a private home before they were combined into an orientation center. Visitors here will see a large collection of local artifacts, including furniture, costumes, and portraits.

All the buildings are owned by the society, and many still have their original furnishings. At the **Abraham Hasbrouck House** (1692) the dark rooms include a cellar-kitchen, which was the heart of village social life, and a built-in Dutch bed. Other houses of the period include the **Bevier-Elting House,** distinguished by a long well sweep and covered walk for the convenience of the ladies; the **Freer House,** with its mow door, which made it easier to move provisions into the attic; and the **Dubois Fort,** which is reputed to be haunted by a headless lady. Possibly the most interesting house is the **Jean Hasbrouck House,** which once served as a store and tavern. Downstairs you'll find a bar and grill (with the real grill, which could be pulled down to protect the bottles from thieves), as well as a jambless fireplace with its curtainlike decorations; upstairs there is a massive brick chimney, the only one of

Gomez Mill House, the oldest surviving Jewish homestead in North America

JOSEPH PUGLISI

its type in the United States. Several other buildings are also open to the public, including the reconstructed **French Church,** the Federal-style **LeFevre House,** and the **Deyo House,** a remodeled 17th-century home. There are two tours; the longer one may not be suitable for children, but it shouldn't be missed by anyone interested in history.

The **Huguenot Path** is a self-guided tour along the river and Huguenot Street; call 845-255-0100 for a brochure and guide.

Hurley Patentee Manor (845-331-5414). Take Route 209 south to Hurley; follow signs to Old Route 209 and the manor house. Summer hours; call for tour information. Admission fee. This National Historic Landmark is a combination of a Dutch cottage, built in 1696, and a 1745 Georgian manor house. The manor was the center of the Hurley Patent, a 96,000-acre land grant that included the land between Woodstock and New Paltz but that today has been reduced to the 5 acres surrounding the house. The house is privately owned and has been restored to its original condition. The owners display many fine antiques from the 17th to the 19th centuries, including a chair once owned by Sir William Johnston and a desk with a secret drawer. The basement of the house has one of the few indoor animal pens still in existence and is also the display area for Hurley Patentee Lighting, a company that crafts handwrought reproduction lighting fixtures. The owners are friendly and well versed in local history, so don't miss out on their tour. Children will enjoy the attic museum in particular.

Locust Lawn, Terwilliger House, Little Wings Wildlife Sanctuary (845-255-1660 or 255-1889), Route 32, outside Gardiner. Open May through September, Wednesday through Sunday 9:30–4. Admission fee. These three sites are within minutes of each other, and all are administered by the Huguenot Historical Society of New Paltz. Locust Lawn, a Federal-style mansion, was designed by a Newburgh architect and built in 1814 for Col. Josiah Hasbrouck, a Revolutionary War veteran. The elegant white Federal-period mansion has a magnificent three-story central hall and still houses a fine collection of 18th- and 19th-century furniture and decorative arts, as well as several portraits by the American folk painter Ammi Phillips. Since Locust Lawn remained in the Hasbrouck family until the 1950s, when it was donated to the society, many of its original furnishings remain. Also on the site are outbuildings typical of a farm of that era, and visitors can see the carriage house, smokehouse, and slaughterhouse. One rare artifact found here is the great oxcart that was used to transport supplies to the beleaguered army at Valley Forge.

Down the road from Locust Lawn stands the **Terwilliger House,** built in 1738 and left almost untouched over the last two and a half centuries. This is a fine example of the architectural style used by the area's Dutch and French Huguenot settlers. Built of stone, with a center hall and great fireplace, the house has been furnished in the style of the era. Outside, visitors may follow a cleared path over Plattekill Brook to a small graveyard where family members and their slaves were buried.

In the **Little Wings Wildlife Sanctuary** there are several nature trails to be explored, and more than 30 species of birds have been sighted on and near the refuge's pond. The magnificent wildflower garden is especially lovely in spring, when lady's slippers, Dutchman's breeches, and wake-robin bloom. Bring a picnic lunch and enjoy the afternoon.

HISTORIC SITES

Gomez Mill House (845-236-3126), Mill House Road, Marlboro. Open Wednesday, Saturday, and Sunday 10–4; Thursday and Friday by appointment. From November through April open by appointment only. Admission fee. This site offers visitors a chance to view the oldest surviving Jewish homestead in North America as well as a unique cultural landmark. Built in 1714 as a sawmill and trading post, the site was named after the Gomez family, which supplied traders roving the upstate New York wilderness. Later owners were farmers, boatmen, members of Continental Army, writers, and painters; Dard Hunter (1913–1919) was a paper-mill owner whose mill is still in working condition

The Mohonk Mountain House

(you can buy handmade paper in the gift shop). The site has also served as a home, inn, and school, and the buildings interpret the many personalities who have lived and worked there.

Hudson River Maritime Museum and Rondout Landing (845-338-0071), located at the foot of Broadway in Kingston. Open daily, except Tuesday, May through October 11–5; call for a special-events schedule. Admission fee. For almost two centuries, the Hudson River was a major water highway between New York City and Albany. One of the ports of call along the way was the Rondout Landing in Kingston, once a bustling area of boatyards and rigging lofts that echoed with steam whistles and brass ships' bells. But when shipping on the Hudson fell into decline, so did the fortunes of the Rondout. Then, in 1980, the Hudson River Maritime Museum was opened with the goal of preserving the heritage of the river. The museum has since restored several riverside buildings as well as several historic vessels, and visitors can now see a working part of the Hudson's legacy. There is an exhibit hall that features shows on marine history. Outside there is an ever-changing display of river vessels, including the 1899 steam tug *Mathilda* and the cruise boat *Indy 7*. Visitors to the landing have also included the presidential yacht *Sequoia* and the sailing ships *Clearwater* and *Woody Guthrie*. Special weekend festivals are held throughout the year, including a Harvest Festival in October, a Shad Festival in May, sailing regattas and gatherings of antique wooden boats, and tours to the **Rondout Lighthouse.** This satellite museum is open from May through October, and offers visitors a glimpse into a way of life that once was typical of Hudson River lighthouse keepers and their families.

At the Saugerties Lighthouse visitors can enjoy the Ruth Glunt Nature Preserve and at low tide walk out to the historic site. Open April through November, weekends and holidays 2–5; follow Main Street to its end, turn right, and follow the road to the preserve parking. The site is also accessible by boat from the Route 9W boat-launch area.

Kingston Urban Cultural Park Visitors Center (845-331-7517 or 1-800-331-1518), 308 Clinton Avenue, Kingston. Open daily 11–5 May through October; from November through April open Monday through Friday 1–5; call for tour information. Free. New York State has designated Urban Cultural Parks as the interpreters of urban settings of particular historic interest; Kingston's is known for its importance in the history of transportation. The center is located in the Stockade area (once surrounded by walls of tree trunks 13 feet high) and offers orientation displays that cover Kingston from 17th-century Dutch settlement to the present. Directions for self-guided walking tours are available, and guided tours may be arranged by appointment. While uptown, you may also want to stop by the **Volunteer Firemen's Hall and Museum,** 265 Fair Street, open May through October, Friday and Saturday 10–4. The museum is in an old firehouse where antique fire apparatus, memorabilia, and period furniture are on display.

Mohonk Mountain House (845-255-1000), 6 miles west of New Paltz. Take Route 299 west over the Wallkill River, turn right at the MOHONK sign, then bear left and follow the road to the gate. Open year-round; call ahead for skiing and hiking information and special-events weekends. A use fee is charged. When Alfred and Albert Smiley built this resort in 1869, they were determined to preserve the surrounding environment and offer gracious accommodations to visitors from the city. Guests here could hike the nearby Shawangunks, take a carriage ride around the manicured grounds, or enjoy the carefully tended flower beds. There was a lake for ice skating, as well as croquet lawns; the hotel itself was furnished with the best of the Victorian era: acres of polished oak paneling and floors, hidden conversation nooks, and homey, overstuffed furniture. Mohonk has endured the last century with timeless grace, and today visitors will find many things unchanged. The resort is still dedicated to preserving the natural world, and the gardens have won awards for their beauty. Mohonk sits next to a trout-stocked lake that becomes the focus of special winter carnival weekends. There is a stone tower atop the mountain that offers a six-state view on sunny days. Hikers, birders, horseback riders, and cross-country skiers will find Mohonk unequaled. Day visitors are welcome, but it takes more than a day even to sample all of the surprises at Mohonk; plan at least a long weekend if possible.

JOSEPH PUGLISI

The historic Old Dutch Church in the uptown area of Kingston dates back to 1659.

Old Dutch Church (845-338-6759), 272 Wall Street in the uptown area of Kingston. Hours vary; visitors must call ahead for tours. Free. Organized in 1659, the Reformed Protestant Dutch Church of Kingston has served the people of the area continuously ever since. The present building was built in 1852; its bluestone exterior is in the Renaissance

Revival style, and the windows were made in the Tiffany studios. Local tradition once held that the bell was cast from silver and copper items donated by the congregation, and that one of the steeples (from an earlier church that stood on the site) may have been haunted by a goblin. Inside, you will see bronze statues as well as artifacts from the 1600s onward. Take time to walk through the churchyard and view the fine examples of early gravestone art (Gov. De Witt Clinton's gravesite is located here). In spring thousands of yellow and red tulips planted in honor of the Netherlands line the church walks.

Opus 40 and **The Quarryman's Museum** (845-246-3400). Follow Route 212 west from Saugerties; Opus 40 is located on Fite Road, off Glasco Turnpike. Open May through October, Friday and Saturday 10–4; Sunday and holiday Mondays noon–5. Admission fee. In 1938 artist Harvey Fite's bluestone quarry outside Saugerties was merely the source of material for his sculpture. But as work on the individual pieces progressed, Fite realized that the terraces and steps he had created as a backdrop for the sculpture had themselves become the focus of his work. Naming the site Opus 40 because he believed it would take 40 years to complete, Fite set about creating a vast environmental work that would eventually contain 6 acres of steps, levels, fountains, pools, and paths. Each of the hundreds of thousands of bluestone pieces was hand cut and fitted, and the 9-ton central monolith was lifted into place with a boom and winches. Today Opus 40 is open to the public as an environmental sculpture and concert site. Fite, who had studied theology and law and worked as an actor and teacher, also built a museum to house his collection of quarrymen's tools and artifacts. The museum offers a rare glimpse into a lost way of life.

Senate House (845-338-2786), 312 Fair Street, Kingston. Open April through October, Wednesday through Saturday 10–5, Sunday 1–5. Call ahead for a special-events schedule. Admission fee. When the New York State government was forced to leave New York City during the Revolution, it sought safety upstate. The house in which the men met was built in the 17th century by a Dutch settler, Wessel Ten Broeck, and was partially burned by the British in 1777. After numerous additions and changes to the building, the house has been restored to reflect its part in history. Visitors can see several rooms, including the kitchen with its kitchenware and huge fireplace, and the meeting room in which the state constitution was hammered out. There is a special tour of the lovely rose garden in June, when the flowers are in full bloom. A second building on the site, the **Loughran House,** was added in 1927, and it houses a museum with historic displays and changing exhibits that reflect the story of Kingston. One room is given over to the works of John Vanderlyn, a Kingston native who was considered one of the finest painters of 19th-century America. This site offers special events including concerts, slide shows, and lectures throughout the year; a Dutch Christmas is also celebrated.

Visitors to the Senate House in Kingston, the state's first capitol, can tour this room where New York's first Senate met on September 9, 1777.

SCENIC DRIVES

Ulster County has hundreds of miles of well-maintained roads, coupled with some of the most spectacular scenery in the Hudson Valley. It doesn't matter if you travel in autumn, with all the riotous color, or in winter, with its icy beauty—Ulster will always surprise.

For a drive that offers history as well as scenery, start at **Kingston** (exit 19 off the NYS Thruway) and go south along **Route 209.** This is one of the oldest roads in America—the Old Mine Road, which was a trading route between upstate New York and Pennsylvania in the 17th century. As you pass by Hurley, Marbletown, and Stone Ridge, you will see acres of fields planted with sweet corn, the area's largest agricultural crop. The architectural styles of the homes range from Dutch stone to late Victorian, and you'll see many farm stands in summer and autumn. At Route 213 head east through High Falls, along the old Delaware and Hudson Canal. Stop in at the High Falls Co-op if you like natural foods, or just continue down the road that follows the canal. At Route 32 you can head south into New Paltz and explore the old stone houses or head north back to Kingston.

For a second scenic route from **Kingston** take **Route 9W** south along the Hudson River. At West Park you may want to follow the signs to Slabsides, once the writing retreat of naturalist John Burroughs; it's on your right, down across the railroad tracks (park at the bottom of the hill and walk up). Back on Route 9W, continue south and take Route 299 west through New Paltz, then follow Route 44/55 for some fine overlook sites. At Route 209 head back north past old Dutch farms and stone houses to Kingston.

From Kingston you can also follow Route 28 to Route 28A around the **Ashokan Reservoir,** a special treat in autumn. Follow the signs to the pump station and walk around the fountain or have a picnic—it is a fairly uncrowded, undiscovered area. However, since New York City watches its watershed area very, very carefully, be wary of where you park, hike, or stop. The NO PARKING and NO STOPPING signs are serious.

For an unusual drive, take the Hudson Valley Pottery Trail to studios in Accord, High Falls, and Stone Ridge. Call 845-687-0636 for a map brochure.

You can also take a self-guided driving tour through three centuries of European settlement in the Kingston area. Call 1-800-331-1518 for a guide, or pick one up at the exit 19 Thruway kiosk. The tour covers the Rondout, Uptown, and Stockade areas of Kingston, which are filled with history and homes dating back to the 17th century and Dutch "ownership." What's unique about this tour is that you can tune your car radio to the suggested frequencies and drive while you listen to the narratives!

WINERIES

The Hudson Valley has become an important center of wine production in New York, and visitors are welcome to stop at many of Ulster County's wineries. They range in size from tiny "boutique" wineries to full-sized vineyards complete with restaurants, bottling plants, and cellars. Wherever you go, however, you will find people who love their work and are willing to share their expertise and wines with you. Some of the vintners offer formal guided tours; others just have a showroom and tasting area. You may want to call before you go—there are special events, concerts, and tours throughout the season, and hours may change when the harvest begins. Most of the sites are free, as are the tastings, but there may be admission charged to special events.

Adair Vineyards (845-255-1377), Allhusen Road, New Paltz. Open daily May through December, 11–6. The vineyard has an old Dutch barn and offers tastings, tours, and picnics. The picture-perfect Ulster site looks as if unchanged through the centuries.

Baldwin Vineyards (845-744-2226), Hardenburgh Estate, Pine Bush, is located on a 200-year-old estate where more than 40 acres of pastures, vineyards, and woodlands are open for strolling. Open daily June through October, weekends in winter, and by appointment. Award-winning wines can be tasted (including a strawberry-flavored wine that tastes like summer), and lunch is served in a gourmet café overlooking the vineyards.

Benmarl Wine Company (845-236-4265), 156 Highland Avenue, off Route 9W south of Marlboro. Open daily year-round noon–5. Visitors can enjoy guided tours, wine tastings, a stop at the gallery—the founder was an illustrator—or lunch in the **Bistro,** serving food à la France.

Established in the early 19th century, the winery overlooks the Hudson River.

Brimstone Hill Vineyard (845-744-2231), Brimstone Hill Road, Pine Bush. Open year-round, but call for hours; tours and tastings available May through October. French-style wines are the specialty, and the wineshop is also open for browsing.

Regent Champagne Cellars (845-691-7296), 200 Blue Point Road, Highland. Open weekends year-round, daily from March through December. Champagnes and cheese are offered along with tastings, and special events include dances, tours, Oktoberfest, Christmas festivals, and concerts.

Rivendell Winery (845-255-2494), 714 Albany Post Road, New Paltz, specializes in chardonnay and is open every day, rain or shine, for tours and tastings. There are special events throughout the summer. There's also a retail shop on-site. Call for detailed directions and an events schedule.

Whitecliff Vineyard & Winery (845-255-4613), 331 McKinstry Road, Gardiner, is the newest vineyard in the region and produces European-style wines.

Windsor Vineyards (845-236-4440), 104 Western Avenue, Marlboro. The wineshop and tasting room are open year-round here. New York and California wines and champagnes are stocked.

Woodstock Brewing Company (845-331-2810), 20 St. James Street, Kingston. Open year-round; call for hours. Beer lovers will want to stop by, tour this microbrewery, and sample one of the few beers made in the Hudson Valley. Hudson Lager, Big Indian Porter, and other fine-tasting brews are produced here, and visitors will learn a lot about the science and art of good beer.

Smaller wineries that offer premium wines, tastings, and tours include **El Paso Winery** (845-331-8642), Route 9W, Ulster Park; **Magnanini Farm Winery** (845-895-2767), 501 Strawridge Road, Wallkill; and **West Park Wine Cellars** (845-384-6709), Burroughs Drive, West Park. This last winery produces fine chardonnays, and visitors can enjoy using a lovely picnic area overlooking the Hudson River Valley.

TO DO

BICYCLING

Mountain bikes can be rented at **Overlook Mountain Bikes** (845-679-2122), 93 Tinker Street, Woodstock. In New Paltz try **Cycle Path** (845-255-8723), 138 Main Street; and **Catskill Mountain Bicycle Shop** (845-255-3859), 3 Church Street.

The Wallkill Valley Rail Trail is 12.2 miles of linear park between the New Paltz–Rosendale and the Gardiner–Shawangunk town lines. In the late 19th century the Wallkill Valley Railroad transported produce and dairy products from Ulster County to New York City. It also served

JOSEPH PUGLISI

A bridge over the Wallkill River on the 12-mile Wallkill Valley Rail Trail in New Paltz

as a commuter railroad. In 1977 the railroad took its last freight run. In 1983 all the ties and rails were removed and community volunteers cleared the trail. The rail trail officially opened to the public for recreational use in 1993. Enjoy a walk, jog, or bike ride along this scenic trail, maintained and managed by volunteers. Motorized vehicles are prohibited, except for those used by handicapped persons. Open dawn to dusk. Write to the WVRT Association, Inc., P.O. Box 1048, New Paltz, NY 12561 for a brochure.

BOAT CRUISES

The Hudson runs the length of Ulster County, and visitors can select from several companies that cruise the river. Even if you don't know port from starboard, there are tours that take all the work but none of the fun out of a river trip. One warning: It can be very breezy and cool out on the river; bring a hat, scarf, and sweater unless the day is blazing hot.

The Rondout waterfront at the end of Broadway in Kingston

Great Hudson Sailing Center (845-338-1557), Rondout Landing, Kingston, is open from mid-May through October and offers day and sunset sailings with wine and cheese.

The Rip Van Winkle (845-255-6515; 255-6618 for credit card orders only), at Rondout Landing, Kingston, offers cruises on a roomy ship that features plenty of seating, rest rooms, and a snack bar. Because the river tends to be less choppy than the ocean, the ride is smooth and pleasant. Cruise season is May through October, weather permitting, and music is provided on some trips. Day cruises to West Point and back depart daily.

Hudson Rondout Cruises (845-338-6515), Rondout Landing, Kingston, is the perfect choice if you are in the mood for a short trip. The boat sails to the **Kingston Lighthouse,** where passengers disembark for a tour, then continues south to the **Esopus Meadows Lighthouse.** Cruises run daily June through October, with special events like dinner and brunch sailings.

North River Cruises (845-679-8205), Rondout Landing, Kingston, is run by Capt. John Cutten. His boat, the *Teal,* fitted with rich wood and brass, takes you back to a time of genteel river travel but offers all the modern amenities. Available for private charters and corporate parties.

FISHING

Ulster County offers fishing enthusiasts a chance to try their luck in scores of streams, a reservoir, and the great Hudson River. The waters are well stocked with a variety of fish—trout, bass, pike, pickerel, and perch are some of the more popular catches. Fishing areas are well marked, and New York State licenses are required, as are reservoir permits. Call the **Department of Environmental Conservation** (845-255-5453), New Paltz, for information.

Some of the better-known fishing streams in Ulster County include Esopus Creek (access points along Route 28, west of Kingston), Rondout Creek (access point on Route 209, south of Kingston), Plattekill Creek (access near Route 32 in Saugerties), and the Sawkill (access along Route 375 in Woodstock). Most of the main access points are indicated by brown-and-yellow state signs; many also have parking areas. If you are uncertain about the stream, ask; otherwise, you may find yourself on the receiving end of a heavy fine. Holders of reservoir permits will want to try the Ashokan Reservoir (Route 28A, west of Kingston), with 40 miles of shoreline and trout, walleye, and bass lurking beneath the surface. The Kingston City Reservoir requires a city permit for fishing, but it is worth the extra effort.

GOLF

Ulster County golf courses can be by turns dramatic, relaxing, and colorful, and the areas that offer golf cater to a wide range of skills and interests. Hotel courses are usually open to the public, but it is recommended that you call ahead, since they schedule special events and competitions.

In Ellenville **The Nevele Grand Golf Course** (845-647-6000), Route 209; and the **Shawangunk Country Club** (845-647-6090), Leurnkill Road, have championship golfing.

Mohonk Mountain House (845-255-1000), New Paltz, maintains lovely greens and fairways high above the valley (see *To See—Historic Sites*).

New Paltz Golf Course (845-255-8282), 215 Huguenot Street, New Paltz.

Kingston is home to **Green Acres Golf Course** (845-331-2283), Harwich Street; **Jeto's Miniature Golf and Driving Range** (845-331-2545), Sawkill Road; and the **Ascot Driving Range** (845-339-6395), Esopus Avenue.

HANG GLIDING

Mountain Wings Hang Gliding Center (845-647-3377), 150 Canal Street, Ellenville, features hang gliders and ultralights.

HIKING

Ulster County has some of the best hiking in the Hudson Valley, with views that go on for miles and trails that range from an easy walk to a hard day's climb. The following suggestions for afternoon or day hikes provide magnificent vistas, but it is recommended that you use maps, available locally, in order to make your hike as safe as possible.

Belleayre Mountain (845-254-5600), in Highmount, has a marked cross-country ski trail that provides a nice walk in the woods, and a hike to the summit will reveal a sweep of mountains below.

Fly-fishing on Esopus Creek near Shandaken

Frost Valley YMCA and Conference Center, Route 47 from Route 28 in Big Indian, has hundreds of acres to explore.

For a variety of walks in the woods on nicely graded trails, don't overlook **Mohonk Mountain House,** Mountain Rest Road, New Paltz; and **Minnewaska State Park** (845-255-0752), Route 44/55, New Paltz. Both are day use only and charge a fee. The Shawangunk trails found at both sites are excellent, although somewhat crowded on summer weekends. Mohonk has 128 miles of paths and carriage roads to hike, and there are some first-rate spots for rock climbing as well (see *Rock Climbing*).

Overlook Mountain, in Woodstock, is a moderate walk up a graded roadbed. From Tinker Street at the village green take Rock City Road to Meads Mountain Road, which leads to the trailhead, just across from the Tibetan monastery (see *To See*). The summit takes about an hour to reach, depending on how fast you travel the 2-mile ascent. You will pass the ruins of the Overlook Mountain House on the way up and find a lookout tower and picnic tables at the top; the view of the valley and river is incomparable.

Vernooy Kill Falls in Kerhonkson can be reached by taking Route 209 to Lower Cherrytown Road, then bearing right and continuing 5 miles to Upper Cherrytown Road. In another 3 miles you'll see the parking lot on the right and the trailhead on the left. The trail is just over 3¹/₂ miles up and back.

With lots of back roads to explore, walkers might enjoy a trek along Route 212 in Woodstock. Start in the center of town and travel west toward Bearsville or along parts of Route 209 near Stone Ridge (park and begin in town). Hurley, on Route 209 south of Kingston, also has pretty streets and byways, with many historic homes along the way. Although more a walk than a hike, the **Huguenot Path** is a self-guided tour along the river and Huguenot Street; call 845-255-0100 for a brochure and guide.

See the **Wallkill Valley Rail Trail** under *Biking*.

PICK-YOUR-OWN FARMS

For a listing of farms and orchards that offer pick-your-own apples, pumpkins, berries, and other produce, see "Farm Stands and Pick-Your-Own Farms" under *Selective Shopping*.

ROCK CLIMBING

Those who want to learn rock climbing (a special sport in the Shawangunks region) should contact **High Angle Adventures** (845-658-9811 or 1-800 777-2546), New Paltz, which has full-day instruction with some of the best climbers in the East; and Jim Munson at **Mountain Skills** (845-687-9643), Stone Ridge, where instruction and guided climbs can be arranged. At **The Inner Wall** (845-255-ROCK), Eckerd's Plaza, Main Street, New Paltz, you will find an indoor rock climbing gym that is open year-round.

TUBING

Very popular in the area, tubing isn't so much a sport as it is a leisurely pursuit. It doesn't take any special skills and can be done by just about anyone. All you do is rent a huge, black inner tube, put it in the water, and hop on for rides that last anywhere from 1 to 3 hours. Maneuvering can be done with your hands, and proper tubing attire consists of shorts and a T-shirt, or a bathing suit, with old sneakers. A life jacket is recommended for those who are not strong swimmers. Although most of the waters are not very deep, they are cold and the currents can be swift. The tubing season runs from the first warm weather until the last— somewhere between late May and early September. You will have to leave a security deposit for the tubes, and rental does not include extras like life jackets or "tube seats," which keep you from bumping along the rocky bottom; some sites will arrange to transport you back after the trip. Tubes and gear, including helmets, may be rented at **F-S Tube and Raft Rental** (845-688-7633), Main Street, Phoenicia; **Town Tinker Tube Rental** (845-688-5553), the granddaddy of tubing services, with a well-stocked headquarters at Bridge Street, Phoenicia; and **Rubber Ducky Tube Rental** (845-688-7877), just off Route 28, at the Hayloft Restaurant, Shandaken.

A trailhead off Route 214, between Phoenicia and Hunter

WINTER SPORTS

CROSS-COUNTRY SKIING

Ulster is a good place for cross-country enthusiasts. When valleys, meadows, and fields receive a cover of snow, new trails are broken and old ones rediscovered. **Belleayre Mountain** (see *Downhill Skiing*) has several marked, ungroomed trails that cover 4 miles. They follow the old Ulster and Delaware Turnpike and even pass an old family cemetery. Lessons are available (call 845-254-5600 to schedule), and rentals are offered just across the road from the trails. There is no fee and no charge for parking or use of the lodge. Expert "skinny skiers" can purchase lift tickets and use the mountains.

Frost Valley YMCA. Take Route 28 in Oliverea to Route 47 and go 15 miles. Twenty miles of groomed trails wind in and out of lovely forests and alongside streams. The trails are color-coded, and there is a warming hut. A small use fee is charged; call for lesson and rental information.

Lake Minnewaska, Route 44/55 near New Paltz, has 150 miles of cross-country trails for everyone, from novices to advanced skiers.

Mohonk Mountain House (845-255-1000), in New Paltz, has 35 miles of carriage-road trails opening onto views of distant mountain ridges, glens, and valleys. Trails are color-coded and mapped, and there is a use fee. Rentals and refreshment sites available; call before you go.

Williams Lake Hotel (845-658-3101), Rosendale, has excellent cross-country skiing for the beginner and for skiers with young children. Great lake views.

DOWNHILL SKIING

Downhill skiing in Ulster County offers the best of all worlds: country surroundings and challenging slopes that are convenient to cities like Albany and New York.

Belleayre Mountain (845-254-5600) is the largest downhill ski area in Ulster; follow Route 28 west from Kingston to Highmount, at the western edge of the county. Open daily Thanksgiving through March, 9–4. Owned by New York State, Belleayre has a top elevation of 3,365 feet and full snowmaking capabilities, and is the only ski area in the state that has a natural division: The upper mountain is for intermediate and expert skiers; the lower mountain is for beginners and intermediates. There is plenty of free parking, and a courtesy shuttle runs all day. At the upper mountain 16 trails are serviced by snowmaking equipment, triple and double chairlifts; new equipment makes the wait shorter and gets you to the slopes more quickly. Runs range from intermediate to extreme expert. For those who want even more of a challenge, there is a complete racing program, including clinics, competitions, and coin-operated starting gates. The ski school at Belleayre is outstanding, with patient, capable instructors who can teach the youngest beginner or help advanced experts polish their skills. Snowboards are allowed on certain trails (rentals, sales, and instruction are available), and there are special events all season. The Upper Lodge is a huge, welcoming log building with a fieldstone fireplace, bar, ski shop, nursery, cafeteria, lounge area, and outside deck; the Lower Lodge has a cafeteria and ski shop. Both offer rental equipment, rest rooms, and locker areas. Belleayre has great children's programs (including the SKIwee program), and a fully equipped nursery; call for reservations before you go. It also sponsors inexpensive learn-to-ski days, ski clubs, special events, and other activities throughout the season, and it's very family and service oriented.

ICE SKATING

Town of Saugerties Kiwanis Ice Arena (845-246-2591, 845-246-5890), Washington Avenue Extension and Small World Way, Saugerties. Open fron early November through March. This enclosed ice skating rink, while not heated, is a great place to skate every day from approximately 8:30–6. There are a series of 1½-sessions and the cost for adults is only $3.00; $1.00 for students; 5 and under skate for free. Hours vary, so call

View of Trapps from Mohonk

for a schedule. Rental skates are available and there is a heated changing area and bathroom facilities.

The Nevele Grande Ice Rink (800-647-6000), Ellenville. This rink is open to the public from Thanksgiving through March. For those who love skating outdoors, this covered rink is the place to go. Hours vary, so make sure to call for the schedule. There are usually two sessions: 10 AM–1 PM and 2–5 PM. The cost is $7.00, but if you take a lesson with Heidi Graf, an excellent instructor who has been at the hotel for decades, that fee is waived. Rental skates are available and if you have your own skates, they do a first-rate job of sharpening the blades.

GREEN SPACE

Ice Caves, Route 52, Ellenville. Permits are required to visit the Ice Caves area north of High Point, west of the High Point Carriageway and south of the Smiley Road. Groups visiting the Ice Caves must be limited to no more than 12 people. The area is environmentally sensitive, and The Nature Conservancy asks that hikers take care to stay on the trails. To reduce any potentially damaging impact to the trail area, particularly to delicate mosses, hike in early spring when there is still a protective snowpack. To obtain a permit contact The Nature Conservancy, Eastern New York Chapter, 200 Broadway, 3rd floor, Troy, NY 12180 (518-272-0195).

Kingston Point Beach and Hudson River Landing Park (845-679-5297). Take Broadway to the end, turn left, and follow East Strand (which becomes North Street) 1 mile to the park. The beach is open year-round, dawn to dusk. Park hours vary with special events, and admission is charged. Kingston Point Beach offers a nice view of the river; there is swimming in summer and a small playground, and visitors can watch sailboards and sailboats at play. The Hudson River Landing Park, a privately owned site on the river, hosts special events such as flea markets and country fairs year-round.

Minnewaska State Park (845-255-0752), Route 44/55 (P.O. Box 893), New Paltz. Open daily from 9 AM until dusk most of the year. Hours are adjusted seasonally and posted each day at the entrance. Located on the dramatic Shawangunk Mountain Ridge, this park offers spectacular mountain views, waterfalls, and meadows. Lake Minnewaska itself is surrounded by a network of woodland trails and carriageways that are excellent for hiking, horseback riding, and cross-country skiing. The paved carriageways make for fine biking. You can take a leisurely 2-mile walk around the lake, which is a nice way to get oriented in this large park. Swimming is permitted at the sandy beach area, and there is a lifeguard on duty. Another good place to swim in the park is Lake Awosting, approximately a 3-mile walk from the entrance. Minnewaska is a day-use area only; no camping is permitted. There are several fine places to picnic, some with raised portable grills. Those who visit in November and December should be aware that hunting is permitted in certain outlying areas of the park.

The Mohonk Preserve (845-255-0919 or 255-1000), Mountain Rest Road, New Paltz. Open daily year-round, dawn to dusk. Admission fee. This 5,600-acre nature preserve is owned and operated by a private nonprofit environmental organization. It surrounds 2,000 acres owned by the Mohonk Mountain House resort. From the visitors center 26 miles of hiking trails and 19 miles of wider carriage roads stretch out in all directions. Maps are available. The trails are ideal for cross-country skiing and walking. From the tower at Sky Top, the highest point along the trails (1,500 feet above sea level), you can see six states on a clear day (New York, New Jersey, Pennsylvania, Connecticut, Massachusetts, and Vermont). Sky Top is about 2$\frac{1}{2}$ miles from the visitors center. The tower was built in 1920 as a memorial to Albert Smiley, one of the founders of Mohonk Mountain House, which opened in 1870. The preserve offers some of the most scenic views in the Hudson Valley.

Sam's Point and Dwarf Pine Ridge Reserve (845-647-7989), Route 52, Ellenville. Preserve open year-round, dawn to dusk. Open daily May through November. Parking fee. It is suggested that visitors wear comfortable shoes and bring a sweater. The park and lookout point are circled by a road that offers wide views of Ulster and the surrounding counties, but it's at Sam's Point that you'll want your camera. Formed by glaciers, the point is a little less than ½ mile above sea level and offers a flat viewing area from which you can see five states on a clear day. There are safety walls, but you'll feel suspended over the valley below; if you don't like heights, don't stop here. Sam's Point supposedly got its name from a trapper who, fleeing a Native American war party, jumped over the edge and landed safely in some trees. Nature trails lead to a dwarf pine barrens. The trails are well marked, and tours are self-guided with signs and brochures. A walk will take you past chasms and tunnels and around incredible balanced rocks. Explore at your own pace and enjoy the natural surroundings.

Shale Hill Farm and Herb Garden (845-246-6982), 6856 Hommelville Road, Saugerties, just off Route 32. Gardens open spring and summer, shop open year-round; call for hours. This farm is a perfect stop for flower fanciers and herb lovers—the extensive gardens bloom with color and fragrance, and the owner, Patricia Reppert, is an expert in herb lore and use. The shop carries herbal products, plants, gifts, and antiques, and special workshops are offered on weekends (wreath making, cooking, and the like). A nice spot to stop and select some additions to your garden.

LODGING

Many of the bed & breakfasts in Ulster County are tucked away down private roads or are off the beaten path and in private homes. They are sometimes difficult to contact as well, since they do not always have separate listings in local telephone directories. The most up-to-date listings may be obtained by calling the Ulster County Public Information Office (1-800-DIAL-UCO), or by writing to that office at P.O. Box 1800 TG, Kingston 12401.

The Alpine Inn (845-254-5026), Alpine Road, Oliverea 12410. ($$) A pristine mountain lodge nestled on a hillside near the base of one of the tallest peaks in the Catskills, this inn will appeal to those who enjoy exploring the outdoors. Complete with an Olympic-sized pool. Breakfast, lunch, and dinner are served. Twenty-two rooms with private bath, private balcony, and air-conditioning. Children are welcome. Open year-round.

Audrey's Farmhouse Bed and Breakfast (845-895-3440), 2188 Brunswyck Road, Wallkill 12589. ($$) This pastoral spot offers visitors a relaxing getaway. There are five guest rooms (three with private bath; two share a bath), each with air-conditioning and magnificent mountain views. Guests can use the in-ground pool in the warm-weather months, and some rooms have a Jacuzzi and fireplace. A gourmet breakfast is served. Pets are welcome. Open year-round.

Bed by the Stream (845-246-2979), 7531 George Sickle Road, Saugerties 12477. ($$) This peaceful lodging is located on 5 acres of streamside property and offers an in-ground pool and creek swimming. Marked hiking trails are available nearby, and Hunter Mountain and Ski Windham are only a short drive away (see *To Do—Downhill Skiing* in "Greene County"). Bed by the Stream offers one master suite, two rooms with private bath, and two rooms that share a bath; all have queen-sized beds, cable TV, and views of Blue Mountain. A country breakfast is served on the porch overlooking the stream; children are welcome.

Birchcreek Inn (845-254-5222), Birchcreek Road, Pine Hill 12465. ($$) This inn is in a remote but wonderful spot, with a sign indicating its location just off Route 28. More than 100 years old, on 23 private acres, the estate combines the rustic and the refined for an informal yet elegant ambience. Every guest room has a private bath. Check out the Champagne Room for a special occasion: It's huge, as is its luxurious bathroom. There is also a lovely cottage outside the main house with a fireplace and kitchenette.

Black Lion Mansion Bed and Breakfast (845-338-0410), 124 West Chestnut Street, Kingston 12401. ($$$) This Kingston landmark has been magnificently restored to its former Victorian splendor. The spectacular views of the Hudson River will delight visitors, as will the gracious and luxuriously appointed bedrooms filled with fine antiques. Enjoy afternoon tea on the terrace, or in the parlor by the fireplace in cooler weather. Choose a two-room suite or one of six large bedrooms, all with private bath and cable TV.

Bluestone Country Manor (845-246-3060), P.O. Box 144, West Camp, 12490. ($$) Built in the 1930s on a hilltop in the Catskills, this meticulously restored and maintained estate features an imported brick exterior, hardwood floors inlaid with teak, a gracious stairway, and a screened-in front porch. Guests begin their day with a full country breakfast served in the main dining room or in an intimate setting by the fireplace. Four rooms all have private bath, and there is a carriage house with kitchenette.

Cafe Tamayo Bed and Breakfast (845-246-9371), 89 Partition Street, Saugerties 12477. ($$) The official name of this establishment is Upstairs at Cafe Tamayo, Bed and Gourmet Breakfast, and that about says it all. Located above the Cafe Tamayo, an outstanding dining spot (see *Dining Out*), the bed & breakfast features private baths and a gourmet breakfast prepared by chef-owner James Tamayo. The café is a short walk from the antiques shops and boutiques of the village and a short drive from Woodstock, Kingston, and the main ski areas.

Captain Schoonmaker's Bed and Breakfast (845-687-7946), Route 213, High Falls 12440. ($$$) A fine spot for antiques lovers, this 18th-century house will make you feel as if you are stepping back into an earlier time. Schoonmaker's has been featured in many publications, and the hostess serves a seven-course breakfast that should hold you until dinner. Two rooms have private bath; two rooms share a bath. All rooms have a private balcony overlooking a stream. Children under the age of 12 permitted weekdays only. Open year-round.

Cedar Heart Lodge (845-658-8556), 22 Hillcrest Lane, Rosendale 12472. ($$) This recently restored 50-year-old lodge has seven guest rooms, all with private bath. Enjoy rustic elegance in a lovely setting at a reasonable price. Full breakfast is served to all guests. The dining room offers dinner Thursday through Saturday 5–10, Sunday brunch 11–2.

✍ **Copper Hood Inn and Spa** (845-688-2460), Route 28, Shandaken 12480. ($$) Tucked away alongside a well-known fishing stream, the Copper Hood is really an intimate, full-service spa. In addition to fine dining, the inn offers one of the few indoor heated pools in the region; Jacuzzi, massage, and herbal wraps; hiking trails; and, of course, fishing. All 20 rooms have private bath. Children are welcome. Open year-round.

Deerfield (845-687-9807), RD #1, The Vly, Stone Ridge 12484. ($$) Once a boardinghouse, this turn-of-the-19th-century building has been renovated for modern overnight guests. The rooms are airy and light, and there is a nice mix of antiques and country throughout the inn. You'll find more than 30 acres to explore, and antiques shops and points of interest are within a short drive. Guests can enjoy an in-ground pool, a Steinway piano, and a large gourmet breakfast. Two of the six guest rooms have private bath; the other rooms share two baths.

The Emerson Inn & Spa (845-688-7900), 146 Mount Pleasant Road, Mount Tremper 12457. ($$$) This luxurious establishment—with 24 individually and lavishly decorated rooms and suites—is reminiscent of European country manor hotels. You'll find a full-treatment spa, a pool, and fitness facilities. The personal amenities and attention to detail will please the most discerning guests. Gourmet restaurant on the premises for guests only. Open year-round.

Fox Hill Bed and Breakfast (845-691-8151), 55 South Chodikee Lake Road, Highland 12528, approximately 5 miles from exit 18 off the NYS Thruway. ($$) Wander through the woods, sit by the garden pool and feed the colorful koi, or just relax in your room. There are two suites and a separate guest house—a cottage with queen-sized bed, private bath, fireplace, and brick patio with a view of the pond. All rooms are air-conditioned and have TV and VCR. There is an in-ground pool. Open year-round.

The Guesthouse at Holy Cross Monastery (845-384-6660), Route 9W, P.O. Box 99, West Park 12493. ($$) This monastery has spectacular views of the Hudson River and provides a rather unique bed & breakfast experience. The reasonable per-person fee per night includes a room and three meals served in a large dining room with the monks. On some weekends special educational programs are offered; you can write or call for a schedule of events. Open year-round.

Hudson Valley Resort and Spa (1-888-9HUDSON), 400 Granite Road, Kerhonkson 12446. ($$$) Set on 400 acres between the Catskills and Shawangunk Mountains, this newly renovated 300-room luxury resort features magnificent views, a European-style health spa, indoor and

JOANNE MICHAELS

The Inn at Stone Ridge and Milliways Restaurant

outdoor pools, exercise equipment, tennis courts, and a Jacuzzi, as well
as an 18-hole golf course. Travelers will discover a balance between
classic charm and modern comfort during a stay here. Minnewaska
State Park with its world-famous hiking trails and rock climbing cliffs is
close by. Two fine restaurants—**Bentley's American Grill** (regional
cuisine) and **Sansui,** a Japanese restaurant and sushi bar—are on the
premises. Open year-round.

The Inn at Stone Ridge (845-687-0736), Route 209, Stone Ridge 12484.
($$$) For a romantic getaway, this gem should be at the top of your list.
It's beautiful year-round but particularly so in spring, when the flowers
around the stone swimming pool are in bloom. The former Hasbrouck
House is an 18th-century stone mansion set on 40 acres and amid gar-
dens. There are six newly renovated suites. Listed on the National
Register of Historic Places, the inn is open all year; a first-rate restau-
rant, Milliways, is found on its first floor (see *Dining Out*).

Inn the Woods (845-338-2574), P.O. Box 624, Woodstock 12498. ($$) Unwind at this serene country retreat surrounded by 100 blissful wooded
acres. This B&B is also an oxygen day spa, and an oxygen chamber and
sauna are available for guests by appointment. The two guest rooms
share a large living room, dining room, kitchen, and bath. A healthful
gourmet breakfast is served. For those who like to jog or walk on
wooded paths, this is an ideal find. Open year-round.

Jingle Bell Farm (845-255-6588), 1 Forest Glen Road, New Paltz 12561.
($$) This stone house, over two centuries old, is furnished with fine
country antiques and offers visitors more than 12 acres to explore. In

The parlor of the Mohonk Mountain House

summer take a dip in the landscaped pool. The farm, complete with horses, is a short drive from skiing, fishing, and shopping. An elegant retreat serving a full breakfast; four rooms, all with private bath. Children not permitted.

Locktender's Cottage (845-687-7700), Route 213, High Falls 12440. ($$$) The Locktender's Cottage is a romantic getaway situated alongside the Delaware and Hudson Canal in the center of picturesque High Falls. The Victorian cottage once served as a lodging for the canawlers, the sturdy men who manned the barges; today it is owned by John Novi, the chef and proprietor of the DePuy Canal House, right across the road (see *Dining Out*). The deluxe top-floor suite has a kitchenette, Jacuzzi bath, and air-conditioning; the bedrooms on the lower floor have air-conditioning and private bath. Four-star dinners are served at the Canal House, and the cottage is within minutes of many local activities. Open year-round.

The Lodge at Catskill Corners (877-688-2828, 845-688-2828), 5368 Route 28, Mt. Tremper 12457. ($$$) Located minutes away from Belleayre Mountain and the town of Woodstock, this luxurious lodge, opened in 1997, features contemporary Adirondack-style decor in all 27 rooms. The spacious private suites offer wet bar, refrigerator, and whirlpool bath, and all accommodations have cable television, telephones, and data ports for computers. Guests can enjoy streamside dining at the Catamount Cafe next door (see *Dining Out*).

Minnewaska Lodge (845-255-1206), at the intersection of Routres 299 and 44/55, Gardiner 12525. ($$$) This contemporary 26-room mountain lodge is nestled on 17 acres at the base of the spectacular Shawangunk Ridge. The lodge successfully combines the ambience of a bed & breakfast with the conveniences of a fine hotel. All rooms have private decks and mountain views. Guests may enjoy the fitness center on the premises, as well as hiking in the nearby Mohonk and Minnewaska State Park Preserves.

Mohonk Mountain House (845-255-1000), Mohonk Lake, New Paltz 12561. ($$$) This National Historic Landmark is a mountaintop Victorian castle that stands in the heart of 22,000 unspoiled acres. Dazzling views are everywhere, and serene Mohonk Lake adds to the dramatic setting. Although the hotel offers a museum, a stable, modern sports facilities, and many outdoor activities, the place is still very much the way it was more than a century ago (it is still managed by the same family). Midweek packages are available, and special-events weekends are held throughout the year (see *To See—Historic Sites*). Activities are offered for children ages 2–12. Of the 291 rooms, 140 have a working fireplace and 200 have a balcony; all have private bath. Rates include three meals a day; men must wear jackets for the evening meal (see *Dining Out*). Open year-round.

Mountain Meadows Bed and Breakfast (845-255-6144), 542 Albany Post Road, New Paltz 12561. ($$) This lovely country home nestled in the foothills of the Catskills is a fine place for people who enjoy a casual atmosphere, lounging by the pool, relaxing by the fireplace, or playing a game of pool in the recreation room. The spacious landscaped grounds offer croquet, badminton, and horseshoes. All three rooms have private bath, central air-conditioning, and a king- or queen-sized bed. Located only 4.5 miles from NYS Thruway exit 18. Open year-round.

The Nevele Grande Hotel (845-647-6000 or 1-800-647-6000), Route 209, Ellenville 12428. ($$$) This beautifully maintained, full-service resort with nearly 700 rooms has been in business since 1901. The facilities are first-rate and include a par-70 golf course, an Olympic-sized ice rink (open October through April), an indoor and outdoor pool complex and fitness center, tennis courts, and riding trails. During the winter months there are cross-country ski trails and downhill slopes with snowmaking. There are always scheduled activities for children, and from late June through Labor Day there is a day camp program for kids 3–10.

Nieuw Country Lloft (845-255-6533), 41 Allhusen Road, New Paltz 12561. ($$) This cozy, 18th-century Dutch stone house has six fireplaces, beamed ceilings, and wide-plank floors. Three bedrooms (one with fireplace) are dressed up with period furniture and quilts, and the country breakfast is a hearty way to begin a day. Locally produced wines are offered in the evening. Walkers will enjoy the on-site nature trails; many outdoor activities are located a few minutes' drive from the inn. Three rooms share a bath. Children not permitted. Open daily year-round.

Onteora, The Mountain House (845-657-6233), Pine Point Road,

The Saugerties Lighthouse Bed and Breakfast

Boiceville 12412. ($$) Onteora has the most spectacular mountain views of any B&B in the Catskills. Located 1 mile off Route 28, it was the estate of Richard Hellman, the mayonnaise mogul. There are five bedrooms, all with cathedral ceiling and private bath. Breakfasts are made to order, with requests taken the evening before. Children over 12 are welcome. Open year-round.

🖉 **Pine Hill Arms** (845-254-9811), Main Street, Pine Hill 12465. ($$) First opened in 1882, the Pine Hill Arms now caters to skiers. The cozy bar is where everyone meets after the lifts close and where hot spiced wine and great snacks are served. There is also an outstanding greenhouse dining room (see *Dining Out*). All 30 rooms have private bath. Children are welcome. Open year-round.

🖉 **Rocking Horse Ranch** (845-691-2927; 1-800-64-RANCH outside New York State), 600 Route 44/55, Highland 12528. ($$$) This family-owned and -operated ranch resort has offered a variety of vacation packages for over 20 years. A stay includes two sumptuous meals and horseback riding on acres of trails. During the summer months there is waterskiing and boating on the lake. The ranch has heated indoor and outdoor pools, saunas, a gym, a petting zoo, and daily organized activities for kids. Open year-round.

🖉 **Rondout Bed and Breakfast** (845-331-8144), 88 West Chester Street, Kingston 12401. ($$) This late-19th-century house is close to Kingston's restaurants, museums, and river landing, and guests will enjoy the personal attention as well as the location's convenience. Hearty breakfasts may include waffles and homemade maple syrup, and evening refreshments are served by the fireplace. Well-behaved children welcome. Four rooms, two with private bath. Open year-round.

Saugerties Lighthouse Bed and Breakfast (845-247-0656), 168 Lighthouse Drive, Saugerties 12477. ($$) Treat yourself to a unique, romantic experience—sleep in a renovated lighthouse. Watch the boats pass by and see the stars from your bedroom window. The lighthouse keeper will prepare a hearty breakfast in the morning. Two upstairs rooms share a bathroom on the third floor. Travel light, since it's a 10-minute walk from the parking area. Open May through October.

Shandaken Inn (845-688-5100), Route 28, Shandaken 12480. ($$$) With only 12 rooms (9 with private bath), this inn is a cozy mountain retreat. It is open weekends only, and the rate includes breakfast and an excellent French country dinner.

Sparrow Hawk Bed and Breakfast (845-687-4492), 4496 Route 209, Stone Ridge 12484. ($$) This recently renovated brick Colonial, originally a 1770 farmhouse, features four unique air-conditioned guest rooms, all with private bath. A full gourmet breakfast is served fireside in the dining room or on the outdoor patio. Enjoy afternoon tea in the spacious great room, with its cathedral ceiling and balcony library. Open year-round.

Twin Gables: A Guest House (845-679-9479 or 679-5638), 73 Tinker Street, Woodstock 12498. ($$) The architecture and furnishings of the 1930s create a relaxed, easy ambience at this guest house; its service and hospitality have earned it a reputation for comfort and affordability. There are nine guest rooms, and a living room and refrigerator are available to visitors. Twin Gables is only a short walk from restaurants, shopping, galleries, and entertainment. The New York bus line stops right in front, so it's a great spot for those traveling to Woodstock without a car. Some rooms are air-conditioned; both private and shared baths are available. Children are welcome at the owner's discretion. Open year-round.

✎ **Ujjala's Bed and Breakfast** (845-255-6360), 2 Forest Glen Road, New Paltz 12561. ($$) Innkeeper Ujjala Schwartz has renovated this charming Victorian frame cottage surrounded by apple, pear, and quince trees on $3\frac{1}{2}$ acres. The house is bright and cheery, with skylights and lots of plants, and a full breakfast with homemade whole-grain breads, fruit, and vegetarian specialties is included. Four rooms, two with private bath and two that share a bath. All rooms are air-conditioned; one has a sauna, another, a fireplace. Children are welcome. Open year-round.

✎ **Val d'Isere Bed & Breakfast** (845-254-4646), Route 28, Big Indian 12410. ($$$) This inn has lovely mountain views. Bus travelers can disembark just outside the inn's doors, so it's an excellent choice for people who want to get away but don't have a car. Fishing, hiking, and skiing are nearby.

Continental breakfast is served, and the restaurant offers fine French country dinners. There are five rooms, each with private bath. Children are welcome. Open year-round.

Whispering Pines Bed & Breakfast (845-687-2419), 60 Cedar Hill Road, High Falls 12440. ($$) This secluded contemporary B&B has skylights and is surrounded by 50 acres of private woods. There are four plush bedrooms, all with private bath, one with Jacuzzi and fireplace. There is a lovely library. Open year-round.

✍ **Wild Rose Inn Bed & Breakfast** (845-679-5387), 66 Rock City Road, Woodstock. ($$$) Enjoy an elegant Victorian ambience in the heart of town. The five rooms are all beautifully furnished with antiques and all have air conditioning, cable television, and whirlpool baths. A gourmet Continental breakfast is served. Children are welcome and a portacrib is available.

Woodstock Country Inn (845-679-9380), 27 Cooper Lake Road, Woodstock 12498; call for directions. ($$) This quiet, elegant inn is located in the countryside outside Woodstock, yet it's near enough that a short drive will bring you to all the cultural action the village is famous for. The inn, which once belonged to an artist, has been restored and filled with antiques, and has charming nooks to relax or dream in. Four rooms, all with private bath; there is a lovely in-ground pool with magnificent mountain views. Special midseason rates. Open year-round.

✍ **Woodstock Inn on the Millstream** (845-679-8211), 38 Tannery Brook Road, Woodstock 12498. ($$) This is almost a motel—efficiency units are available—but it has its own special charm. Set right on a brook, the inn gives you the option of enjoying breakfast waterside or in the sun room. There is a porch for rocking, and a short walk brings you to the village green. Children are welcome. Open year-round.

WHERE TO EAT

DINING OUT

✍ **Armadillo** (845-339-1550), 97 Abeel Street, Kingston. ($) Open for lunch daily except Monday; dinner served from 4:30. Tex-Mex Southwest cuisine from an enormous menu includes great ribs, fajitas, and chicken specialties; make sure you try the grilled tuna with lime marinade and wasabe mustard. A nice touch: Crayons are provided so you can draw on the paper tablecloths.

Bear Cafe (845-679-5555), Route 212, Woodstock. ($$) Open daily (except Tuesday) for dinner at 5. This is a French American bistro that serves a range of entrées, from grilled fish and chicken to steak sandwiches and pasta dishes. There is a nice view of Sawkill Stream from the dining area. Be sure to make a reservation, since this is one of the best restaurants in the area, and it is always busy.

Benson's (845-255-9783), Route 208 and Route 44/55, Gardiner. ($$) Open

A covered bridge in Rifton

daily for dinner at 5. Blessed with a panoramic view of the Shawangunk Mountains, the building that houses this restaurant dates back to the early 1860s, when it was used by farmers for cattle auctions. Since 1974 it has been an elegant restaurant owned by the Benson family. It specializes in fine Continental cuisine. We strongly recommend the duck.

Blue Mountain Bistro (845-679-8519), Route 212 and Glasco Turnpike, Woodstock. ($$) Open for dinner Tuesday through Sunday 5–10. This cozy spot is a terrific place to stop for lunch after shopping in town. The Mediterranean cuisine includes imaginative items like salmon in parchment paper and pita bread with herbed chicken, mozzarella, sun-dried tomatoes, and mushrooms served with a green salad. Another popular dinner entrée is the 7-hour leg of lamb with red wine, garlic, and fresh rosemary. The freshest local produce is used whenever possible, and the chef has his own salad and herb garden in summer.

Brickhouse Restaurant (845-236-3765), 1 King Street, Marlboro. ($$) Open Tuesday through Sunday for dinner 5–10. Located in a historic building, this restaurant offers a romantic atmosphere with beautiful dark wooden walls and floors, velvet-covered chairs, and antique furnishings. The New American cuisine includes popular dishes like jumbo curried chicken dumplings for an appetizer, and shrimp over fettuccine with garden vegetables for an entrée. On weekday evenings there is a fixed-price three-course dinner that includes a glass of wine. Live jazz on Saturday night.

Cafe at Woodstock Lodge (845-679-3213), 77 Country Club Lane, Woodstock. ($$) Open Sunday through Thursday 5–10, Friday and Saturday until 11. Excellent northern Italian cuisine featuring homemade pasta as well as a number of veal dishes, including osso buco.

Cafe Tamayo (845-246-9371), 89 Partition Street, Saugerties. ($$) Open for dinner Wednesday through Sunday 5–10; Sunday brunch 11:30–3. A popular bistro, housed in a renovated 1864 landmark building, Cafe Tamayo serves home-style American and international cuisine and features such specialties as country pâté with spicy red cabbage, garlic, and green chili; braised duck legs with mole sauce; and cassoulet. Children are welcome.

Le Canard-Enchaine (845-339-2003), 276 Fair Street, Kingston. ($$) Open daily. Enjoy a classic French dinner in a casual bistro atmosphere—experience a touch of Paris in Kingston. A variety of the freshest fish is available daily, or choose from four classic duck entrées. The freshly baked pastries are excellent, and so are the café au lait and cappuccino. A good choice for either lunch or dinner.

Catamount Cafe (845-688-7900), The Resort at Catskill Corners, Route 28, Mount Tremper. ($$) Open daily for dinner 4–10; Sunday brunch 10:30–2:30. Savor international farmhouse cuisine (comfort food from the Catskills) featuring fresh meat and fish, as well as farm-raised game, particularly grilled and rotisserie dishes. Dine in a Catskill Forest Preserve setting, in a cozy lodge situated on the banks of the Esopus River. A few of the specialties of the house are cedar-planked salmon on steamed spinach with mashed potatoes and lime butter sauce; strip steak charbroiled with a three-peppercorn demiglaze; and pan-seared fillet of venison with port wine–exotic mushroom sauce and chestnut-herb spaetzle.

Clove Cafe (845-687-7911), Route 213 and Mohonk Road, High Falls. ($) Open for lunch Friday 11:30–3:30; brunch Saturday and Sunday 9–4; dinner Wednesday through Sunday from 5. Serving American cuisine with a European touch. Excellent steaks, hamburgers, and fish. Breads are baked fresh on the premises.

Coal & Steam Restaurant (845-888-5080), Route 209, Wurtsboro. ($$) Open Tuesday through Sunday noon–9. New American cuisine, with fresh fish, filet mignon, prime rib, and rack of lamb the specialties.

✍ **DePuy Canal House** (845-687-7700 or 687-7777), Route 213, High Falls. ($$) Open Thursday through Sunday for dinner at 5; Sunday brunch 11:30–2. If you want a spectacular meal on a special occasion, make certain you dine at this establishment, which is housed in an 18th-century stone house that was once a tavern. Try the rabbit pâté with pignoli, and the chocolate date truffle in Sabra mole for dessert. Dinner is prix fixe: three courses, $30; four courses, $42; seven courses, $54; plus an à la carte menu every night except Saturday.

Emiliani Ristorante (845-246-6169), 147 Ulster Avenue, Saugerties. ($$) Open daily for dinner from 5. Some of the finest northern Italian cuisine you'll find anywhere is served in this informal yet elegant establishment. The pastas are made on the premises, and all dishes are made to order.

Harvest Cafe (845-255-4205), 10 Main Street, Water Street Market, New Paltz. ($$) Open daily, except Tuesday, 11–8; brunch buffet available on

John Novi, chef/owner of the DePuy Canal House

weekends 10–1. Organic American and vegetarian cuisine with imaginative specialties including a salmon BLT with herb mayonnaise on a
fresh-baked roll, Oriental soba noodle salad with a soy ginger vinai-
grette, and a barbecued pork burrito with chive sour cream and carrot
slaw. Outdoor patio dining in the warm-weather months.

The Inn at Woodland Valley (845-688-5711), Route 28, Phoenicia. ($$)
Open Monday through Thursday 4–10, Friday through Sunday noon–
11. This is a good place to go for a hearty meal after hiking in the
Phoenicia area. The standard American favorites—including steaks,
burgers, pasta, and fish—are served in a cozy atmosphere.

Little Bear Chinese Restaurant (845-679-8899), Route 212, Woodstock.
($$) Open daily for lunch and dinner noon–10:30. Sit along the Sawkill
stream and enjoy fine Chinese cuisine prepared by Chef Kuo of Hunan,
China. There is a dim sum brunch Sunday noon–4, and Tuesday night
is sushi night.

Locust Tree Inn (845-255-7888), 215 Huguenot Street, New Paltz. ($$)
Open for lunch Thursday and Friday 11:30–2:30; dinner Wednesday
through Sunday 5:30–10; Sunday brunch 11–2. Located in an 18th-
century stone house, this casual country restaurant has a fireplace in
every dining room. The contemporary international cuisine here
features imaginative fish and pasta dishes, but there are also steak and
seafood entrées for those who prefer more conventional fare.

The Loft (845-255-1426), 46 Main Street, New Paltz. ($$) Open daily
11:30–11:30. The regional American fare here is first-rate. Try the
grilled marinated Gulf shrimp for an appetizer and the Loft island duck
(duck breast marinated and topped with an orange and ginger brandy

glaze, served with wild rice and an array of steamed vegetables). The lunch menu includes pasta dishes, salads, excellent soups, and sandwiches. Fine food at reasonable prices.

Loretta Charles Natural Wood Grill (845-688-2550), 7159 Route 28, Shandaken. ($$) Open for dinner daily, except Monday, from 5. Saturday and Sunday lunch is served noon–2:30. Contemporary American cuisine featuring wood grilled steaks and seafood.

Luke's Grill (845-254-4646), Route 28, Big Indian. ($$) Open daily (except Wednesday) at 5. Specialties at this casual French restaurant are excellent pâtés, baby rack of lamb, and chicken with maple sauce. For dessert, the chocolate mousse with hazelnuts is a treat. Children are welcome.

Marcel's (845-384-6700), Route 9W, West Park. ($$) Open Thursday through Sunday for dinner 5–10. This is a romantic and cozy spot, with a fireplace, dimmed lights, and fine French food. Try the rack of lamb, pasta with seafood, and chicken Provençal. Not recommended for children.

Mariner's Harbor (845-691-6011), 46 River Road, Highland. ($$) Open daily March through late November for dinner at 4. Enjoy a seafood dinner with a view of the Hudson. There are daily fish specials like farm-raised catfish, grilled tuna, stuffed flounder, and Long Island bluefish; exceptional shellfish dishes, such as lobster tails, scallops, and clams; and excellent homemade desserts. Outdoor seating in summer.

Marlee's Grill (845-679-0888), 295 Tinker Street, Bearsville. ($$) Open for dinner daily except Wednesdays, 5–11. Sunday brunch served 10:30–3. Reservations suggested on weekends. This is the place to go if you love grilled fish, as we do. Excellent yellow fin, salmon, swordfish, and sea bass. For those who prefer turf, there is grilled sirloin and an array of pasta dishes. The portions are generous and the prices are moderate.

Milliways (845-687-0736), Route 209, Stone Ridge. ($$) Open Wednesday through Sunday for dinner from 5. Enjoy fine regional American cuisine in this stone house that dates back to the 18th century (see *Lodging*). The owner, Dan Hauspurg, travels the country in search of the right foods to serve here. He changes the menu every two weeks to include items from the Pacific Rim, Mississippi Delta, and Hudson Valley. Our favorite is the Chesapeake crabcakes.

Mohonk Mountain House Restaurant (845-255-1000), Mountain Rest Road, New Paltz. ($$$) Open daily for breakfast 8–9:30; lunch served 12:30–2; dinner 6:30–8. Jackets are required for men during the evening meal. It is necessary to make a reservation for any meal at Mohonk or you cannot get in the gate. The regional American favorites here change seasonally. Breakfast and lunch are served buffet style. There is a four-course meal at dinner. Guests can walk around the grounds before or after their meal, and the views are magnificent any time of year (see *Lodging*).

Mountain Gate Restaurant (845-679-5100), 4 Deming Street, Woodstock. ($$) Open daily for dinner. A fine selection of Indian dishes is served here, including vegetarian meals and traditional Tandoori chicken. There is a fixed-price buffet on Wednesday night.

New World Home Cooking (845-246-0900), 1411 Route 212, Saugerties. ($$) Open daily for dinner 5–11; lunch Monday through Friday noon–2:30. Eating here is like taking a tour of America's finest and funkiest restaurants. The house specialties are Jamaican jerk chicken, Thai mussel stew, and black sesame-seared salmon. The emphasis is on peasant flavors, and the colorful, casual ambience reflects the many cultures represented on New World's menu.

Northern Spy Cafe (845-687-7298), Route 213, High Falls. ($$) Open daily (except Wednesday) for dinner 5–10; Sunday brunch 11–3. "International soul food" is the way the chef, a Culinary Institute graduate, describes the imaginative fare in his informal eatery. He takes pleasure in adding interesting touches to traditional favorites from around the world. One popular entrée is the Moroccan-style chicken with ginger and cilantro. Desserts include a Northern Spy pie named after the apples from the orchard in back of the restaurant. You can enjoy dinner at the bar or on the terrace in warm weather.

Pine Hill Arms (845-254-9811), Main Street, Pine Hill. ($$) Open daily for dinner 5–11; open for lunch Saturday noon–4; open daily noon–4 in July and August. Closed Wednesday. The best steak fries in the region aren't the only reason to dine here—this old stagecoach stop also serves great grilled chicken, fish, and steaks in the greenhouse dining room. The spot is cozy, and the desserts are out of this world (try the cream cheese brownie with chocolate sauce and ice cream or the chocolate mousse pie).

Portobello (845-338-3000), corner of Fair and John Streets, Kingston. ($$) Open for lunch Monday through Friday 11–3; for dinner Monday through Saturday 5–10; closed Sunday. Portobello specializes in northern Italian cuisine. The freshly made pastas are first-rate, and so are the salads.

Reginato Ristorante (845-336-6968), Leggs Mill Road, Lake Katrine. ($$) Open for lunch Monday through Friday 11:30–2:30; dinner Monday through Saturday 5–10, Sunday 1–10. Enjoy homemade northern Italian specialties in a relaxed atmosphere.

✍ **Reservoir Inn** (845-331-9806), Route 1 and Dike Road, West Hurley. ($$) Lunch Tuesday through Saturday 11:30–2; dinner Tuesday through Sunday 5–11. Consistently good family fare at reasonable prices is offered in a cozy atmosphere. Italian specialties include pizza and pasta as well as early-bird specials on weekdays before 6 PM.

Riccardella's Restaurant (845-688-7800), Main Street, Phoenicia. ($$) Open Wednesday through Saturday 4:30–10, Sunday 2–10. This Italian restaurant offers diners fine food in an informal atmosphere.

✍ **Roadhouse Grill** (845-334-9383), 14 Thomas Street, Kingston. ($) Open Sunday through Thursday 11:30–9, Friday and Saturday until 10; closed Tuesday. This is the place to go for barbecue. The chefs here burn hickory logs in a specially designed pit oven to achieve perfectly done meats. They are known for their steaks, ribs, and chicken. The Roadhouse marinated steak is steeped in garlic, ginger, sesame, molasses—and the rest is a house secret. The burgers, chili, salads, and tater toppers are also house specialties.

🖋 **Ship Lantern Inn** (845-795-5400), Route 9W, Milton. ($$) Open for lunch Tuesday through Friday noon–2; dinner Tuesday through Saturday 5–10, Sunday 1–8. This charming old restaurant has nautical decor and serves Continental cuisine. The food and service are consistently excellent. House specialties include fresh fish, mignonette of beef Bordelaise, and Saltimbuca Romana. Children are welcome.

Ship to Shore Restaurant (845-334-8887), 15 West Strand, Kingston. ($$) Open daily for lunch and dinner. The specialties here are steaks and seafood. One of our favorite dinner entrées is the 16-ounce boneless New York sirloin with peppercorn butter. For lunch, there's the salmon club or grilled portobello mushroom burger with roasted red peppers and fresh mozzarella. Take a walk after your meal along the Rondout.

Terrapin Restaurant (845-331-3663), 250 Spillway Road, West Hurley. ($$) Open for dinner Wednesday through Sunday 5:30–10. Extraordinarily fine contemporary country dining created by a former chef of the French Culinary Institute. An innovative menu includes southwestern and Asian flavors, fresh seafood, vegetarian dishes, and terrific steaks. Be sure to make a reservation on weekend evenings.

Toscani and Sons Restaurant (845-255-2272), 119 Main Street, New Paltz. ($$) Open for lunch Thursday through Saturday 11–2:30; dinner Tuesday through Saturday 5–11, Sunday 1–8. This is the place to enjoy what the Toscani family calls *cucina casalinga,* home-style cooking. This small restaurant has a bustling atmosphere. Don't pass up the fried calamari or the four of twelve styles of mozzarella cheese appetizer for which the delicatessen is renowned. The giambotte (fresh homemade sausage roasted with peppers, potatoes, onions, olive oil, and spices) is superb; the cappuccino is first-rate.

The Would Restaurant (845-691-2516), 120 North Road, Highland. ($$) Open for lunch Monday through Friday 11:30–2; dinner daily 5–10. A former gin mill once known as the Applewood Bar, this informal restaurant is becoming renowned for its high-quality creative cooking. There is a mix of international and New American cuisine with several unique touches. The Oriental chicken salad with roasted almonds and Chinese noodles is popular for lunch. The dinner menu includes grilled lamb chops on roasted walnut-mint pesto with Mediterranean vegetable compote. The pastry chef bakes focaccia and pesto bread as well as great desserts—try the flaky apple pie spiced with cinnamon, or the raspberry-chocolate brûlée.

EATING OUT

The Alternative Baker (845-331-5517), 35 Lower Broadway, Kingston. ($) Open Thursday through Monday 8–6, Sunday until 4. You will find dairy-free, sugar-free, wheat-free, and organic baked goods here, in addition to standard favorites like brownie fudge cake. The focaccia, buttermilk scones, and muffins are popular with local residents. A good stop if you want to pick up a snack or pack a picnic lunch.

Ann Marie's Gourmet Marketplace (845-246-5542), 216 Main Street, Saugerties. ($) Open daily 7–7. This bustling café-bistro is known for fantastic homemade wraps, burritos, lasagne, frittatas, and potato pancakes. They make their own turkey and roast beef and have an array of coffees and teas.

The Bakery (845-255-8840), 13A North Front Street, New Paltz. ($) Open 7 AM–8 PM (until 6 from November through March). The bagels, ruggelach, and butter cookies are first-rate, and this is a popular place with local residents. The outdoor café is surrounded by gardens and provides a pleasant ambience for those who want to relax and enjoy a treat from the coffee bar. Overstuffed sandwiches, salads, and intriguing pasta dishes are a few of the options for lunch.

Bluestone Country Foods (845-679-5656), 54C Tinker Street, Woodstock. ($) Open daily 10–8. Tasty vegan, wheat-free, and organic dishes; fresh pasta; and naturally sweetened desserts are the highlights here. Children are welcome, and there is outdoor seating in warm-weather months.

Bread Alone Bakery (845-679-2108), Route 28, Boiceville; also located on Tinker Street, Woodstock. ($) Don't miss this bakery, renowned for its fantastic bread—Norwegian farm, mixed grain, Swiss peasant, Finnish sour rye, and others—all baked in a wood-fired oven. Stop in at the pastry section, have a cup of tea or coffee, and satisfy your craving for something sweet and rich.

Brio's (845-688-5370), Main Street, Phoenicia. ($) Open daily 7 AM–10 PM. This luncheonette is a good place to stop for an overstuffed sandwich, outstanding chili, or snack. The breakfasts here are fantastic, and there are 10 kinds of pancakes served. A popular place with local residents. Kids love the spaghetti and meatballs.

Catskill Mountain Coffee (845-334-8455), 906 Route 28, Kingston. ($) Open daily 8–4. Enjoy organic coffee, homemade desserts, and soups in this smoke-free "coffeehouse." On many weekend evenings there are extended hours for live music, so call for the schedule.

Coyote Cafe American Cantina (845-382-2233), 1300 Hudson Valley Mall, Ulster Avenue, Kingston. ($) Open daily 11 AM–2 AM. The salads, burgers, sandwiches, and pasta dishes are served with generous portions of Southwest slaw and crispy fries. The sizzling fajitas and chargrilled quesadillas are exceedingly popular. There are also a few vegetarian dishes to choose from.

Cynfres (845-336-5088), Lohmaier Lane, Lake Katrine; Route 375, West Hurley (845-679-5580); and Cherry Hill Center, New Paltz (845-255-8500). ($) This bakery boasts some of the finest cakes in the region. Lunch is served weekdays 11:30–2:30.

Brio's in Phoenicia is a popular eatery among local residents

🖊 **Deising's Bakery & Coffee Shop** (845-338-7503), 111 North Front Street, Kingston. ($) Open daily at 7 for breakfast and lunch. Deising's has excellent pastries, breads, and other baked goods (try the cream napoleons). The coffee shop offers large, overstuffed sandwiches; fresh, rich quiches; and hearty soups and salads—all made fresh daily.

Dot's Diner (845-338-5016), 275 Fair Street, Kingston. ($) Open daily 7 AM–5 PM. Try the chicken souvlaki with Greek salad or the vegetable souvlaki. Another chef's specialty is the Philly cheese steak. There are great triple-decker sandwiches, burgers, omelets, and hot sandwiches served with homemade gravy, fries, and coleslaw. A good stop for lunch or breakfast.

Downtown Cafe (845-331-5904), 1 West Strand, Kingston. ($) Open daily, except Tuesday, 10–10. This Italian bistro is a good place to stop if you want a cappuccino or a sandwich after touring the Rondout area. One of our favorites is the grilled chicken with fresh mozzarella and roasted red peppers. Dinner entrées include risotto with porcini mushrooms and salmon with capers and artichokes in white wine sauce.

The Egg's Nest (845-687-7255), Route 213, High Falls. ($) Open daily 11 AM–2 AM. Located in a former parsonage, this cozy restaurant with funky decor has homemade soups, great sandwiches, and a special crispy-crusted *praeseau*. Children welcome.

La Florentina (845-339-2455), 604 Ulster Avenue, Kingston. ($) Open weekdays 11:30–10, weekends 4–11 PM. Excellent pizza and other baked specialties. A traditional wood-fired oven is used. Even the cheeses are homemade, and there are outstanding dishes such as pizza with veal and broccoli (the dough is yeast-free). Try the grilled seafood from the new brick seafood grill—the choices range from Dijon shrimp kabob and salmon with vegetables in a garlic and lemon sauce to grilled swordfish. Great Sicilian and other Italian desserts include cannoli, ices, and layer cake. Children welcome.

Gadaleto's Seafood Market and Restaurant (845-255-1717), 246 Main Street, Cherry Hill Shopping Center, New Paltz. ($$) Open daily, except Sunday, 8 AM–9 PM. Enjoy fresh fish, shrimp, clams, crabs, or lobster in this informal eatery. A great place to get takeout as well.

Gateway Diner (845-339-5640), Washington Avenue, Kingston. ($) The standard diner fare is fresh and well prepared. Murals adorn the walls, and the diner, open 24 hours, is convenient to exit 19 off the NYS Thruway.

The Golden Ginza (845-339-8132), 24-28 Broadway, Kingston. Open daily for lunch, Monday through Friday, 11–2:30; dinner is served daily, 2:30–10. Enjoy all types of Japanese cuisine, including tempura, teriyaki, sushi, and sashimi. Children will love watching the flames rising from the grill at the center of the table if you order hibachi dinners prepared Benihana style. There's a sushi bar for those who enjoy this delicacy, and everything is prepared fresh.

Gypsy Wolf Cantina (845-679-9563), Route 212, Woodstock. ($) Open daily (except Monday) for dinner from 5. This is an authentic Mexican cantina with colorful decor and a festive atmosphere. The chips and salsa are first-rate, and the Gypsy Wolf platter includes a little of everything to put in your tortillas.

Heaven (845-679-0011), 17 Tinker Street, Woodstock. ($) Open daily Sunday through Friday 9–4, Saturday 9–5. Chef Oliver Kita, a graduate of the Culinary Institute and formerly a pastry chef at the Russian Tea Room, has created a marvelous eatery in the middle of Woodstock. Sample the rainbow chicken salad on a French baguette or the fresh turkey breast with avocado sprouts on double-grain bread. The cold pasta dishes are first-rate, and so is the salad bar. Don't miss the outrageously chocolatey brownies.

Catskill Corners kaleiodscope

JOSEPH PUGLISI

Italian Supreme (845-255-7313), 52 Main Street, New Paltz. ($) Open daily (except Tuesday) 11–10. This restaurant serves hearty Italian pizza, pasta, deli specialties, and excellent calzones. A giant hero, up to 10 feet long, is sold by the foot. Good for kids.

Jane's Homemade Ice Cream (845-338-8315), 305 Wall Street, Kingston. ($) Open Monday through Friday 9–6, Saturday 10–5; closed Sunday. Homemade ice cream is the specialty, along with cakes, cookies, and scones. Breakfast and lunch are served, and there is a variety of soups, salads, sandwiches, and vegetarian specialties.

Landau Grill (845-679-8937), 17 Mill Hill Road, Woodstock. ($) Open daily 9 AM–midnight. Interestingly prepared, reasonably priced American cuisine. Try the Chinese chicken salad wrap for lunch. Roast duck and meat loaf are popular dinner entrées. There's a full bar and outdoor patio dining in the warm-weather months.

Lydia's Country Deli (845-687-7157), Route 209, Stone Ridge. ($) Open daily 6 AM–4 PM, Sunday until 5. The chicken, macaroni, and potato salads are delicious, and worth picking up for a picnic lunch.

Main Course (845-255-2600), 232 Main Street, New Paltz. ($) Open daily (except Monday) for lunch and dinner 11:30–10. Unusual spa cuisine and contemporary American dishes including grilled fish and home-made pasta are the offerings here. Casual and relaxing.

Main Street Bistro (845-255-7766), Main Street, New Paltz. ($$) Open daily for breakfast, lunch, and dinner 8 AM–9 PM. Fresh pastas, gourmet salads, and sandwiches and burgers of all kinds are served in a casual atmosphere. The pastries and baked goods are outstanding. More than 60 types of beer and wine to choose from.

✎ **Maria's Bazar** (845-679-5434), Tinker Street, Woodstock. ($) Open daily 6:30 AM–8 PM, Sunday until 7:30 PM. Maria is well known for her home-cooked Italian specialties. Excellent salads, fresh pastas, homemade soups, and outstanding pastries are here; vegetarians will find many selections. Children are welcome.

Nekos Luncheonette (845-338-8227), 309 Wall Street, Kingston. ($) Open daily, except Sunday, 7–3. This family-owned and -operated all-American diner offers a huge menu of classic favorites, including home-cooked pastrami, hot turkey with french fries and gravy, and first-rate chicken salad sandwiches. The portions are generous and the prices are reasonable.

✎ **Plaza Diner** (845-255-1030), New Paltz Plaza, New Paltz. ($) Serving patrons for over 20 years, the diner is open 24 hours daily. For breakfast, the French toast and pancakes can't be beat. The service is fast and the food reliable.

Raccoon Saloon (845-236-7872), Main Street, Marlboro. ($) Lunch served daily 11:30–2:30; dinner Tuesday through Sunday 5–9. Some of the best burgers in the region, along with excellent fries, chicken, soups, and salads. A casual stop for lunch or dinner.

Rosendale Cafe (845-658-9048), 434 Main Street, Rosendale. ($) Open Monday 5–11 PM, Tuesday through Sunday 11–11. This vegetarian restaurant offers a variety of soups, salads, sandwiches, and pasta dishes. Try the tempeh reuben or Fakin' Bacon FLT. The nachos, chili, and burritos are also tasty. Organic coffees and homemade desserts. There's music on most weekend evenings.

✎ **Spotted Dog Restaurant** (845-688-7700), at Catskill Corners, Route 28, Mount Pleasant. ($) Open Monday, Wednesday, and Thursday noon–7; Friday, Saturday, and Sunday until 9:30. Closed Tuesday. Located approximately 20 miles west of NYS Thruway exit 19, this place is built like a Victorian firehouse. Children especially will enjoy dining inside a real fire truck with fire equipment all around. Reasonable prices for family fare, which includes burgers, salads, sandwiches, and hearty soups.

✎ **The Stairway Café** (845-246-7135), 346 Route 212, Saugerties. ($) Open daily 7 AM–11 PM. Rafael and Barese, Italian immigrants from Argentina, have made this establishment a popular eatery among local residents. Located just across the highway from the New York State Thruway entrance (heading north), it is also a convenient stop for travelers. Traditional diner favorites with a home-cooked touch. Childen will love the desserts.

Stella's Italian Restaurant (845-331-2210), 44 North Front Street, Kingston. Open Wednesday through Saturday 5–10 PM for dinner only. For some of the best Italian home cooking, including baked lasagna, eggplant parmesean, and spaghetti and meatballs, this is the place to go. A local favorite, it's been open for several years and offers a child-friendly menu.

Sweet Sue's (845-688-7852), Main Street, Phoenicia. ($) Open daily 7–3; closed Wednesday. This is a great breakfast and lunch place with more than a dozen types of pancakes (including fruited oatmeal) and French toast (including walnut-crunch). Everything from muffins to soups and all desserts is homemade here. A casual, truly outstanding café. Nice for children.

West Strand Grill (845-340-4272), 50 Abeel Street, Kingston. ($$) Open daily, except Monday, from 3 PM. This restaurant, located in a renovated building that was once a synagogue dating back to 1892, serves contemporary American favorites such as herb-grilled rack of lamb, ginger pan-fried sea bass, and West Strand grilled primavera pasta. There is patio dining overlooking the Rondout waterfront. Live music every weekend.

Winchell's Pizza (845-657-3352), Reservoir Road and Route 28, Shokan. ($) Open daily 11:30–9:30. Unusually tempting pizzas with a thick crust, and creamy homemade ice cream for dessert. Great salad bar.

Wok n' Roll Japan (845-679-3484), Mill Hill Road, Woodstock. ($$) Open weekdays, except Wednesday, 5–11 PM, Saturday noon–11, Sunday noon–10. Enjoy the Tokyo-style sushi bar, tempura and noodle dishes, and the area's most extensive collection of rice wines. The chef's 35 years of culinary experience are evident, particularly in dishes like chicken teriyaki, which is the best we've had anywhere. Sushi lovers will be pleased with the high quality of the food as well as the presentation and reasonable prices.

Also see Michael's Candy Corner in *Selective Shopping*.

ENTERTAINMENT

Maverick Concerts (845-679-8217), Maverick Road just off Route 375, Woodstock. Open July and August; call for concert schedules. Admission fee. Founded in 1916 by author Hervey White, the Maverick Concerts were to be a blend of the best that chamber music and the natural world had to offer. White wanted to encourage other "maverick" artists, and attracted some of the premier string and wind players to this glass-and-wood concert hall. The small building seats only 400, but many people enjoy hearing the concerts from the surrounding hillside, a setting that was White's idea of perfection. The concerts are known as the oldest chamber series in the country, and they are still attracting the best chamber groups in the world, among them the Tokyo, Mendelssohn, and Manhattan String Quartets and the Dorian Wind Quintet.

River Arts Repertory at Byrdcliffe Theatre (845-679-2100). From Woodstock take Rock City Road to Glasco Turnpike; go approximately 1 mile; Byrdcliffe Road is on the right. Performance schedules vary. Admission fee. Built in the early 20th century in reaction to the artistically poor industrial revolution, this cluster of buildings has remained a refuge for visiting artists. The theater hosts a variety of performances each summer and is home to River Arts Repertory, which offers original and experimental plays with professional casts that include some big names. The **Bird on a Cliff Theatre Company** (845-679-5979) offers a free Shakespeare festival in the park each summer.

Also see the Kleinert Arts Center, below.

SELECTIVE SHOPPING

IN WOODSTOCK

The Kleinert Arts Center and Crafts Shop (845-679-2079), 34 Tinker Street, is housed in an 18th-century building in the middle of town. The center is a showcase for the visual and performing arts, with gallery shows and concerts presented throughout the year. The **Rare Bear** stocks antique and new teddy bears, **Anatolia** has Turkish kilims, and **The Gilded Carriage** carries a wide selection of kitchenware, pottery from around the world, and children's toys. Stop in at **Bazar** and **Bluestone Country Foods** for a snack or the makings of a gourmet picnic. Don't miss any of the side streets either, where tiny shops are tucked away in corners.

If you like gardening, after you leave Woodstock take a short drive to **Smoky Mountain Garden Art** (845-331-6257), 375 Spillway Road, West Hurley, where you will find a huge selection of concrete garden ornaments, statues, fountains, and birdbaths, along with unique, one-of-a-kind pieces.

KINGSTON SHOPPING

Amazing Threads (845-336-5322), 2010 Ulster Avenue (Route 9W), Lake Katrine, just north of Kingston. Closed Sunday. This shop sponsors workshops in the vanishing needle and fiber arts year-round. It is also a must-see for lovers of wool and fiber, and carries fine buttons, books, weaving, sewing and spinning equipment. A plus: The owners are patient teachers and incredibly knowledgeable about even the most complicated sewing machine. Call for special class schedules, workshops, and demonstrations.

AmeriBag Adventures (845-339-8033), 291 Wall Street. Their patented

Healthy Backpack is seen in the finer catalogs, but a stop at the shop will give you dozens of styles, sizes, and colors to choose from. They also make leather and fabric luggage, and prices at the store make the trip a bargain. Open Monday through Saturday 10–5.

Collector's Tea Pot (1-800-724-3306), Foxhall Avenue. Here is where you will find teapots of all shapes, themes, and sizes. Everything from vampires to painting easels, Dorothy and the Wicked Witch to Queen Victoria and Mark Twain, has made its appearance in the form of pots, cookie jars, and canisters. The shop is really the mail-order office of the business, and not a retail outlet. If you love teapots, however, take a chance and stop by—or just call for a catalog.

Marcuse (845-339-6468), 319 Wall Street. Open daily. Fine crafts, from glass to paintings, are found in this elegant shop. Many local artists are represented here, and the selections are unique and often exquisite.

Michael's Candy Corner (845-338-6782), 773 Broadway, Kingston. Open year-round, this is one of the few shops that manufacture candy canes. Tours are limited to the holiday season, when groups are welcome, but you can stop in anytime and purchase an unusual handmade confection.

Piddily Links Too, on Broadway opposite Colonel Chandler Drive. Another wholesaler, but this one has shop hours and regular holiday sales (Mother's Day, Valentine's Day, Christmas, and more). Definitely worth the trip for the sales; the jewelry is Victorian in style, lavish with crystals, pendants, and beads, and carried in boutiques nationally.

Three Geese in Flight (845-338-CELT), 275 Fair Street. Open by chance or appointment. Irish, Welsh, Scottish, Manx, Breton—all the Celts are here, in book and music form. A great place to browse, with old and new publications.

ANTIQUES

Ever since the 17th century people in Ulster have been accumulating things, which now turn up as valuable antiques. But even if you don't collect rare furniture, you can enjoy hunting down that special collectible vase or a colorful quilt. Auctions are listed in the local newspapers, and yard sales bloom each weekend like dandelions. There are many antiques shops throughout the county, but the following centers offer several dealers under one roof and give browsers a wide selection. And since no listing of a center's stock is ever comprehensive, visitors will never know what treasures they may find.

Acorn Antiques Craftsmen's Gallery (845-688-2100), Route 214, Phoenicia, has Mission and Mission-style collectibles and antiques.

Barking Dog Antiques (845-687-4834), High Falls; and **Cat House Antiques,** 136 Bruceville Road, are fun places to browse. Open year-round.

Catskill Mountain Antique Center (845-331-0880), Route 28, Kingston, has all types of furniture, collectibles, and textiles. Open year-round.

The Country Store Antique Center (845-255-1123), Route 44/55, Gardiner, has furniture and country collectibles.

Saugerties Antiques Center and Annex (845-246-3227) is located in the downtown Partition Street antiques district. Open daily year-round.

Skillypot Antique Company (845-338-6779), 41 Broadway, Kingston, is a co-op of 25 dealers who offer lamps, furniture, glassware, and collectibles. Open year-round.

Woodstock Cottage & Camp Antiques (845-679-6499), 62 Tinker Street, has great old stuff that reminds everyone of a vacation in the mountains.

Kingston is also the base for **Festival Promotions** (845-331-8852 or 338-7113), which sponsors several excellent large antiques shows at the Kingston Armory; call for schedules.

BOOKSTORES

Alternative Books (845-331-5439), 35 N. Front, Kingston. A fine used bookstore that offers readings by local authors.

Ariel Booksellers (845-255-8041), 3 Plattekill Avenue, New Paltz, is a 20-year-old full-line bookstore specializing in local books, carefully chosen remainders, and books for SUNY classes.

Barner Books (845-255-2636), 69 Main Street, New Paltz, has a large selection of used books and first editions.

Blue Mountain Books and **Editions** (845-679-5991), Route 28, Boiceville; watch for sign on road. Editions is open daily 10–5; Blue Mountain Books is open Friday through Sunday. Two bookstores specializing in everything from rare first editions and manuscripts to good used books. Plan to spend time here if you are a bibliophile.

Esoterica (845-255-5777), 81 Main Street, New Paltz, is a first-rate New Age Book and gift shop.

The Hope Farm Press and Bookshop (845-246-3522), 252 Main Street, Saugerties. This is the place to go if you love regional books, although they have a wonderful array of used books as well. We feel it is the best selection of local titles anywhere in the upper Hudson Valley. The owner, Richard Frisbie, is usually in the store to answer questions or help you find whatever you are looking for.

Pages Past (845-339-6484), 103 Tammany Steet, at East Chester Street, 0.25 mile from Routes 9W and 32. Fine and rare books, many on the Hudson River and Catskills region, with a nice selection of antique children's publications.

FARM STANDS AND PICK-YOUR-OWN FARMS

Some Ulster County farms are still owned by the families that founded them; others have been cultivating the same site for centuries. The harvest season here stretches from early-summer strawberries to late-fall pumpkins and even some holiday greenery. Some farm stands offer freshly baked pies and cakes, while others have recipes for you to take home, along with food and other regional goodies. Pick-your-own farms and stands let you do the work as well as giving you the choice of what you want in the basket. Most of these stands provide containers, but if you bring your own, the price is usually lower. However you decide to gather in the harvest, the following is just a sampling of places to try.

The two **Gill Corn Farms** (845-331-8225), Hurley Mountain Road and on Route 209, both outside Kingston, are open May through November. Both farms are in sweet corn country, and that's what they specialize in, although a wide variety of other fruits and vegetables is offered, including several pick-your-own crops.

Davenport Farms Market (845-687-7446), Route 209, Stone Ridge, open April through November, has an extensive selection of local produce, including raspberries, grapes, corn, apples, pumpkins, and melons. There is also a second market at the Kingston traffic circle.

Dressel Farms (845-255-0693), 271 Route 208, New Paltz, open from the first Thursday after Labor Day through Thanksgiving. Closed Sunday and holidays. You can pick your own apples and pumpkins here, surrounded by magnificent views of the Shawangunk Mountains. The farm is also open during June for strawberry picking.

Barthels Farm Market (845-647-6941), farther south on Route 209, in Ellenville, is open May through November. You can pick your own strawberries and select fruits and vegetables from the stand.

The final stop on Route 9W is in Port Ewen at **The Apple Bin,** the Nemeth Orchards shop, where many varieties of local corn, fruit, and apples are offered; you'll also find an excellent selection of baked goods. Open April through December.

Alyce & Roger's Fruit Stand (845-688-5615), Route 28, Mount Tremper. A dazzling array of local produce is found here, and there are lots of jack-o'-lanterns come October.

Wilklow Orchards (845-691-2339), Pancake Hollow Road, Highland. (From Exit 18 off of NYS Thruway, turn right on Route 299. Go 2.3 miles, turn right on New Paltz Road. Go approximately one mile and make a right on Pancake Hollow Road. It's another mile to the orchard.) One of the oldest family-run pick-your-own farms, in business for more than a century, open from 9–5 every day from September 1st through October 31st. There are ten varieties of apples, as well as pumpkins, for picking. Because weather conditions make it difficult to predict exact harvest dates, do call for information about the crops available. The kids will enjoy the farm animals.

Some local fruit farms that specialize in pick-your-own fruits include: **Kelder's Farm & U-Pick** (845-626-7284), Lower Whitefield Road, Accord, with berries, pumpkins, and barnyard animals (to visit, not pick); **Mr. Apples Low-Spray Orchard** (845-687-9498), Route 213, High Falls, with several varieties of apples and cider; **Moriello's Apple Hill Farm** (845-255-0917), Route 32, New Paltz; **Minard Farms** (845-883-5755), off Ohioville Road, Clintondale, with apples, cider, picnic areas, and a hayride; **Clarke Westervelt Fruit Farm** (845-795-2270), 182 Clarke's Lane, Milton, with apples; and **Wright's Farm** (845-255-5300), Route 208, Gardiner. At **Smoked Fish & Honey** (845-679-

4514), 189 Wittenburg Road, Bearsville, the trout, shrimp, and salmon are cured with a traditional hot-smoking method that uses no preservatives or chemicals. They also stock fresh ginseng roots, honey, bee pollen, and organic coffee. Herb lovers will want to stop at **Tweefontein Herb Farm** (845-255-7024), 4 Jenkins Lane, New Paltz, for the organic herbs and a visit to the bird sanctuary. **Butterfly Hill Herbary** (845-744-3040), Route 52 (91 Main Street) Pine Bush, offers herbs and classes.

A few larger farm markets that are worth stopping at: **Adam's Fairacre Farm** (845-336-6300), on Route 9W in Lake Katrine; **Hepworth Farms** (845-795-2141), on Route 9W in Milton; and **Wallkill View Farm** (845-255-8050), on Route 299 in New Paltz. The produce and baked goods here are first-rate.

SPECIAL EVENTS

February through March: Maple tours take place in late winter (usually February or early March) when the sap begins to run. There is absolutely nothing to match the fragrance of steamy maple syrup. At **Arrowhead Maple Syrup Farm** (845-626-7293), Route 209, Kerhonkson, tours are offered daily noon–5; dairy tours are offered the rest of the year. **Lyonsville Sugarhouse and Farm** (845-687-2518), County Route 9, offers tours; call ahead for schedules.

May and September: **Woodstock/New Paltz Art and Crafts Fair** (845-679-8087), Ulster County Fairgrounds, off Libertyville Road; follow Route 299 to the turnoff and signs. Shows are held Memorial Day and Labor Day weekends, Saturday through Monday 10–5. Admission fee. This huge arts fair offers more than just booths of crafts; some of the region's finest artists are on hand each year to exhibit their works. Working craftspeople demonstrate their skills, which have included quilting, scrimshaw, weaving, etching, and broom making. There is even a children's center with things to do and exhibits of young artists' works. Furniture and architectural crafts, craft supplies, entertainment, food, and health care products are all on display and/or sale, and there are plenty of snack stands. There are tents on-site, but dress appropriately for the weather—it can get very hot, both inside and out.

May through August: **Belleayre Music Festival** (845-254-5600), Belleayre Ski Center, Route 28, Highmount. Call for ticket information. This new music festival has been attracting outstanding performers to its mountain setting. The likes of the Cleo Laine, Juice Newton, Pete Seeger, Jay Ungar and Molly Mason, the West Point Military Band, and Glimmerglass Opera alumnae have entertained thousands, and the festival keeps growing. There are seats under a tent and lawn for the weather-wary, and the evening concerts offer a cooling summer's night of entertainment.

September: **Hudson Valley Garlic Festival** (845-246-3642), Cantine Field, Saugerties, late September. Free. Visitors won't have to use a map to find this festival; the nutty fragrance of garlic attracts tens of thousands to the one-day affair, where garlic-flavored foods—from pizza to ice cream—await the connoisseur. Crafts vendors and entertainment enliven the day, and there are lots of garlic vendors and culinary information on hand as well. An unusual and really fun day, regardless of how much garlic means to you.

October: **The Burning of Kingston Reenactment** (845-331-7517). In 1777, the British invaded and burned the city of Kingston. Now the city reenacts the battle, complete with British and American troops and period music, crafts, food, and entertainment, including a colonial dance. The battle takes place the first weekend in October, but call for specific times and events.

October: **Belleayre Mountain Fall Festival and Concerts** (845-254-5600). Highmount is just off Route 28, about 40 miles west of Kingston; watch for signs to the upper lodge. Open 10–5. Free (there is a charge for the ski lift). Held Saturday and Sunday of Columbus Day weekend, this festival attracts thousands of leaf-peeping visitors. The fun goes on all day and includes bands, crafts, entertainment, German food and beer, chicken barbecues, and ski equipment sales. The festival is well run, and the site has magnificent views of the mountains. Wear appropriate clothing and get there early; it is held rain or shine.

October: **Mum Festival** (845-246-2809), Seamon Park, Route 9W, south of Saugerties. Open dawn to dusk. Park is free; admission fee to festivals. For the entire month of October, Seamon Park is one big chrysanthemum celebration. Thousands of mums bloom throughout this 17-acre park, and the display of yellow, lavender, and rust flowers in shaped beds is breathtaking. Weekend festivals offer music, entertainment, and food, and there is a parade on opening day.

October: The **Haunted Hudson** is the theme for Halloween goings-on at the **Rondout Lighthouse** (Kingston, at the foot of Broadway). Set sail from the Hudson River Maritime Museum and learn about the ghostly inhabitants who still haunt the region each October. Reservations are required; call 845-338-0071.

October: A haunted hayride and haunted house may be just the way to spend an eerie evening in the Catskills. At **Headless Horseman Hayrides** (Route 9W, Ulster Park; 845-339-BOOO), visitors will meet up with some scary denizens of the region. Rides take place weekends throughout October, and reservations are required. Ask about the scare factor if you are taking children along.

Also see Hurley under *Villages* for descriptions of Hurley Stone House Day and the Hurley corn festival, and see *Selective Shopping* for holiday tours at Michael's Candy Corner.

V. Delaware County

One of the largest counties in New York (about the size of Rhode Island), Delaware County is a region of rolling meadows, curious cows, and tiny towns that look as if they were plucked from a 19th-century picture book. More than 64,000 acres are state owned and have been proclaimed "forever wild." This foresight has resulted in an area that is a paradise for anglers, hunters, hikers, bikers, walkers, and those who just enjoy rural charm and an old-fashioned way of life coupled with modern convenience and an easy drive.

Much of the charm of Delaware County comes from the strong influence of the 19th century, which turns up in local architecture and community get-togethers. Towns throughout the county are filled with homes and commercial buildings of Federal, Queen Anne, Gothic Revival, and other styles; drive along the back roads and you'll find dairy farms and mountain views nearly unchanged for a century and more. From the winter pancake breakfasts to the holiday open houses, from county fairs to summer auctions, the region brings back a sense of community celebration that has been lost in much of modern life.

GUIDANCE
    Delaware County Chamber of Commerce (607-746-2281 or 1-800-642-4443), 114 Main Street, Delhi 13753; www.delawarecounty.org.
GETTING THERE
    Delaware County is most easily reached by taking the New York State (NYS) Thruway, exit 19 at Kingston, to Route 28 west (PINE HILL sign), and following Route 28 into the county. Route 30 intersects with Route 28 in Margaretville.
MEDICAL EMERGENCY
    Margaretville Memorial Hospital (845-586-2631), Route 28, Margaretville.

TO SEE

Delaware County Historical Association (607-746-3849), Route 10, 2 miles north of Delhi. Open May through October; hours vary. Admission fee. A fascinating site comprised of historic buildings that have been donated, purchased, or just rescued from neglect, where visitors

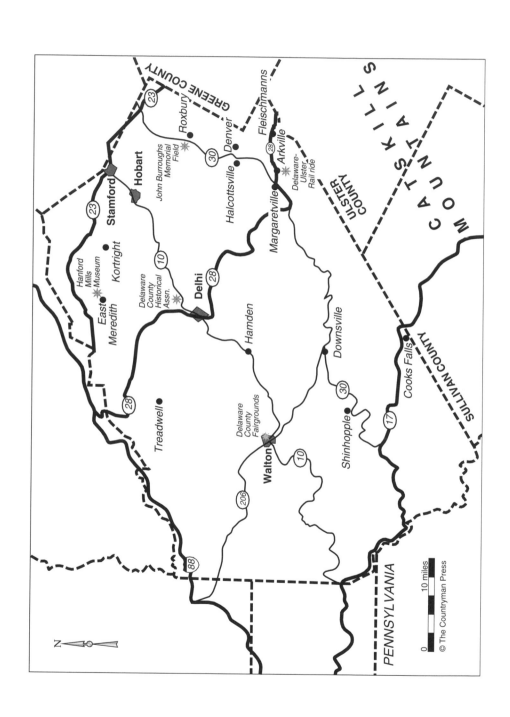

JOSEPH PUGLISI

Hanford Mills Museum

can get a taste of life in rural America during the 19th century. The main building houses a library and exhibit hall, where changing displays of farm tools, household goods, folk art, and crafts are offered each season. There are additional interpretive exhibits that focus on different aspects of farm life in several of the other buildings. The **Gideon Frisbee House,** a 1797 example of Federal-style architecture, once served as a tavern, county meeting room, post office, and private home. The interior has been restored to reflect the changes in life from pioneer days to the period just before World War I. Decorative arts and furniture collections include Belter chairs, woven rugs, souvenir glassware, and a chair that tradition holds was used at the Constitutional Convention. The Frisbee barn houses a collection of farm implements and a permanent exhibit titled "It's a Fine Growing Time," which guides the visitor through the joys and hard work of a farmer's year. Other buildings include the gunsmith's shop, the schoolhouse (still in use for educational programs), a tollhouse, a farm lane, and even a family cemetery. Special events include a farm festival at which you can enjoy demonstrations of old-fashioned rural skills.

Hanford Mills Museum (607-278-5744). Take Route 28 to the intersection of Routes 10 and 12 in East Meredith; follow the signs. Open May through October, with some special events in the off-season; hours vary. Admission fee. Once the industrial center of the surrounding farm country, the mill has today been restored to its clanking and chugging past. Flour, lumber, wooden goods like butter tubs and porch posts, and electricity (courtesy of nearby Kortright Creek) were all produced at Hanford Mills, one of the few remaining industrial mills of the last century that are still in use. Visitors will see lathes, jigsaws, and other machines used to produce woodenware, along with the pulleys and belts that were once the staples of manufacturing. Inside the mill itself, a series of catwalks and walkways winds through the workrooms, where museum interpreters are still hard at work; downstairs, the enormous metal reconstruction of the original wooden waterwheel is turned by the millpond waters. Throughout the site, water-generated electricity powers lightbulbs and other machines, a reminder of the time when light didn't come with the simple flick of a switch. Also on the site is the **Gray Barn,** in which there are agricultural and farm equipment displays, a shingle mill, the millpond, and the mill store, where local crafts are sold. Hanford Mills hosts several special events each year, including fly-fishing clinics at the millpond, Independence Day complete with ice cream and speeches, and late winter's Ice Harvest Day (when the ice is cut and stored for the summer ice cream social).

HISTORIC SITES

✎& **Delaware and Ulster Railride** (845-586-DURR), Route 28, Arkville. Open late May through October; schedules vary. Entrance to the site and depot is free, but admission is charged for the ride. The Catskill Mountains were once a daily stop for tourist and milk trains from New York City, but when the service stopped in the 1960s, many believed the echo of a train whistle was gone forever from the valleys. The railride has resurrected some of the favorite trains that rattled along the tracks, and there is no better way to sample the fun of old-time travel than to hop aboard any of the vintage cars. Try the *Doodlebug,* also known as the *Red Heifer,* one of the few self-propelled trains still at work. Or take some photos of the farms and homes, wave at the cows, and enjoy the open-air observation car. The conductor may tell a tale or two about train history; special events, held throughout the summer, include a costumed train robbery, a fiddler's get-together, Halloween ghost trains, foliage runs, and more. All the tours begin at the restored Arkville Depot, and you'll find a gift shop, snack caboose, rest rooms, and wheelchair access on-site.

John Burroughs Memorial Field. Take Route 30 north through Roxbury

JOSEPH PUGLISI

Delaware & Ulster Railride

and follow signs. Open year-round, weather permitting. Free. Although this is not an "active" site, the former writing studio and grave of nature writer John Burroughs is worth the stop. A friend of Teddy Roosevelt, Henry Ford, and Thomas Edison, Burroughs is a respected American nature writer whose many essays spoke of Delaware County, the Catskills, and the Hudson Valley. Today his writing nook, **Woodchuck Lodge,** is maintained by his family (it is opened on an extremely limited basis, although you can view the site from the road). Just up the road is Memorial Field—which contains Boyhood Rock, where Burroughs spent many hours observing the natural world—and the Burroughs grave site. This is a quiet spot with a breathtaking view of the Catskills, a lovely place to sit and enjoy the same scene that inspired a great author.

SCENIC DRIVES

Delaware County offers the driver many lovely views and well-maintained main roads, but—as in any other rural area—some of the back roads can be tricky in bad weather, four-wheel drive or not. Dirt roads are charming, but even the toughest truck can become bogged down in mud or snow along them. Deer and other wildlife are also a problem, especially at night, so be aware and don't rush.

If you want to see dairy farms, cornfields, the county seat, and the Pepacton Reservoir, start in **Margaretville** and follow Route 28 to

Delhi (the town square once made the cover of the *Saturday Evening Post*). Then take Route 10 south to Walton, Route 206 east to Downsville, and Route 30 back to Margaretville. The roads are well marked, and you will pass two covered bridges along the way, one near Hamden, the other outside of Downsville. This drive also takes you past farm stands (some let you choose your produce and put your money in a box), including Octagon Farms near Walton, where an eight-sided house has been made into a bed & breakfast (see *Lodging*). Legend has it that the ghost of a young woman killed in a carriage accident roams the road at night. If you have the time, you can detour through Delhi and follow the signs west to Franklin on the Franklin Turnpike, a winding road that offers beautiful vistas in summer.

A second county drive follows part of the old turnpike, which was a major stagecoach route through the area. From **Margaretville** follow Route 28 west to Andes and then to Delhi, then take Route 10 north to Stamford, make a right onto Route 23 and drive to Grand Gorge, and, finally, turn right onto Route 30 and head south back to Margaretville. If you have a chance, stop in Stamford and look at some of the grand homes that made this village a popular turn-of-the-19th-century resort area and gave it the name Queen of the Catskills.

If you wish to drive up **Mount Utsayantha,** follow Route 23 east to Mountain Avenue; the twisty road is accessible in spring, summer, and fall, and the views are beautiful. Call the Department of Environmental Conservation (607-652-7364) for more information about this drive or hike. The headwaters of the Delaware River East Branch rise alongside Route 30 between Grand Gorge and Roxbury, and the road back to Margaretville passes through farm country.

TO DO

AUCTIONS

If it seems that everything is auctioned off in Delaware County, don't be surprised—it is. Cows, puppies, cabbages, eggs, Shaker chairs, Irish pewter, even antique coffins have all shown up in the hands of auctioneers. Auction lovers don't need to plan ahead; just pick up a copy of the local newspaper and look for a sale. Some auctions are weekly institutions, attended by locals and weekenders alike; other auctions are specialty sales for real estate or farm equipment; still others are one-time-only house sales, where the contents of a home can include some surprises.

Country auctions are fun, but there are some tips. Get there early: You have to examine the goods before the sale and sign up for a card or paddle. Bring a chair for outdoor auctions, and a hat or umbrella depending on the weather. Most auctions advertise that they accept "cash or good checks"; in the latter case, this can be tricky if you are from out of state or not known to the auctioneer; call ahead for information. Don't buy anything you can't carry, unless you plan to make shipping arrangements. And finally, know what you're bidding on: Don't buy the overstuffed armchair because you thought you were getting the Tiffany lamp.

Every Saturday night at 7, year-round, **Roberts' Auction** (845-254-4490), Main Street, Fleischmanns (park in the lot or along the street), sells everything from fine antiques to a better grade of junk. Auctioneer Eddie Roberts keeps the sale moving, and you'll never be bored. The crowd is a good, often lively mix of local people and visitors; there are rest rooms and a snack bar. Get there early, since many seats are reserved and the others go fast.

McIntosh Auction Service (607-832-4829), Old Creamery, Route 28 north to Route 6, Bovina (watch for signs for Bovina Center), has Saturday auctions at 6:30 PM year-round. There is plenty of parking here, both behind the barn and in the field, not far from the cows. The Creamery is heated in winter and has a rest room and snack bar. Seats go fast, and auctioneers Chuck McIntosh and Bob Burgin keep everyone happy with quick sales and good humor. Everything from furniture to blackberries to fine antiques is sold here, and the setting is country at its best. They also do many on-site auctions throughout the summer.

CANOEING

The best canoeing in Delaware County is along the western border near Pennsylvania, but canoeing, like all other water sports, should not be attempted unless you are familiar with the rivers. Both the Delaware and Susquehanna can be treacherous, especially in spring or after a heavy rain. Your best bet is to use one of the canoe outfitting services, which will provide you with the right equipment, maps, and even a shuttle service.

Al's Sport Store (607-363-7135), Shinhopple, is a clearinghouse for canoe and fishing information.

Also in Shinhopple is **Peaceful Valley Campsite** (607-363-2211), which offers limited outfitting services.

DeNys Canoe Sales (607-467-2303), Deposit, also rents canoes for day trips.

FARM STANDS

When the harvest begins in early summer with strawberries and flowers, farm stands begin to blossom along the roadsides as well. In Delaware County there are many farm stands where you can pick out the produce, bag it, and leave the money for the owner. Other stands are a bit more formal, but they all stock the best local fruits, vegetables, maple syrup, and honey. Days and hours of operation vary widely with the season and the stock, and some crops, including strawberries, seem to disappear after only a few days, so the best way to find local produce is to watch for roadside stands or stop and ask at the nearest town. This is

Take the kids to a pick-your-own farm in the autumn.

also savvy farm country; in the past few years county agriculture has "grown" to include specialty crops such as blue potatoes and garlic, which often turn up on Manhattan's trendiest restaurant plates.

The largest and best produce market in the county is the **Pakatakan Farmer's Market,** held every Saturday from the week before Memorial Day to Columbus Day starting at 9 AM. It's found at the Kelly Round

Barn on Route 30 north of Margaretville. Free admission. Vendors offer everything from fresh trout, organic produce, and bouquets of wildflowers to fine crafts and home-baked pies. Selections change with the seasons, and there is plenty of food on hand to sample for breakfast and lunch.

Mac's Farm Stand is located on Route 28 near Delhi, just before the turn into the town. The stand stocks a wide variety of produce throughout the summer and into apple season.

Roxbury Gardens Stand can be found roadside on Route 30 just south of Roxbury Village. Choose your produce, then leave your payment. Selections vary with the season, although you'll generally find great corn, melons, squash, apples, and tomatoes.

Octagon Farm Market, Route 10, Hamden, sells its own fruits and vegetables, along with lots of other local offerings, and has a large selection of apples and excellent cider in fall.

Honey lovers may want to check out **Herklotz Apiaries** (607-829-8687), Merrickville Road, Franklin (open year-round), for its selection of sweets, candles, and other honey-related items. **Crescent Valley Apiaries,** New Kingston Road, Bovina (watch for signs), also stocks honey from its hives, as does **Ballard Honey,** Main Street, Roxbury.

Because the tree-tapping season is so changeable, maple syrup lovers should call the Delaware County Chamber of Commerce (607-746-2281) for up-to-date information on farms that offer sap season tours; the chamber also publishes a farm bounty map.

FISHING

Delaware County is crisscrossed by the East and West Branches of the Delaware River and by the Susquehanna and Beaverkill Rivers, and served by the Cannonsville, Pepacton, and Schoharie Reservoirs, making fishing a popular sport in this region. New York State fishing licenses are required. They are easy to purchase in most towns; check with the town clerk or at the village offices. For reservoir fishing, special permits are required—call the **Environmental Protection Agency** offices at 607-363-7501 for information on permits and maps. Stream fishing areas open to the public are indicated by brown-and-yellow wooden signs along the streams and rivers; most areas offer off-road parking as well. Detailed maps are available where you purchase your fishing license and at town office. Riverfront property may be posted or off-limits as part of the New York City water supply, so the maps should be consulted; heavy fines could result from illegal fishing. Further information on specific fishing areas can be obtained by calling 1-800-642-4443 (outside New York State) or 1-800-356-5615 (in New York State).

GOLF

Golf enthusiasts will appreciate the courses in the Delaware County area, where the lush greens of summer and the blazing trees of autumn provide everyone—duffer and hacker alike—a lovely setting in which to play. Green fees vary depending on the season and the length of the membership, so call for specific information.

Hanah Country Inn and Golf Resort (845-586-2100), Route 30, Margaretville, has an 18-hole course, practice greens, and a driving range. There is also a golf school on the premises.

Shepherd Hills Golf Course (607-326-7121), Golf Course Road, Roxbury, has a hilly 18-hole course with beautiful views of the countryside.

State University of New York (607-746-4281), off Route 28 near Delhi (follow signs), has a course that is used as a training area for students in the turf management program. It's a small gem and rarely overcrowded.

Stamford Golf Club (607-652-7398). Take Route 10 to Taylor Road in Stamford. Complete facilities, 18 holes, and a driving range.

Meadows Driving Range (845-586-4104), Route 28, Margaretville. Those who just want to practice their techniques should head here, where there is also miniature golf for the kids (and putter-challenged adults).

HIKING AND BIKING

A large part of Delaware County is part of the "forever wild" park system in New York State, and as such has not been developed with easy-to-use trails or tourist-related sites. Many of the existing hiking trails are for experienced hikers only, and some require overnight stays in simple trail huts; those who would like detailed trail information should contact the New York Department of Conservation at Bear Spring Mountain (607-865-6161). Marked bike trails are also scarce in Delaware County, although many of the roads listed under *Scenic Drives* can be navigated safely by bicycle. In fact, just about any road should lead to lovely vistas and scenic overlooks, but bike rentals are hard to come by.

Ski Plattekill (1-800-GOTTA-BIKE), Plattekill Mountain Road, Route 30, Roxbury. Open 10–5 April through November on weekends and holidays; July through Labor Day on Friday, weekends, and holidays. Admission fee. This outstanding mountain bike area offers equipment rentals, a chairlift ride to the summit, and more than 60 miles of trails. Beginners shouldn't be wary of trying mountain biking here, since a package deal provides a bike, lift ticket, helmet, and 1-hour lesson with guide; riders can then enjoy the excercise all day. Sanctioned races are held throughout the season, and the site has dining and camping facilities. This is a great weekend stop anytime in summer, and even more so during leaf-peeping season.

LODGING

Bed & breakfasts provide a special way to see Delaware County, and most are moderately priced and offer package rates as well. Call before you go, since many are booked for holiday weekends and special events. For information, call 1-800-DEL-INNS.

Bella Vista Ridge (607-746-2553), Route 10, Hamden 13782. ($) An

Italianate home set above the surrounding farmland looking across to the mountains. Guests can visit the gift shop or walk into town. Nearby are fishing, hiking, swimming, and places of historic interest. Six rooms share three baths. Full breakfast. Open year-round.

Breezy Acres (607-538-9338), Route 10, Hobart 13788. ($$) This is right in the heart of farm country, so guests may take a stroll before breakfast to check out the scenery. The owner is a quilt collector, and the walls of this B&B are decorated with an array of colorful quilts. In the warm-weather months breakfast is served on a lovely brick patio surrounded by gardens. Only three rooms, but all have private bath. Full breakfast. Open year-round.

Carriage House (607-326-7992), Main Street, Halcottsville 12438. ($) This Victorian house, more than 100 years old, still has many of its original furnishings; it is run by the builder's granddaughter, whose homemade breakfast breads and muffins are local favorites. Sherry and herbal tea are offered to guests in the afternoon. The house is set in a tiny hamlet that lies along the Delaware River, and there are many places to stroll the country lanes. Four rooms share two baths. Children welcome. Open year-round.

The Country House B&B (607-832-4371), Box 109, Bramley Mountain Road, Bovina Center 13740. ($) Built circa 1840, this 600-acre working farm features hand-stenciled walls and lovely wooden floors. Hiking, fishing, and swimming are available on the property, and guests can enjoy a full breakfast on the front porch or in the gazebo, weather permitting. Three guest rooms, all with private bath. Open year-round.

Hanah Country Inn (845-586-2100), Route 30, Margaretville 12455. ($$$) A full-service resort, the inn has a championship 18-hole golf course (see *To Do—Golf*), health club, tennis courts, swimming pool, fishing stream, and restaurant. Golfers should note that a nationally recognized school is held at the inn every summer. All rooms have private bath. Children welcome. Open year-round.

The Inn at Cup and Chaucer (607-865-7083), 20 North Street, Walton 13856. ($) This restored 1895 Victorian home features a bookstore with a café and gallery on the first floor. The original floors, woodwork, and stained-glass windows make this a cozy place to relax. Four rooms with private bath. Full breakfast served. Open year-round.

Margaretville Mountain Inn (845-586-3933), Mountain Road, Margaretville 12455. ($$) This restored 11-bedroom Victorian home was built as a boardinghouse and functioned as a working farm. It offers a spectacular view of the New Kingston Valley from the old-fashioned veranda. It's just a short drive from town. A full breakfast is served in an elegant dining room, outdoors in summer. Six rooms, all with private bath. There are limited facilities available for children and pets; call ahead for information. Nonsmoking environment. Open year-round.

Octagon Bed and Breakfast (607-865-7416), Route 10, Walton, 13856. ($)

This bed & breakfast is in a historic octagonal house built in 1855; it is also opposite the farm stand run by the owners. This is one of the only eight brick octagonal houses in America. The farmer's breakfast served here is hearty and may include pancakes and sausage or eggs and waffles. Four rooms share 1½ baths. Children welcome. Open year-round.

The Old Stageline Stop B&B (607-746-6856), Box 125, Turnpike Road, Meridale 13806. ($$) Enjoy a carefree stay in a 1900s farmhouse that was formerly a dairy farm and is set high on a hill with magnificent views. The rooms are decorated with country furnishings. A full breakfast is served in the sun-filled dining room or on the porch, weather permitting. Rooms with private or shared bath available. Open year-round.

Rambling Rose B&B (607-865-8366), RD #1, Box 47, River Road East, Walton 13856. ($) A century-old farmhouse with renovated rooms on 150 scenic acres on the West Branch of the Delaware River. Guests can hike and fish on the property and have a full breakfast while enjoying views of the countryside. There is one large bedroom with a private bath, and two rooms that share a bath. Open year-round.

🐾⌇ **River Run** (845-254-4884), Main Street, Fleischmanns 12430. ($$) This restored 20-room house has seven guest rooms with either private or shared bath. The yard slopes down to the river, and guests can walk into town (there's a great country auction only minutes away every Saturday night; see *To Do—Auctions*). The unusual aspect of this inn is that it welcomes both children and pets (just give the innkeepers some notice about the four-footed family members). Breakfast is hearty and healthy, and the inn has lots of antiques, stained glass, and old-fashioned comfort to offer visitors. For two consecutive years, this inn was the recipient of the Catskill Service Award for best accommodations in the Belleayre region.

Silver Maples (607-746-3516), DeLancey 13752; call for directions. ($$) Open September through May only. You may want to schedule a visit in very early spring, when the farm is busy with maple syrup production. Of course, breakfast features the local sweetener, and guests can take country walks, fish, swim, or shop nearby. Four bedrooms share two baths.

Swallow's Nest B&B (607-832-4547 or 516-887-2358), RR #65, Box 112, Bramley Mountain Road, Bovina Center 13740. ($$) Set in the midst of the Catskills, this 1840 farmhouse tastefully blends the past and present. Relax on the porch by the pond or brook. Full gourmet breakfast. Hiking, fishing, horseback riding, and skiing are all nearby. Private or shared bath available. Open year-round.

Victoria Rose (607-363-7838), Main Street, Downsville 13755. ($$) A lovely Queen Anne home, filled with antiques and country touches, where guests enjoy breakfast, tea, and evening snacks. Four rooms, each with private bath. Open year-round.

WHERE TO EAT

DINING OUT

The Old Schoolhouse Inn (607-363-7814), Upper Main Street, Downsville. ($$) Open daily (except Monday) for lunch 11:30–2:30; for dinner 5–9. Brunch is served Sunday 11:30–2:30. This restaurant is housed in a renovated schoolhouse that dates back to 1903. In a Victorian-style dining room hearty portions of standard American favorites are the mainstay. The French lobster, prime rib, and seafood medley are the most popular entrées, and the homemade desserts are first-rate. Thanks to a local taxidermist, a grizzly bear, buffalo, and bison decorate the bar!

EATING OUT

Casual is the word for Delaware County restaurants, where moderate prices are the rule at dinner. Hours and days of operation vary with the seasons, so it is smart to call ahead. In general, reservations are not needed, except for holiday weekends.

Aiello's (607-865-6707), 5 Bridge Street, Walton. ($) Open every day for lunch and dinner 11–9. This Italian American establishment is renowned for serving the best pizza and prime rib around and is a favorite with local residents. Everything here is homemade. The owner tells us that this is one of the few places in Delaware County where the eggplant is fresh, not frozen!

Cafe on Main (845-586-2343); located in the Commons, Main Street, Margaretville. ($$) Open daily for lunch; dinner from 5 PM Thursday through Monday. A relaxed place to watch the world go by on Main Street (or shop between courses), this café serves excellent light fare and many regional Italian specialties. Dinner reservations are recommended, and you can arrange to take out any of the delightful meals.

The Cheese Barrel (845-586-4666), Main Street, Margaretville. ($) Open daily 9–5. An excellent selection of snacks and cheese is found in this shop, and the dishes are great for takeout and picnics. The homemade soups are satisfying. There is a dining area.

The Flour Patch (845-586-1919), Bridge Street, Margaretville. Open Tuesday through Sunday 7–2. Here you'll find the best "made from scratch" muffins in the Catskills—plain, simple, hearty, along with great bagels and sandwiches.

The Hidden Inn (607-538-9259), Main Street, South Kortright. ($) Open for dinner Monday through Saturday 5–9, Sunday noon–7. This quiet country inn in a pastoral setting features an international menu. The specialty of the house is prime rib, but you will also find that the lamb, duck, and seafood entrées are tasty. (Four rooms are available for overnight accomodations.)

Leo's (607-538-1611), Route 10, Main Street, Hobart. ($) Open Monday through Saturday for lunch and dinner 11–10. Closed Sunday. The

Continental cuisine here is varied and the pizza is quite good. A local haunt that offers a little bit of everything.

The **Square Restaurant** (845-586-4884), Binnekill Square, Main Street, Margaretville. ($$) Open Thursday through Saturday for lunch at noon; dinner served Tuesday through Sunday from 5:30. A casual, relaxing restaurant, The Square has windows and a dining deck overlooking a small stream. The food has a Swiss touch, and the veal dishes are particularly good. Venison is served in-season, and there are excellent daily specials. Everything is cooked to order. Children are welcome.

T. A.'s Place (607-865-7745), 249 Delaware Street, Walton. ($) Open daily for breakfast, lunch, and early supper 6 AM–7 PM. Old-fashioned American favorites like meat loaf and mashed potatoes, grilled pork chops and marinated chicken breasts, are the specialties here. Everything is homemade.

ENTERTAINMENT

West Kortright Centre (607-278-5454, or write Box 100, East Meredith 13757). Take Route 28 to East Meredith, then follow signs to the center, which is in West Kortright; or follow signs from Route 10, 2 miles north of Delhi near Elk Creek Road. Open July through September; performance schedules vary. Admission fee. Nestled in a hidden valley, the West Kortright Centre is housed in a charming white-clapboard, 1850s church that was rescued from neglect by dedicated volunteers. Stained-glass windows and kerosene chandeliers glow in the twilight. The center offers unique performances throughout the summer, with concerts and special events for every taste, from bluegrass to zydeco, performance art to dance. Concerts are held both outdoors, in the green fields, and inside, where guests are seated in unique rounded pews; the lawn is often dotted with preconcert picnickers. The intimate setting makes all events a delight, and you may just bump into the evening's featured performer as he or she warms up in the churchyard.

SELECTIVE SHOPPING

Delaware County has several unique crafts and specialty shops, although you can find good shopping in just about every village. Arkville is home to a lively flea market on Route 28 every Saturday and Sunday from spring through autumn, weather permitting. It begins at 9 AM.

Rocko! (845-586-3978) at Main Street (just west of the traffic light) has a wide selection of fine jewelry, minerals, and geologic collectibles (including a dinosaur egg!).

Paisley's Country Gallery (845-676-3533), Route 28, Andes, has an amazing collection of baskets from all over the world. Blown glass is created at **Sweetwater Glass Studios and Gallery** (845-676-4622), Fall Clove

Road, Andes, with ornaments, goblets, and glasses the specialties.

Parker House Gifts (607-746-3141), Main Street, Delhi, is a cornucopia of fine jewelry, gifts, and tableware.

Purple Mountain Press (845-254-4062), Main Street, Fleischmanns, publishes and stocks a large number of books about the Catskills and New York regional history, though it is not open to the public; call for the catalog.

On Main Street in Margaretville the **Commons** houses a number of specialty shops, including **Home Goods** (the best kitchenware and specialty shop in the Catskills), **Franklyn Clothing,** and **Kicking Stones,** with its fine antiques and quirky collectibles. Across the street the **Village Homemaker** (845-586-3620), featuring hundreds of fabrics and calico gift items, is a quilter's delight located in a beautifully restored landmark building.

SPECIAL EVENTS

Since Delaware County is still a rural area, the special events here tend to take place during the "better-weather" months, from early spring until autumn. For specific dates and times, unless otherwise noted, contact the **Delaware County Chamber of Commerce** (607-746-2281).

June: The **Arkville Fair** is held on Route 28, complete with parade, marching bands, entertainment, crafts, and food.

July: The week of July Fourth ushers in the **Firemen's Field Days** at the village park in Margaretville, where a carnival, rides, entertainment, games of skill (and chance), and food concessions keep everyone busy. At the Andes Presbyterian Church, Route 28, Andes, the **Strawberry Festival** is celebrated each July Fourth weekend. July also brings the four-day **Lumberjack Festival** (1-800-467-3109), Riverside Park, Deposit, which includes fireworks, an art show, antique cars, raft races on the Delaware River, a walking tour of historic homes, a carnival, and lots of food, along with demonstrations of lumberjack skills. The **Peaceful Valley Bluegrass Festival** (1-800-467-3109), Downsville, features some of the best in traditional music. Dozens of bands perform all weekend, and there are square dances, jam sessions, and food concessions. Held on a 500-acre farm, the festival is great for families or anyone who wants to have a chance to bring along a banjo, guitar or mandolin. There are camping facilities but spaces are limited, so call ahead.

August: The charming village of Franklin hosts **Old Franklin Day** on Main Street, with sales, open houses, displays, and special events. Call the Delaware Chamber of Commerce for dates and times.

August: The Delaware County Fair (607-746-2281), at the fairgrounds off Route 10 in Walton (follow signs), runs the second week of August. Open daily 9 AM–10 PM. Admission fee. Part of the agricultural and social life of Delaware County for more than a century, this is one of the last of the truly agricultural county fairs in New York State. Each year hundreds of 4-H members gather to show off their prize goods, including sheep, pigs, cows, horses, and rabbits. The finest local produce is displayed and sold, and the handiwork building bursts with the colors of hundreds of quilts, afghans, and doilies. The celebration begins on Main Street with a parade, and visitors will enjoy the show of the best livestock and the latest farm equipment and agricultural news, demonstrations, and other "country stuff." Sample some milk punch served by the Delaware Dairy Princess and her court; try your hand at games of skill and chance; let the kids have fun on the carousel and Ferris wheel (a delight at night). You probably won't bid on the livestock, but you will enjoy the demolition derby with its action and noise, the tractor pulls, the horse shows, and the popular animal dress-up days. Don't worry about going hungry here: The pancake and pie tents, the sausage sandwiches, and the antique popcorn wagon—itself on the National Register of Historic Places—will take care of the greatest appetite.

September: **Woodstock Film Festival** (845-679-4215), P.O. Box 1406, Woodstock, New York, 12498. This event lasts for four days (call for exact dates) and features independent films, workshops, and lectures by renowned directors, critics, and actors, and offers an exciting selection of films. www.woodstockfilmfestival.com

VI. Greene County

Greene County offers the perfect outdoor experience any time of year. In winter dramatic, snow-filled gorges yield to gray and white fields, and cross-country skiers may come across bear tracks; others can fly down the slopes at Hunter, Ski Windham, and Cortina Valley, which provide some of the best downhill skiing in the East. In spring bright wildflowers cling to wind-scraped rocks, and visitors to the county can watch (or join in) the Spring Rush, a running, biking, and canoeing competition. Each June a tour of homes, farms, and estates is held to benefit the county historical society. Summer celebrates its warmth with the gifts of icy brooks for tired feet and a flood of cultural festivals. This is a fine time of year to visit North and South Lakes and Kaaterskill Falls. Autumn is a season to wonder at the colors that transform the hills and towns into paint pots full of orange and red—the magic that drew Rip Van Winkle to Catskill still enchants visitors today. Or stop by Thomas Cole's house, the place where the Hudson River School of landscape painting began. Other ghosts haunt Greene County as well; in Leeds, if you walk along a dark country road, you might run into the spirit of the servant girl who was dragged to her death by her master and his horse. You'll find both an Irish Cultural and Sports Center and a tiny Butterfly Museum in the same town—East Durham. There are also hiking trails, museums, country auctions, breathtaking waterfalls, waterfront villages, festivals, and fine restaurants to enjoy.

GUIDANCE

Greene County Promotion Department (518-943-3223 or 1-800-355-CATS), Box 527, Catskill 12414; www.greene-ny.com.

GETTING THERE

Greene County is off exit 21 of the New York State (NYS) Thruway. Routes 23 and 23A run east–west across the county; Route 32 runs north–south. Almost all sites here can be accessed from these roads.

MEDICAL EMERGENCY

Columbia Greene Medical Center (518-943-2000), 159 Jefferson Heights, Catskill.

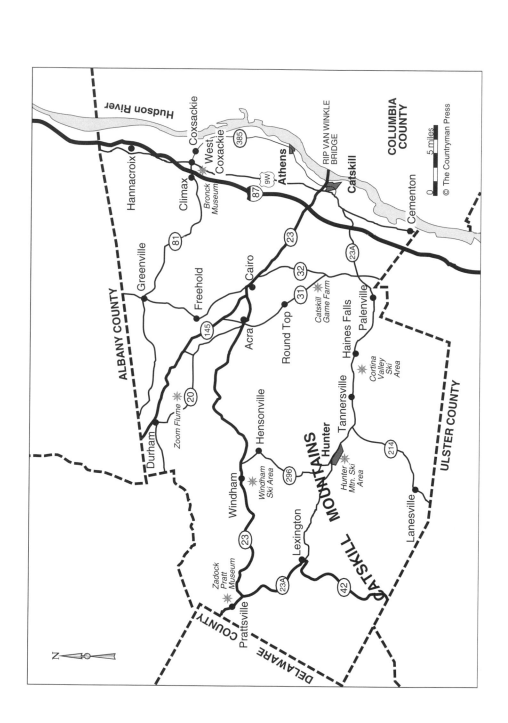

TO SEE

Bronck Museum (518-731-6490 or 731-8862), off Route 9W on Pieter Bronck Road in Coxsackie. Open Memorial Day through October 15; call for hours. There are winter hours for the **Vedder Memorial Library** (call 518-731-1033 or 731-6822 for information). Admission fee. Once home to nine generations of the Bronck family (which also gave its name to the Bronx), the museum's collection traces the history of the Upper Hudson Valley. Visitors should begin with the original structure, a 1663 stone house that contains an Indian lookout loft—from a time when settlers were not welcome. The house was remodeled in the late 18th century, when a wing was added along with fine paneling and fireplaces. Displays include an impressive exhibit of local textiles, looms, and spinning wheels that chronicle the production of Bronck cloth and clothing. The 1738 Brick House was connected to the stone house through the hyphen-hall. This part of the family home is now used to display, among other things, a fine collection of paintings by 18th- and 19th-century artists, including Ammi Phillips, John Frederick Kensett, Nehemiah Partridge, Ezra Ames, Benjamin Stone, and Thomas Cole. Outside is a kitchen, a charming, tiny house itself, set apart from the main house in the style of plantations. The displays here consist of furniture and kitchen tools. Farm buffs will enjoy the three barns that are found at the complex, each representing a different era. The Dutch barn, with its huge beams; the center-pole-supported, 13-sided Liberty Barn, once the storage area for the wheat harvest, now the oldest documented multisided barn in New York; and the Victorian horse barn (called the Antiquarium) each offers the visitor a look at the tolls, carriages, and wagons of the day. A walk through the family and slave cemeteries will bring you even closer to the people who made the Bronck complex a working and living farm. The Bronck Museum sponsors a Greene County house tour each June, when a different area of the county offers a look into the region's many historic homes. Researchers into local history will want to stop at the Vedder Memorial Library, with its extensive collections of Greene County and New York State history.

Cedar Grove (Thomas Cole House) (518-731-6490), 218 Spring Street, Catskill. Open Memorial Day through Columbus Day weekend; hours vary, so call ahead. Admission fee. Thomas Cole, a painter, poet, and essayist, played a significant role in determining how America viewed its landscapes and vistas; his 19th-century paintings helped inspire the land conservation movement, and tourism became an industry as visitors trooped to the Catskills in search of the sites Cole depicted. His family home, Cedar Grove, is open to the public and presents an unusual look into the daily life of a Hudson River painter (in fact, Cole is credited with founding the Hudson River School of landscape art). The graceful Federal-style house and gardens still look off to the Catskill

Mountains, and a locust tree that Cole mentioned in his writings remains outside the front entrance. Inside, interpretive exhibits introduce the visitor to Cole and his family, the Catskills region, artists such as Asher B. Durand and Frederic Church, and the Hudson River School. Several small oils and sketches by Cole are on display, along with family heirlooms including his aeolian harp (a wind-powered musical instrument), sketching stool, paint box, and Bible; you'll also see leaves from his journal and his traveling trunk. Outside on the grounds, you can stop and see the family's Greek Revival privy (with a front door for family and a back door for servants), and Cole's "Old Studio," which once served as slave quarters. There are lectures and events scheduled throughout the summer, and visitors can take a short walk to the Cole family gravesite.

Zadock Pratt Museum and **Pratt's Rocks** (518-299-3395), Route 23, Prattsville. Open Memorial Day through Columbus Day, Wednesday through Sunday 1–4. Admission fee. Call ahead for group tours. Born in 1790, genius businessman Zadock Pratt started out as a harness maker and soon went into the leather tanning business. He became such a prominent community leader that the town of Prattsville was named in his honor. His tanning facilities were among the largest in the state, and he built many of Prattsville's homes for his workers (more than 90 percent still stand). In later years Pratt served in both the state and federal governments. Today his home is a museum that shows what life in New York was like in the 1850s. Exhibits focus on the tanning industry and the story of Greene County, with rooms displaying period furniture and decorative arts. In a separate gallery the work of local artists is shown and special events like the holiday decorating show are held. When your visit to the museum is completed, you can stop just outside Prattsville (Route 23 heading west) at Pratt's Rocks, a memorial carved by an itinerant stonemason. The huge stone reliefs show Pratt's son, a favorite horse, and Pratt himself. There is a small picnic area overlooking Schoharie Creek; free.

FOR FAMILIES

Catskill Game Farm (518-678-9595), Game Farm Road, off Route 32, Catskill. Open daily May through October. Admission fee. One of the oldest game farms in the country, the Catskill Game Farm is also the most popular in the East. With more than 2,000 animals such as lions, tigers, and bears to see and enjoy, a visit here should take up several hours. Special shows introduce the audience to animal friends, and the petting zoo is still one of the most popular places for children. There is a small train/tram that transports visitors from one section of the zoo to another (at an additional charge), and an amusement park and picnic and play areas. It's best not to leave young children alone in the petting area, since they may feel overwhelmed by all the friendly deer.

Ted Martin's Reptile Adventure (518-678-3557), Route 32, Catskill.

Open daily 10–7 May 15 through September 15. Admission fee. If snakes and reptiles interest you, visit this intriguing display. You'll find 100 types of rare snakes and reptiles, which have included the yellow spitting cobra, eastern diamondback rattler, and a 15-foot-long African rock python. There are local snakes to wonder at, too, as well as exotic creatures right out of a Rudyard Kipling story, and all are housed in 50 living habitats that duplicate the animals' natural environment. Tour guides are available with lots of reptile rap; reptile shows are held throughout the day. Even people who are frightened of snakes leave here with a better understanding of these remarkable creatures.

Zoom Flume (518-239-4559), just off Route 145, Shady Glen Road, 2 miles north of East Durham. Open late June, weather permitting, daily through Labor Day. Call for hours. Admission fee. Billed as an "aquamusement park," this playground is set in the Shady Glen canyon, a natural formation of steep walls and running water. The Raging River Ride and the Zoom Flume let you slosh and slide your way down the canyon; there's also a pool, a game area, and the Soak-A-Buddy section— great for splashing a friend or two. Look for nature trails, scenic overlooks and waterfalls, and a restaurant with an observation deck for drying out.

SCENIC DRIVES

Mountains, deep gorges, valleys, and waterfalls can all be seen during a leisurely drive through Greene County, and a tour can take all day or only a few hours, depending on the number of stops you want to make. Some of the roads are narrow and winding, though, so use the designated parking areas to take in scenic views. And be careful to check driving conditions if you take a ride in winter or early spring.

Some lovely parts of the county can be seen by taking Route 42 north over the Deep Notch, which is cool even on the hottest days. At Route 23A head east through Hunter, Haines Falls, and Palenville. Along the road you will see Hunter Mountain, breathtaking waterfalls, winding streams, and the Amphitheatre, a natural, bowl-shaped rock formation. Follow Route 23 into Catskill, where you can pick up the NYS Thruway at exit 21.

Another tour starts at the junction of Routes 23A and 23C; follow **23C east to Jewett.** The large and elegant homes lining the roads and tucked into the hills were part of Onteora Park, a "cottage" colony where many wealthy families summered during the 19th century. The junction of Routes 25 and 23C shelters the Old Stone Church, in which there are some lovely murals. (The church is closed in winter.) At County Route 17 head south to Route 23A, where you can pick up the scenic drive above, into Catskill.

To see some exceptional churches, begin on Route 23A in **Jewett Center.** Here you will see the St. John the Baptist Ukrainian Church and the Grazhda, which were constructed in the traditional style using large beams and wooden pins instead of nails. The interior of the church

St. John the Baptist Ukrainian Church, an architectural gem, in Jewett Center

is decorated with wood carvings and panels, and the education building has displays relating to Ukrainian history. There are concerts and arts shows held in the Grazhda (call 518-263-3862 for information). On Route 23A in Hunter you will find Our Lady of the Snows, one of the oldest Catholic churches in the Mountaintop region. Continue on Route 23A to Haines Falls, where you'll find the grotto of Our Lady of the Mountain. This shrine was constructed in the 1920s and recalls the miracle at Lourdes. The grotto is open to the public. Continue on 23A to Palenville, where the Gloria Dei Episcopal Church is open for tours on Saturday. Then take Route 23A to Route 32 north into Cairo, then Route 24 to South Cairo. There you will find the Mahayana Buddhist Temple (518-622-3619), a retreat complex complete with Chinese temple, dragon decorations, and fine artwork. The walkways are open to the public year-round. From South Cairo, you can take Route 23B east to the NYS Thruway.

TO DO

AIRPLANE TOURS

With its rolling meadows and steep mountain heights, Greene County is a wonderful place to see from the window of an airplane. Recreational flights add some excitement to a vacation, and a call to the **Freehold Airport** (518-634-7626), in Freehold, will put you in touch with pilots. This is a full-service airport (right next to cornfields and a plant nursery) that offers pleasure flights, an art gallery, lessons, and a chance to view antique aircraft.

BIKING

Enthusiasts looking for an interesting way to spend a summer or autumn day may want to make tracks to **The Bike Shop at Windham Mountain Outfitters** (518-734-4700), Route 296 and South Street, Windham, where you can hire a guide—or purchase trail maps and rent a mountain bike to ride the trails by yourself. Then head to **Ski Windham** (518-734-4300), Route 23, Windham, for a chairlift ride and views of a lifetime.

FARM STANDS AND PICK-YOUR-OWN FARMS

Greene County is filled with farm stands: big ones, little ones, and specialty stands that carry everything from maple syrup to mushrooms.

Bennett's Berry Patch (518-756-9472), Independence Lane, Hannacroix, is open June and July and has strawberries only.

Black Horse Farms (518-943-9324), Route 9W, Athens, is open June through December and stocks everything from herbs to apples, all locally grown.

At the **Kaatskill Cider Mill** (518-678-5529), Route 32, Catskill, apples, cider, maple syrup, and honey make this one sweet stop for regional-food lovers. Open year-round.

Maple Glen Farm (518-589-5319), Scribner Hollow Road, East Jewett, offers tours of its maple syrup production area. The farm is open all year for sales. In early spring don't pass up a stop here.

At **Osborn Mushroom Farm** (518-731-8730), Route 9W, Coxsackie, you can buy fresh mushrooms. Open year-round.

Story Farms (518-678-9716), Route 32, Catskill, allows you to pick your own strawberries, peas, and tomatoes, but it also offers a lot of other local produce. Open year-round.

Traphagen's (518-263-4150), Route 23A, Hunter, offers gourmet, flavored honeys, and candy. Open year-round.

Apples for the picking are the specialty at **Henry Boehm's** (518-731-6196), County Road 26, Climax, open September through February; and at **Sunset Orchards** (518-731-8846), Route 81, Climax. **Duncan's Farmstand and Cider Mill** (518-622-8400), Route 23B, Cairo, has local goodies and produce to take home to dinner. Open daily except Wednesday through the summer.

Also see Catskill Mountain Foundation and Dutchman's Landing under *Entertainment.*

FISHING

Fishing in Greene County can mean a lazy day spent pondside or an exciting, nerve-ripping hour fighting a sturgeon in the Hudson. There are more than 58 streams that shelter wild trout here, as well as lakes, ponds, and, of course, the Hudson River. A state fishing license is required in Greene County, and town permits are also needed for the Potuck Reservoir in Catskill and the Medway Reservoir in Coxsackie. Permits and licenses can be obtained at many of the bait-and-tackle and sports shops across the county, as well as in town clerk's offices and the county clerk's office in Catskill. Seasons and limits vary with the species of fish; check with the **Department of Environmental Conservation** (845-256-3000) for specifics. In Greene County public fishing areas are marked by yellow signs; parking spaces are available, although they're sometimes limited. If you want to catch one of the more than 150 species of fish that are found in the Hudson River—shad, perch, herring, and sturgeon among them—you may want to use the public boat ramps that can be found in Athens, Coxsackie, and Catskill. Route 23A will take you past Rip Van Winkle Lake in Tannersville, Schoharie Creek, and the Schoharie Reservoir, all of which are great fishing areas. Route 145 leads to Lower Catskill Creek, Upper Catskill Creek, and Ten Mile Creek, while Route 296 provides access to the Batavia Kill boat launch and the East Kill Trout Preserve. BASSmaster invitational fishing tournaments have been held in Greene County; information may be obtained by calling the **Greene County Promotion Department** (518-943-3223).

GOLF

The greens of Greene County require widely varying levels of skill, but no one who picks up a club will leave the region disappointed. The following establishments are open to the public. It is suggested that you call before you go to determine hours and availability.

Nine-hole golf courses in Greene County include: **Blackhead Mountain Country Club** (518-622-3157), Round Top; **Rainbow Golf Club and Motel** (518-966-5343), Route 26, Greenville, which also offers vacation apartments just off the course, as does the **Sunny Hill Golf Club Resort** (518-634-7698), Greenville; the lovely **Rip Van Winkle Country Club** (518-678-9779), Route 23A, Palenville; **Christman's Windham House** (518-734-4230), Route 23A, Windham, one of the oldest inns in the region; the gracious **Windham Country Club** (518-734-9910), South Street, Windham; and the **Colonial Country Club** (518-589-9807), Route 23A, Tannersville, where the views go on forever.

HIKING

Greene County provides some of the best hiking and views in the Catskill region. You don't have to be a seasoned hiker to enjoy a day

JOSEPH PUGLISI

Diamond Notch Falls, five miles north of Phoenicia, off Route 214

walking on the clearly marked trails. The magnificent vistas have inspired Thomas Cole and other Hudson River painters.

Although the **Escarpment Trail** runs from Kaaterskill Creek on Route 23A to East Windham on Route 23 (24 miles in all), there are several short hikes along the path to Kaaterskill High Peak, North Point, and Mary's Glen. The trails in the North Lake area are renowned for their waterfalls and fantastic views of the entire Hudson Valley. **Kaaterskill Falls** and the **Catskill Mountain House** are particularly noteworthy sites. The easy-to-find entry point for these trails is at the junction of Route 23A and Kaaterskill Creek on the north side of the highway. These hikes are usually very popular on summer weekends, so you might want to go during the week to avoid the crowds. North Lake and good campgrounds are nearby for those who want to take a swim or stay overnight.

For more experienced and adventurous hikers, there is the **Devil's**

Path, named for its steepness and relative isolation. The path passes over much rugged terrain, particularly Indian Head Mountain, and includes the Hunter Mountain Trail and West Kill Mountain Range Trail. To reach the trailhead, turn south off Route 23A at the only light in Tannersville. Continue 1.5 miles to the road's intersection with Bloomer Road. Turn left, and after a short distance bear left onto Platte Clove Mountain Road. Stay on this road for 1 mile to Prediger Road, then go about 0.5 mile farther to find the trail. Each single mountain on the Devil's Path can be hiked in a day or less.

At 4,040 feet **Hunter Mountain** is the second highest peak in the Catskills and is best hiked on the trail that starts on Spruceton Road. To get there, take Route 42 north from Lexington and go 4 miles to Spruceton Road. The trailhead and trail are well defined.

Another pleasant day hike takes you to **Diamond Notch** and **West Kill Falls.** Located 5 miles north of Phoenicia, near Route 214, it is also easy to find. From Route 214 take Diamond Notch Road about 1 mile to a bridge, cross it, and park. The hike is about 4½ miles and should take 4 hours or less.

Highland Flings (1-800-HLF-6665), P.O. Box 37, Windham 12496, specializes in guided hiking and walking tours (especially artists' walks) through the Catskill Forest Preserve and Hudson River Valley. The service will arrange the hikes and accommodations; the guides themselves are charming and versed in history and hiking. **The Mountaintop Historical Society** (518-734-9701; www.mths.org) organizes hiking tours and walks to the historic trails and sites like Poet's Ledge, Kaaterskill Clove, and Echo Lake. Call for a schedule.

WINTER SPORTS

CROSS-COUNTRY SKIING

Greene County is home to some of the best cross-country ski areas in the state. Well over 1000 acres of groomed and ungroomed trails snake their way through the county's forests and fields, and many of the areas are patrolled by Nordic Ski Patrol members.

White Birches Ski Area (518-734-3266), Nauvoo Road, Windham, has 17 miles of groomed, patrolled, and marked trails for everyone from novices to experts; races are sponsored throughout the season.

Winter Clove Inn Nordic Skiing Area (518-622-3267), Winter Clove Road, Round Top, is located on the grounds of a country inn (see *Lodging*), but the facilities, including 400 acres, are open to the public and rentals are available. The same applies to the **Villaggio Resort** (518-589-5000), Haines Falls, with 14 km of trails.

DOWNHILL SKIING

Skiers from beginner to expert will enjoy excellent snow conditions, modern facilities, and some of the best skiing and most spectacular views anywhere in Greene County, which lies right in the New York snow belt, where sudden storms can dump several inches of powder in an hour. Ski season here lasts at least 6 months and slopes are open daily, weather permitting. In addition to their specialty offerings, the following slopes have rentals, baby-sitting and child care services, dining facilities, picnic areas, and ski shops.

Hunter Mountain (518-263-4223), Route 23A, Hunter. Hunter's reputation as the snowmaking capital of the East is well deserved. The three different mountains—Hunter One, Hunter West, and Hunter Mountain—offer skiers of all skill levels a chance to test themselves on nearly 50 different trails. Runs at Hunter can extend more than 2 miles, with vertical drops of 1,600 feet, and there are some extremely difficult areas for the expert. Double, triple, and even quadruple chairlifts cut some of the lines down to size, but this is such a popular area that you should be prepared for crowds on holidays and weekends. Hunter offers ski lessons for all levels and a wide variety of amateur and professional races during the season, including ones for chefs, firemen, snowboarders, and nurses. Hunter also offers 100 percent snowmaking capability, so the season sometimes begins as early as early November and last into May (at least 162 days a year). You will find complete facilities here, including baby-sitting, cafeterias, a lodge, a ski shop, and even a ski museum and art gallery. There is plenty of parking.

Ski Windham (518-734-4300 or 1-800-SKI-WINDHAM), Route 23, Windham, has 33 trails and vertical elevations of 1,600 feet at the base and 3,050 feet at the summit. Trail difficulty ranges from easy to expert, and the longest trail is more than 2 miles long. The Wannabe Wild Snowboard Park is 5-acre-plus area for snowboarders and tubers, with music and lights 4–10 every Friday and Saturday night during peak season, and nightly during holiday periods. A Children's Learning Center offers fun for nonskiers (or tired kids). Windham has won awards for its courtesy services, including valet parking, business meeting rooms with computers, and excellent dining facilities, along with a senior skier development program and lessons in racing, freestyle skiing, and snowboarding. It is also well known for its work with disabled skiers. Mountain bike lovers may wish to inquire about the autumn special events at Windham, when bike rentals are offered and trails are open for the hearty adventurer (see *Biking*).

Ski Cortina (518-589-6500), Route 23A, Haines Falls, has a base elevation of 2,000 feet, the highest in the Catskills, and 90 percent snowmaking capability. The 11 slopes and four lifts serve skiers of all skill levels. The site also offers night skiing and a guest lodge.

GREEN SPACE

Mountaintop Arboretum (518-589-3903), Route 23C, Tannersville. Free. Open year-round, but call about guided tours, offered June through

September. This 6-acre site has hundreds of trees, shrubs, and other plants both native and exotic to the Catskills. Each season brings delights, from the flowering height of spring to the brightly colored autumn foliage. Many of the plants have identification markers, and there are workhops and tours of the site throughout the year. Horticulturists (and those who just want to know "what is that tree?") will enjoy a visit here.

North and **South Lakes** (518-589-5058 or 943-4030). Take Route 23A to County Route 18 (O'Hara Road), Haines Falls. Open daily late May through early December, 9 AM until dusk. Admission fee, with an extra charge for campsites. This recreational area offers breathtaking scenery and a multitude of activities. Visitors can swim in a mountain lake with a clean, sandy beach. Boat rentals and fishing are also available.

A short hike from the lakes is Kaaterskill Falls, one of the highest falls on the East Coast and a popular subject for Hudson River School artists. The area also has a multiuse campground with hookups for recreational vehicles; it is advisable to make reservations early in the season, since this is a popular site and it gets busy on summer weekends. An ideal spot for a family outing.

Point Lookout Mountain Inn Gardens (518-734-3381), Route 23, Mohican Trail, East Windham. Open Thursday through Monday year-round. Free. There are perennial and herb gardens on the mountainside next to this historic inn and restaurant (see *Eating Out*), and seating areas to enjoy. But it's the view that really counts: five states, 180 miles, and 270 degrees. Breathtaking all around.

LODGING

Greene County is an extremely popular resort area, and there are hundreds of B&B inns, motels, and campgrounds. Some of the establishments cater to lovers of Irish, Italian, or Scandinavian life; others offer a full range of camping facilities on lakes and rivers. The following list is only a sampling of what can be discovered throughout the county.

Albergo Allegria Bed and Breakfast (518-734-5560 or 734-4499), Route 296, Windham 12496. ($$$) Step up on the wickered porch here and feel the grace and beauty of days gone by. The Victorian theme is continued throughout this bed & breakfast with antique furnishings and period wallpaper and decorations. A continental breakfast of fresh fruit, home-baked muffins, croissants, and local honey and jams is served daily. In summer enjoy breakfast on the porch. The main lounge, with its overstuffed couches and fireplace, and the library are especially warm and inviting. Four suites and 12 rooms, all with private bath; the Jacuzzi Room is the perfect place to celebrate a special occasion. The inn also schedules cooking seminars throughout the year.

Country Suite Bed and Breakfast (518-734-4079), Route 23; Windham 12496. ($$) This restored farmhouse is only minutes from skiing, shopping, and festivals, and guests will enjoy the country furnishings and antiques. There are five rooms, each with private bath. Reservations suggested. Open year-round.

Eggery Inn (518-589-5363), County Road 16, Tannersville 12485. ($$) Nestled amid the majestic ridges of the Catskill Mountains at an altitude of 2,200 feet, this rustic inn offers sweeping views. The woodburning Franklin stove and antique player piano make for a cozy atmosphere, and the dining room has a handcrafted oak bar and an abundance of plants. During the hearty breakfast you will enjoy an unobstructed view of Hunter Mountain. Dinner is served to groups by prior arrangement only. The 15 rooms all have private bath, telephone, and cable TV. Most rooms have air-conditioning. Open year-round.

Fairlawn Inn (518-263-5025), P.O. Box 182, Main Street, Hunter 12442. ($$) This inn is the epitome of Victorian charm, from the three-story corner turret and wraparound porches to the elaborately designed wallpapered ceilings and cozy brass beds. A stunning grand staircase and wicker-filled lobby are only a preview for the inn's several large common rooms, which provide a variety of settings for quiet contemplation or socializing. Each of the 12 bedrooms has a queen-sized bed and private bath. Homemade granola and yogurt begin a breakfast feast that may include a spinach quiche or stuffed French toast. Special midweek rates. Open year-round.

🖎 **Golden Harvest** (518-634-2305), 356 Golden Hill Road, East Durham 12423. ($$) A nice family place, this inn has a separate two-bedroom apartment for guests, complete with VCR and screened-in porch. The Golden Harvest is located on the site of a former orchard, and the extensive grounds include a duck pond; volleyball, croquet, and horseshoe courts; and reading benches. There are also picnic and barbecue facilities, and a full breakfast is served in the main dining room. Open year-round.

🖎 **Greenville Arms** (518-966-5219), South Street, Greenville 12083. ($$$) Special care is taken to provide a quiet retreat for guests at this gem of a Victorian home built by William Vanderbilt in 1889. Each room is decorated with antiques, and the 7 acres of lush lawns and gardens are a riot of color each spring and summer. Old-fashioned country cooking is the specialty at breakfast, and dinner is by reservation only. Fifteen rooms, all with private bath. Children welcome; open year-round.

Kaaterskill Creek Bed and Breakfast (518-678-9052), Malden Avenue, Palenville 12463. ($) Cozy rooms, a fireplace, and a front porch make this country inn a delight. The view is of the creek and the distant mountains, and guests can enjoy nearby swimming, hiking, skiing, and more. A full breakfast is served in an enclosed gazebo. There are four rooms, one with private bath, three that share one bath.

Mountain Valley Spa (518-263-4919 or 1-800-232-2772), Route 214,

Hunter 12442. ($$) This 15-acre resort at the base of Hunter Mountain is an informal retreat with all the amenities of a full-service spa. Located in the midst of the Catskill Forest Preserve, the spa provides a fitness room, sauna, indoor and outdoor swimming pools, tennis courts, and basketball and volleyball courts. Daily exercise options include aerobics, yoga, hiking, tai chi, dance, and water activities. The daily price is reasonable and includes three vegetarian meals as well as use of all facilities. Some packages include a free massage. Other services are available for an additional fee (facials, body wraps, manicures, and pedicures). Open year-round.

Redcoat's Return (518-589-6379), Dale Lane, Elka Park 12427. ($$$) The picturesque locale of this 1850s farmhouse will delight outdoors lovers. There is fishing in nearby Schoharie Creek and skiing at nearby Hunter Mountain. Open year-round.

River Hill (518-756-3313), Box 253, New Baltimore 12124. ($$) Away from it all—but not too far away—this restored historic home has spacious grounds, and there are spectacular Hudson River views from its rooms. Guests are welcome to enjoy the downstairs, which includes a living room with fireplace and grand piano. Breakfast is served on the terrace or in front of the fireplace in the dining room. Two rooms, each with private bath. Open year-round.

Scribner Hollow Lodge (518-263-4211), Route 23A, Hunter 12442. ($$$) For people who enjoy a full-service lodge; the main building offers private rooms, and town houses can also be rented. Every room is different, and the lodge has a sauna, a whirlpool, and an unusual grotto swimming pool. The Prospect Restaurant, an excellent establishment (see *Dining Out*), is on the premises. Open year-round.

Stewart House (518-945-1357), 2 North Water Street, Athens 12015. ($$) A restored Victorian hotel that dates back to 1883, with panoramic views of the Hudson River. Athens is a charming town with a lighthouse (you can see it from room 8). Enjoy a full country breakfast while watching the boats pass by. Five rooms with private bath. Open year-round. Excellent restaurant downstairs (see *Dining Out*).

✿ **The Windham Arms** (518-734-3000), Route 23, Windham 12496. ($$) Take the NYS Thruway to exit 21 to Route 23 west; it's 25 miles to the motel. Only ½ mile from Ski Windham, this establishment combines a country setting with comfortable rooms and spectacular mountain views. It is ideal for families, with a dining room, coffee shop, tennis court, indoor recreation center, and outdoor pool on the premises. It combines the convenience of a motel with the warmth of a country inn. All 55 rooms have TV, telephone, and private bath. Open year-round.

✿ **Winter Clove Inn** (518-622-3267), Winter Clove Road, Round Top 12473. ($$$) Located on 400 acres adjoining the Catskill Forest Preserve, this inn opened in 1830 and is still run by the same family. There are swimming pools, a tennis court, a golf course, cross-country skiing, and

Ski Fest is celebrated at Ski Windham during President's week in February.

even hayrides and a bowling alley. All baked goods are homemade, and many of the recipes have been passed down in the family for generations. Children are welcome. All meals are included in rates unless special arrangements are made in advance. Fifty-one rooms with private bath. Open year-round.

WHERE TO EAT

DINING OUT

The Basement Bistro (518-634-2338), County Route 45, Earlton. ($$) Open for dinner, Thursday through Sunday, 5–8. Sunday tasting-menu brunches are served December through May, 11 AM–2 PM. Reservations required. Closed for the month of January. This unique restaurant gives diners the opportunity to try everything offered. The $32 prix-fixe menu is made up of a dozen courses that change daily, depending on seasonal produce available. Located on a pastoral country road in the basement of a house hand-built by the chef-owner, who lives with his family upstairs, there are only 26 seats in the restaurant. Most dishes are served on one plate, creating a communal dining experience that's particularly enjoyable when there is a large group. The kitchen specializes in a healthful, imaginative style of cooking that uses purees and infused oils instead of butter and cream. Adventurous diners shouldn't pass up this restaurant.

Brandywine (518-734-3838), Route 23, Windham. ($$) Open daily, except Monday, for lunch and dinner at noon. An excellent informal dining spot; the Italian specialties here are superb. Try the rich fettuccine Alfredo, the shrimp Brandywine, or the chicken Scarpariello. Desserts include fantastic cheesecake. There is a bright greenhouse room for dining and cozy booths in the main area. Children are welcome.

Chalet Fondue (518-734-4650), South Street, Windham. ($$) Open weekdays (closed Tuesday) at 4; Saturday at 4; Sunday and holidays at 2. Swiss, Austrian, and German dishes are the specialties here and include veal entrées and a full line of fondues. Children are welcome.

Chateau Belleview (518-589-5525), Route 23A, Tannersville. ($$) Open daily, except Tuesday, at 5. Excellent Continental cuisine and spectacular mountain views are found here, along with candlelight and fine service. Not recommended for children.

La Conca D'Oro (518-943-3549), 440 Main Street, Catskill. ($$) Open weekdays, except Tuesday, for lunch 11:30–2:30 and dinner 5–10; open Saturday 3–10 and Sunday 2–10. The name means "the golden bay," and this unpretentious Italian restaurant serves fine food at exceedingly reasonable prices. The veal entrées, chicken dishes, and homemade mozzarella are house specialties. For dessert, there are excellent cannoli. Children are welcome.

Diamanti's Restaurant (518-678-3173), Route 32A, Palenville. ($) Open every evening, except Wednesday, for dinner 4–9. The reasonably priced Italian cuisine in this establishment attracts travelers and local residents alike. The emphasis is on seafood entrées like *zuppa di pesce.* Both the chicken and veal parmigiana are popular, but we recommend ordering one of the daily seafood specials. All entrées are prepared to order.

Freehold Country Inn (518-634-2705), junction of County Routes 32 and 67, Freehold. ($$) Open daily for lunch noon–3; dinner 4–9. The American cuisine here offers something for everyone with a variety of steak, chicken, pasta, and vegetarian dishes. We suggest that seafood lovers try the fisherman's casserole, a combination of poached salmon, lobster tail, and scallops in a fennel-saffron broth, served over pasta.

Gerardo's Cafe (518-945-2720), Route 385, Athens. ($) Open for dinner Tuesday through Sunday 4–9. The Italian American cuisine here includes a range of fresh pasta, seafood, and veal dishes. The chef's favorite is the southern Italian chicken, which is served over pasta in a sauce with sun-dried tomatoes and capers. All desserts are homemade on the premises; we suggest sampling the chocolate mousse, cake, or cream puffs.

La Griglia (518-734-4499), Route 296, Windham. ($$$) Open daily, except Monday, at 4:30 PM. The bakery is open for coffee and treats at 8 AM—the selection of fine cakes, pastries, cookies, and breads is incredible and worth the trip. Rated one of New York's best restaurants, this elegant inn serves excellent northern Italian dishes. House specialties include osso buco Milanese, roast duck with fig and honey sauce, and pasta. Desserts are prepared by the restaurant's bakery and include chocolate specialties to die for. Children welcome. Reservations suggested.

🖊 **The Prospect Restaurant** (518-263-4211 or 1-800-395-4683), at Scribner Hollow Lodge, Route 23A, Hunter. ($$) Open for dinner Friday through Sunday from 5; breakfast served Saturday and Sunday from 8 AM. Dinner served during the week from Thanksgiving through the end of ski season. Call for hours. Enjoy breathtaking views of Hunter Mountain and the Catskills from just about every table in the dining room. A few of the tantalizing choices are a wild game mixed grill with acorn juniper sauce, apple-braised free-range chicken, and chocolate tartlet with ripe pears for dessert. There are several reasonably priced Wine Dinners throughout the year, featuring some of California's most elegant varietals as well as other wines.

🖊 **Redcoat's Return** (518-598-6379 or 598-9858), Dale Lane, Elka Park. ($$) Open Friday through Sunday for dinner at 6. Providing a taste of England in the Hudson Valley, this inn serves up British dishes including steak and kidney pie, prime rib, and trifle. The surroundings are Old World elegant, and dinner is served in a cozy librarylike dining room with book-lined walls. Children welcome.

Stewart House Restaurant and Bistro (518-945-1357), 2 North Water Street, Athens. ($$) Open for dinner Tuesday through Saturday 5–10; Sunday brunch 11:30–2, dinner 3–10. The bistro serves a limited menu later in the evening as well. New American cooking is featured here, with an emphasis on the freshest seasonal ingredients. The chef uses herbs from his garden along the Hudson River during the warm-weather months. The wood-grilled swordfish is a specialty. All baking is done on the premises, so make sure to sample some of the wonderful pies and desserts, like chocolate torte with raspberry filling.

🖊 **Vesuvio** (518-734-3663), Goshen Road, Hensonville. ($$) Open daily at 4:30. The warm atmosphere and provincial charm make this Italian restaurant a popular stop. Candlelight makes dining elegant, and the specialties include veal and fish, along with outstanding desserts like tortoni and spumoni. Children are welcome.

EATING OUT

Bell's Coffee Shop (518-943-4070), 387 Main Street, Catskill. ($) Open Monday through Friday 8–3. This is an old-fashioned luncheonette with large portions and low prices. The home-cooked turkey sandwich is a favorite among local residents.

Catskill Mountain Chocolate Company (518-734-3769), Route 296, Windham. ($) Open daily, except Wednesday, 10–6. Mouthwatering hand-dipped chocolates in an array of shapes and sizes, jellies, baskets, candies of all kinds. There are also sugar-free chocolate treats for those on a restricted diet.

The Fernwood (518-678-9332), Malden Avenue, Palenville. Open for dinner daily at 5. Standard American favorites are the specialty here. Try the ribs or one of the salads. The Fernwood is known for its excellent margaritas.

Jimmy O'Connor's Windham Mountain Inn (518-734-4270), South Street, Windham. ($) Open daily 11 AM–1 AM. A nice stop for an Irish coffee and a hearty sandwich or a rib-sticking breakfast.

Last Chance Antiques and Cheese Cafe (518-589-6424), Main Street, Tannersville. ($) Open daily at 10 AM. A retail gourmet store, antiques shop, and café all in one. Cheeses, chocolates, quiche, homemade soups, and huge sandwiches make this a great take-out stop.

Mariner's Point (518-943-5352), 7 Main Street, Catskill. ($) Open daily for lunch and dinner noon–11 PM. Located on the Hudson River, this is a great spot for outdoor dining in the warm-weather months. The pizza, hamburgers, and turkey and roast beef sandwiches are popular selections.

Mayflower Cafe (518-943-7903), 355 Main Street, Catskill. ($) This antiques shop, art gallery, and café combined has a delightful ambience and is one of the most memorable stops in the town of Catskill. Just about every square inch is filled with something interesting to ponder. The perfect place to enjoy a cappuccino or an iced tea, accompanied by one of the many mouthwatering desserts.

Point Lookout Inn (518-734-3381), Route 23, Windham. ($) Open for dinner Friday and Saturday 4–10 PM, Sunday 1–10 PM; hours may vary slightly depending on the season. Overnight accommodations available; 14 rooms with private bath. Eat here on a clear day and you can see five states from your dining booth. The food is hearty, with big sandwiches the standouts. The menu is varied with standard American favorites including steaks and seafood.

ENTERTAINMENT

The Catskill Mountain Foundation (518-263-4908), P.O. Box 924, Hunter 12442. This recently formed organization has revitalized the town of Hunter. Stop in at the Catskill Mountain Foundation Bookstore/Gallery or movie theater on Route 23A and pick up a current schedule of events, which include concerts, dance performances, film series, art exhibits, and poetry readings. There is also an organic green market year-round Friday through Sunday, featuring local organic produce, pasta, grains, eggs, cheeses, and other gourmet specialty foods.

Dutchman's Landing (518 943-3223), Catskill Point, Main Street, Catskill. This area once served as a boat landing for the Hudson River craft, and today visitors can enjoy spectacular views of the river and eastern shore. You'll find a farmer's market and crafts market weekends from summer through fall, displays of the river and cultural history of the Catskills, travel information, picnic and dining areas, and entertainment. A great place to start a tour of the region, and one of the easiest access areas to the Hudson River for nonboaters.

Hunter Festivals (518-263-3800), Hunter Mountain, Route 23A, Hunter. Dates vary. Admission fee varies with festival; there is a small parking charge. Although Hunter is known as one of the top skiing mountains in the United States, it is also the site of several music and dance festivals. The shows are colorful and filled with diversity; the foods sold at stands range from pizza to Belgian waffles, bangers and potatoes to fried bread and pumpkin soup. There are festivals celebrating the German Alps, microbrew, Celtic lands, and Native American culture. All offer crafts demonstrations and daylong entertainment. During the festivals the Hunter Sky Ride is in service (additional fee), and the Skiing Hall of Fame (free) offers an interesting look at the men, women, and equipment that helped create American skiing.

Shakespeare on the Hudson (1-877-2-McDUFF), Route 385, 1 mile north of the Rip Van Winkle Bridge. Season runs July and August. Admission fee. Call for hours and a performance schedule. This "theater" is unusual: The audience enjoys a Hudson River view from the intimate (250-seat) amphitheater. Nature plays its role well, offering fireflies, crickets, and other sounds and sights to the Bard's words. Purists beware: the plays are often updated (a recent *Comedy of Errors* featured a swing score). The mixture of New York City and upstate performers, directors, technicians, and musicians makes this a fun outdoor theater evening.

SELECTIVE SHOPPING

ANTIQUES

Greene County offers the antiques lover everything from the funky to the fabulous, with a wide range of shops, auctions, and flea markets. Although many establishments are open all year, their hours tend to be limited in the off-season, so call before you go.

American Gothic Antiques (518-263-4836), Route 23A, Hunter, stocks a wonderful array of antique lamps and accessories.

Some of the finest reverse-painted glass in the world is found right in Greene County, at **The Blue Pearl** (518-734-6525), Route 23, East Windham. Open daily 10–5. Group tours welcome. Located almost at the top of Windham Mountain, this shop offers three floors of fine antiques, jewelry, clothing, and glassware. Ulla Darni's exquisite reverse-painted lamps are here, as are finds from around the world. A café on the premises offers healthy entrées and desserts, and the view outside the window goes on forever. (After you leave the Blue Pearl, continue up the mountain to the Five State Overlook : New York, Vermont, Massachusetts, Connecticut, and New Hampshire are all in view on a clear day. Even if it's not a clear day, you can watch the clouds roll in from across the country!)

The Coxsackie Antique Center (518-731-8888), Routes 9W and 81, West Coxsackie, is open daily with wares ranging from glass and lamps to books and postcards. **The Opera House Antiques Center** (518-945-3224), 21 Second Street, Athens, is open daily (except Monday) 11–6; it's a multidealer shop with small collectibles, furniture, and other finds. **Mooney's Antiques** (518-634-2300), Route 145, East Durham, has flea markets and auctions year-round on Tuesday and Friday; there is also a multidealer shop on the premises. And if all that shopping makes you hungry, stop in at the **Last Chance Antiques and Cheese Cafe** (518-589-6424), Main Street, Tannersville, where you can have a gourmet snack and then buy the furniture out from under the other diners (see *Eating Out*).

ART GALLERIES

Greene County has a wealth of artists and galleries, but many galleries are open only by chance or appointment. For further information on their offerings, contact the **Greene County Council on the Arts** (518-943-3400), 398 Main Street, Catskill 12414. The council also has two crafts galleries that represent regional artists, so ask for a calendar of exhibits and events.

VII. Albany

Long before Albany received its city charter, granted July 22, 1686, by Gov. Thomas Duggan, the settlement was an important river stop and trading center. After Henry Hudson visited the region in 1609, Albany's fertile valleys and abundant game attracted Dutch settlers. Albany was to become a city of tremendous contrast—stagecoaches and steamboats, muddy roads and medical colleges, farmers and politicians. But through a combination of pride, pluck, and foresight, Albany has made the best of it all. A visit to the city today can focus on many things—history, politics, art, architecture—and can be made at any time of year. Spring brings the blossoming of thousands of tulips, pools of color that reflect Albany's Dutch origins. The Pinksterfest, a weekend celebration in May, welcomes the warm weather in the Dutch tradition, and the city parks come alive with fairs and shows. In summer the great Empire State Plaza becomes a unique combination of outdoor park, art gallery, and seat of government, and autumn turns out to be a perfect time to explore the city on foot and discover the tiny side streets that still remain from three centuries ago. Winter ushers in Victorian greenery displays, snow festivals, and the lighting of the state Christmas tree. Whatever the season, be prepared to discover an area where the past and future work together.

GUIDANCE
Albany County Convention and Visitors Bureau (518-434-1217), 52 South Pearl Street, Albany 12207; www.albany.org.

GETTING THERE
Albany is located off exits 23 and 24 of I-87 (Quickway); watch for signs.

MEDICAL EMERGENCY
Albany Medical Center (518-445-3131), 43 New Scotland Avenue.

TO SEE

✐ **The Albany Institute of History and Art** (518-463-4478), 125 Washington Avenue. Admission fee. Open year-round; call for hours. Founded in 1791, this exceptional museum is one of the oldest in the United States, and it is still providing visitors with a chance to see varied, changing exhibits that focus on the Hudson Valley's cultural history. The building

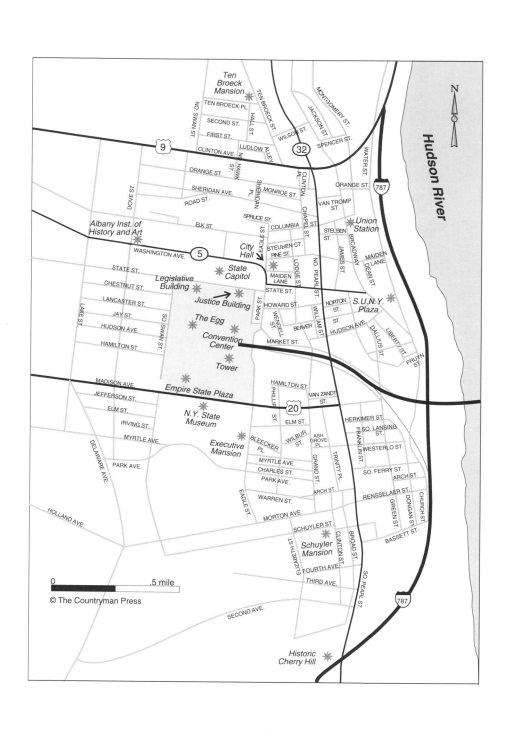

itself is a graceful collection of individual galleries and sweeping staircases, and there is even a small display area in the entrance hall. The institute's collections include fine European porcelain and glass; Dutch furniture, paintings, and decorative arts from the early settlement period in Albany; pewter and silver produced by local smiths in the 18th century; and breathtaking examples of the Hudson River School of painting. The Dutch Room offers an interesting look into early Albany family life. Be sure to see the Egyptian Room on the lower level, where human and animal mummies rest along with some of their prized belongings. Changing exhibits are featured throughout the year, and special events include noontime arts talks, a lecture and slide series, an antiquarian book show, and the colorful holiday Festival of Trees. The gift shop stocks many books about New York State history.

✎ **Albany Visitors Center** (518-434-5132), 25 Quackenbush Square. Open daily 10–4. Free. This site offers guests interactive displays that highlight history and culture in the capital city and provide an overview of the region. The same building is also home to the **Henry Hudson Planetarium,** which features star shows on Saturday at 11:30 AM (children) and 12:30 PM (adults), as well as special school break programs during the year.

✎ **New York State Museum** (518-474-5877), Madison Avenue, Empire State Plaza. To reach the plaza, take exit 23 off the New York State (NYS) Thruway. Pick up I-87 and get off at the Empire Plaza exit. Open year-round (except Thanksgiving, Christmas, and New Year's Day) 10–5. Free. Today it anchors one end of the Empire State Plaza, but the museum has been a part of the state's history since 1836, making it one of the oldest state museums in the country. It is not, however, a dusty old repository with outdated displays of rocks and unidentified bones. This museum is alive with multimedia presentations that allow you to experience everything from a thunderstorm to a Lower East Side pushcart alley of the 1920s. The permanent exhibits include "Adirondack Wilderness," which explores the natural history of that region; "New York Metropolis," which focuses on New York City and the surrounding counties (here you'll find an Ellington-era A train and a set from *Sesame Street*); and displays that focus on Native American life and the Ice Age in the Empire State. Changing exhibits may feature folk art, dinosaurs, giant insects, or contemporary art and fine crafts, and shows are given in the museum's theater. Special events are scheduled all year; you may get to enjoy a Victorian holiday, a children's sleepover in the museum, or even a visit with an American artist. The gift shop is one of the best in any New York museum.

HISTORIC HOMES
Historic Cherry Hill (518-434-4791), 523½ South Pearl Street. Open February through December; call for hours. Admission fee. Built in 1787 by Philip Van Rensselaer in order to replace what was called the

Empire State Plaza in downtown Albany

Old Mansion, this Georgian house was the centerpiece of a 900-acre farm. Cherry Hill remained in the family for five generations, until 1963, and provides the visitor with a rare picture of the growth and care of a home over 176 years. The farm has, of course, disappeared under Albany streets, and the view across the road is of oil tanks instead of orchards, but the house itself still offers a sense of grace and elegance. A visit begins in the basement orientation center, where a wall chart untangles the complicated knot of marriages and relationships that kept Cherry Hill in the family. Upstairs, many of the 31 rooms have not been restored to match one particular period but contain the designs, belongings, and personal touches of their inhabitants. The collections found here are irreplaceable as a record of America's social history. There are more than 150 chairs, more than 30 tables, and thousands (20,000 at last count) of decorative objects, which include 18th-century paintings, 19th-century Oriental export ware, and even 20th-century clothing. Although the house was modernized over the years, things such as heating ducts and plumbing are carefully hidden away. Cherry Hill is a special place, chock-full of New York history and spirit. A holiday tour is offered in December and often features rarely exhibited toys from the museum's collection.

Schuyler Mansion (518-434-0834), 32 Catherine Street. Open April through December, Wednesday through Saturday 10–5, Sunday 1–5.

Admission fee. Once home to Philip Schuyler, a general in the Revolutionary War, the Schuyler Mansion was completed in 1764 on a rolling plot of land known as the Dutch Church Pasture. Schuyler was an important figure during the war, and many well-known statesmen, including Washington, Franklin, and the defeated English general John Burgoyne, visited the mansion over the years. During the war Schuyler's daughter married Alexander Hamilton here, and a kidnap attempt was later made against her by the Tories; a gash on the wooden banister is said to have been made by a kidnapper's tomahawk. The house did not remain in the family after Schuyler's death but passed through a succession of owners before being purchased by New York State in 1912. Although there have been numerous changes to the exterior of the house over the years, including the removal of all the outbuildings, visitors today can still see many examples of 18th-century furniture, glassware, pottery, and art, as well as Schuyler family possessions. An herb garden has been added to replace the original plantings.

Ten Broeck Mansion (518-436-9826), 9 Ten Broeck Place. Open April through December, Wednesday through Friday 2–4, Saturday and Sunday 1–4; closed holidays. Admission fee. Home of the Albany County Historical Association, this Federal mansion was built in 1798 for Gen. Abraham Ten Broeck, who was a member of the Continental Congress and fought in the nearby battle of Saratoga. Once called Arbor Hill, the house now offers a look at the lifestyle of Albany's upper class during the last two centuries. Exhibits include period furniture and decorative items, and the house also contains a wine cellar, which when rediscovered during renovations was found to have a valuable collection of very aged wines!

HISTORIC SITES

Capitol Building (518-474-2418), located at the State Street end of the Empire State Plaza. Open daily year-round, Monday through Friday 9–4, with tours on the hour; Saturday and Sunday there are 10 AM, noon, 2, and 3 PM tours; closed Thanksgiving, Christmas, and New Year's Day. Free. Tours leave from the guide center inside the capitol. This fairytale building, with its red towers and hundreds of arched windows, is one of the few state capitols that aren't topped by a dome. Construction, completed in 1899, took more than 30 years and cost the then unheard-of sum of $25 million. This is where the state senate and assembly meet, and where you'll find the governor's offices once used by Charles Evans, Theodore Roosevelt, Nelson Rockefeller, and Franklin D. Roosevelt. Throughout the building are thousands of fine stone carvings, a tradition that can be traced back to the great churches of the Middle Ages. Many were caricatures of famous politicians and writers; others were of the families and relatives of the artisans; still others were self-portraits of the stone carvers themselves. But the most compelling carvings are the ones that form the Million Dollar Staircase, which took

The state capitol at Albany

years to complete and is the best known of all the capitol's embellishments. Another unusual architectural feature is the senate fireplaces: The huge chimneys did not draw well, so their original function was abandoned in favor of using them as private "discussion nooks." And if you enjoy military history, don't miss the small military museum here; it traces the history of the state militia and National Guard. Flower lovers should make a special point of visiting the **Capitol Park** in spring, when thousands of tulips blaze into red and yellow bloom.

Executive Mansion (518-473-7521), 138 Eagle Street, Albany. Tours are offered Thursday 10–2, but call at least 2 weeks in advance for reservations. This mansion is tucked down a side street just around the block from Empire Plaza. Built in 1850 as a private home, it now serves as the governor's residence. The tour covers the public rooms, which are filled with art from the 18th through the 20th centuries.

WALKING TOURS

There is so much to see in this historic city that a walk down just about any street will give you a glimpse into Albany's colorful past. The following are not specific tours but suggestions for starting points on an Albany exploration.

An example of a 19th-century row-house community, the **Pastures Historic District** is bounded roughly by Morton and Second Avenues and Elizabeth and Pearl Streets. Here you will also find the Schuyler Mansion (see *Historic Homes*) as well as many impressive private homes. The **Mansion Historic District,** bounded by Eagle, Dongan, Hamilton, and Ferry Streets, is a kaleidoscope of building styles, Italianate, Federal, and Greek Revival being only a few. Although the area became run-down earlier in this century, people have been rediscovering the richness of the district, and there is a sense of renewal here. The **Center Square–Hudson Park Historic District,** bounded by South Swan Street, Madison Avenue, South Lake Street, and Spring Street, is the largest historic district. Its centerpiece is Washington Park, a 90-acre area that once served as parade grounds and cemetery. Throughout the park you will find statues, lovely flower beds, and a lake. The district itself has scores of restored houses and commercial buildings.

ART GALLERIES

Many fine publicly and privately owned galleries are scattered throughout the city. At the Nelson A. Rockefeller Empire State Plaza (see *Green Space*), free tours are given to enhance the appreciation of the great treasures found throughout the plaza.

Harmanus Bleecker Center (518-465-2044), 19 Dove Street, has changing displays of the works of regional artists. The center is associated with the Albany Institute of History and Art, so classes and special events are held as well.

Picotte Gallery (518-454-3900), 324 State Street, a small gallery at the College of Saint Rose, offers works by contemporary artists.

Rice Gallery (518-463-4478), at the Albany Institute of History and Art, 125 Washington Avenue (see *To See*), has several different shows each year, including juried exhibits of works by regional artists.

University Art Gallery (518-422-4035), 1400 Washington Avenue, Fine Arts Buildings, State University at Albany, focuses on contemporary art with a variety of changing exhibits, some drawn from the gallery's own holdings, others from the works of both established artists and university students. The gallery's hours change during the year, so call before you go.

GREEN SPACE

Nelson A. Rockefeller Empire State Plaza (518-474-0559). Located off exit 23 of I-87 and bounded by Swan, Madison, State, and Eagle Streets. Open daily year-round. Free. Popularly called the Plaza, this is really a government complex that includes office buildings, a convention center, a performing arts center known as the Egg, a concourse, and the state museum (see *To See*). Built at a cost of more than $2 billion and finished in 1978, the Plaza has fulfilled then-Governor Rockefeller's dream of a government center that would draw visitors and allow them to feel in touch with their state government. Tours of the Plaza are offered several times a day, but you may enjoy walking it yourself. The esplanade area is wonderful to explore, with tranquil reflecting pools, plantings, modern sculpture by artist David Smith, and even a play area known as the Children's Place. An environmental sculpture called *The Labyrinth* offers benches to the weary. The New York State Vietnam Memorial salutes the people who served in that war. Lining the interior halls of the concourse are fine examples of modern art on permanent display—the largest publicly owned and displayed art collection in the country, and it is all the work of New York artists. More than 92 sculptures, tapestries, paintings, and constructions are displayed, among them works by artists such as Calder, Nevelson, Frankenthaler, and Noguchi. Special art tours are offered (call for hours), or stop at any of the tourist booths and ask for the tour brochure. For an above-the-clouds view of the entire mall, take the elevator to the 42nd floor of the Corning Tower. The observation deck, open 9–4, is free, and you can see the Catskills, the Adirondacks, and the Berkshires. Outside near the wide stairway to the New York State Museum, special events are held throughout the summer, among them an Independence Day celebration, concerts, ethnic celebrations, a Tulip Festival, and the Empire State Plaza Farmers Market. First Night Albany, a citywide New Year's Eve celebration, may be enjoyed at the Plaza as well. Children who like to walk will enjoy the activities on the mall.

LODGING

Albany Marriott Hotel (518-458-8444 or 1-800-443-8952), 189 Wolf Road 12205. ($$$) This hotel is near four major shopping malls, a 5-minute drive from the airport, and less than 20 minutes from downtown Albany. Each room in this luxury hotel is equipped with a color television, HBO, and other modern amenities. There are indoor and outdoor pools, a sauna, a whirlpool, and exercise rooms. A continental breakfast is served, and there are restaurants on the site. Open year-round.

The Desmond (518-869-8100 or 1-800-448-3500), 660 Albany Shaker Road 12211. ($$$) The best features of an inn and a hotel are combined at The Desmond, with its period furniture, paintings, handsome wood paneling, and courtyards that bloom with flowers and plants all year. All 323 rooms have custom-made furniture, and guests can use two heated pools, a health club, saunas, exercise rooms, and a billiard room. Open year-round.

Mansion Hill Inn (518-465-2038), 115 Phillip Street 12202. ($$) This bed & breakfast is within walking distance of the state capitol and the downtown business district. Winner of a preservation award, the inn has eight rooms, each with private bath. Choose from a wide variety of dishes on the breakfast menu. Children welcome. Open year-round.

Omni Albany (518-462-6611 or 1-800-THE-OMNI), Ten Eyck Plaza 12210. ($$$) Located in the heart of downtown, near the Capitol

JOSEPH PUGLISI

The Desmond Hotel courtyard blooms with flowers and plants year-round.

Complex and Empire State Plaza, this luxury hotel has 386 recently redecorated guest rooms and 18 suites. You'll find an exercise room, indoor heated pool, and whirlpool. Complimentary airport transportation and free parking are provided; a gift shop, auto rental facilities, and an airline office are on-site. The hotel's restaurant, **Fitzgerald's,** has an excellent and reasonably priced lunch buffet Monday through Friday 11:30–2.

State Street Mansion Bed & Breakfast (518-462-6780), 281 State Street 12210. ($$) This B&B is located in the center of the city's Center Square Historic District, only one block away from the capitol and the Empire State Plaza. Cultural activities, entertainment, and dining are readily accessible. The brownstone dates back to 1889 and has been in business as a guest house for 80 years. There are 12 rooms, all with private bath. A continental breakfast is served. The Bleecker Cafe on the premises serves lunch and dinner daily. Parking is available and included in the room charge.

WHERE TO EAT

DINING OUT

Albany has a wealth of restaurants to choose from, and they offer cuisines from nouvelle to Indonesian. The following were selected for their un-

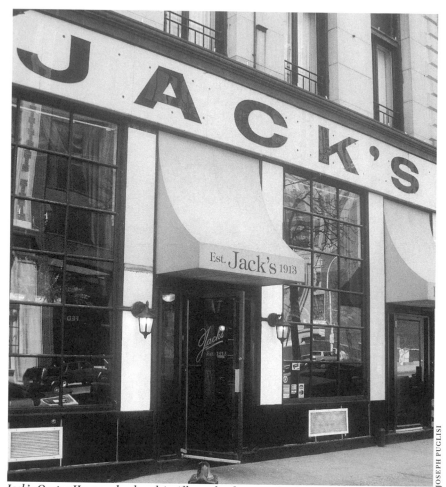

JOSEPH PUGLISI

Jack's Oyster House, a landmark in Albany, has been run by the same family for more than 80 years.

usually good food or interesting surroundings; they provide only a hint of the culinary treasures in the capital city.

Caffe Italia (518-482-9433), 662 Central Avenue. ($$$) Open daily for dinner 5–11. This family-run Italian restaurant is a popular spot with members of the state legislature (there is even a dish or two named after lawmakers). Everything is prepared to order, and the veal and pasta specialties are worth the trip. Reservations required. Not recommended for children.

Conway's (518-489-9999), 492 Yates Street. ($$) Open for dinner daily, except Sunday, 5–10. Housed in what was once an old speakeasy, this restaurant is in the heart of the downtown area. There's a beautiful mahogany bar and a cozy ambience. The food is mostly classic Continental fare; several of the dishes are slow cooked over aged applewood.

Try the shrimp brochette appetizer and the filet mignon *au poivre.* The dessert to try is the chef's passion fruit soufflé for two.

Jack's Oyster House (518-465-8854), 42 State Street. ($$) Open daily for lunch and dinner 11:30–10. This is Albany's oldest restaurant, and for 80 years it has been run by the same family. The steak and seafood are traditions, and the specialties are consistently good. Children are welcome. Reservations suggested.

Matisse (518-436-1415), 137 Madison Avenue. ($$) Open for dinner Tuesday through Sunday 5–10. Framed museum prints adorn the walls in this restaurant, which serves contemporary American cuisine. The fried calamari appetizer and pasta with Maine lobster entrée are two favorites of ours. The steak *au poivre* is excellent. All entrées are accompanied by dill potato cakes and vegetables. For dessert, there are such tempting delights as orange crème brûlée and Amaretto Cake.

Nicole's Bistro at the Quackenbush House (518-465-1111), 25 Quackenbush Square. ($$) Open for lunch Monday through Friday 11:30–2:30; open for dinner daily from 5. Closed Sunday. This restaurant is located in the oldest building in Albany and dates back to the late 17th century. Once an old brick home, it is now a haven with gorgeous gardens in the heart of downtown Albany. Enjoy fine French cuisine, including duck with pear sauce. The food is first-rate, and the building—with its towers and curves—is intriguing. Outdoor dining in the warm-weather months.

Ogden's (518-463-6605), Lodge and Howard Streets. ($$) Open for lunch Monday through Friday from 11:30; for dinner Monday through Saturday from 5:30. Closed Sunday. Enjoy Continental and New American cuisine with such specialties as aged Angus beef with Roquefort sauce and grilled Norwegian salmon with ginger tamari beurre blanc. Salads and sandwiches predominate at lunchtime. The black bean soup has been on the menu for 20 years, and Ogden's is well known throughout Albany for this Cuban-style dish. All breads and desserts are made on the premises, and every dish is prepared to order. An elegant yet casual spot located in a restored turn-of-the-19th-century building with food that is consistently excellent. This is one of the best establishments in the capital.

La Serre Restaurant (518-463-6056), 14 Green Street. ($$$) Open daily (except Sunday) for lunch 11:30–2; dinner from 6. This elegant Continental restaurant is housed in a historic building complete with bright awnings and window boxes full of flowers. The service is superb, and specialties include an award-winning onion soup, bouillabaisse Marseillaise, loin of veal with béarnaise sauce, and steak *au poivre.* Sumptuous desserts are made fresh daily. Children are welcome. Reservations recommended.

The Shipyard (518-438-4428), 95 Everett Road. ($$) Open for lunch Tuesday through Friday noon–3; open daily for dinner from 5:30. This lovely restaurant not only is pretty to look at but also serves excellent Continental and regional American food. Specialties include grilled chicken, lamb, and seafood; everything is fresh and made to order.

Sitar (518-456-6670), 1929 Central Avenue. ($$) Open daily for lunch 11:30–2:30 and dinner 5–10. Indian specialties are prepared to your taste, among them Tandoori and curry dishes and chicken and vegetarian entrées.

Unlimited Feast (518-463-6223), 340 Hamilton Street. ($$) Open Monday through Friday for lunch 11:30–2:30; dinner served Wednesday through Saturday 5–9. Reservations suggested for dinner. Located on a quiet residential block, this charming spot in the city's Center Square area is a tranquil oasis. The eclectic international cuisine makes for an exciting dining experience. Try the Thai chicken with red curry paste and coconut milk, or the duck confit. For an appetizer, don't miss the baked chèvre and roasted garlic with Tuscan toasts. No smoking is permitted in the restaurant.

Yono's (518-436-7747), 64 Colvin Avenue. ($$) Open Wednesday through Saturday for dinner 5:30–10. The taste of Indonesian cuisine is found here, along with Continental specialties. Chicken, vegetarian dishes, and excellent steaks are on the menu. In summer the garden patio is open for dining. Reservations suggested.

EATING OUT

Big House Brewing Company (518-445-2739), 90 North Pearl Street. ($) Open Tuesday through Saturday from 4 PM. Dozens of beers and ales are offered in this lively spot, from Ale Capone Amber Ale to Ma Barker Light. The hearty food includes burgers, sandwiches, steaks, and salads. Tuesdays there are $2 pints; and Thursday is Clambake Night, which includes crab legs, shrimp, clams, steamed potatoes, and sweet corn.

Daleah's Specialty Foods (518-437-1576), 76 Exchange Street. ($) Open Wednesday through Friday 11–4, Saturday 10–3. This is one of the most unusual specialty food stores to be found in the region. It offers a variety of cheeses, pâtés, imported chocolates, smoked fish and meats, wild mushrooms, and breads. You can grab a quick bite or get take-out snacks.

El Loco Cafe (518-436-1855), 465 Madison Avenue. ($) Open Tuesday through Saturday for lunch and dinner 11:30–10. This lively café specializes in Tex-Mex fare and is located in a restored 19th-century building. El Loco is well known for its chili (the heat is up to you) and its large selection of Mexican beer. Even after all the chili and beer you can down, the desserts are still tempting.

Justin's (518-436-7008), 301 Lark Street. ($) Open daily for lunch 11:30–2:30; dinner served from 5; late-night menu available until 1 AM. Located in Albany's answer to Greenwich Village, part of this restaurant dates back to the 1700s, and there has been a tavern or inn on this site ever since. All soups are made fresh daily, and the crab, mussel, and tomato-dill bisques are excellent. There are daily specials and a café menu with gourmet sandwiches. Jazz is featured on some evenings. Not appropriate for children. Reservations suggested.

Mamoun's Falafel (518-434-3901), 206 Washington Avenue. ($) Open daily 11–10. In addition to the vegetarian fare at this Middle Eastern restaurant, there is a variety of chicken and lamb dishes. Try the shish kebob—it's a house specialty.

Miyako (518-482-1080), 192 North Allen Street. ($) Open weekdays for lunch noon–2; daily for dinner 5–10. At this informal Japanese restaurant you can watch the chef prepare your meal on the hibachi table or enjoy the creative fare from the sushi bar.

Quintessence (518-434-8186), 11 New Scotland Avenue. ($) Open daily for breakfast, lunch, and dinner 8 AM–2 AM. This art deco diner bustles with good food and special theme nights, including Italian, seafood, German, and international. A large menu with something for every taste. Children welcome.

SPECIAL EVENTS

February: **Albany American Wine Festival** (518-869-8100) This festival is held at The Desmond hotel, 660 Albany Shaker Road, the first weekend in February. There are tastings, seminars, and dinners featuring wines from all over the country. A one-day pass may be purchased. The lectures are designed to appeal to oenophiles as well as those who want to learn more about wines.

March–April: An unusual way to spend a morning is to take a trip out to the sugarbush and watch maple sap boiled down into rich, sweet maple syrup. Two sugarhouses allow visitors during the season, which usually runs from March into April: **Bassler's Sugarhouse** (518-872-2023), 2180 Becker Road, Berne; and **Sugarbush Farm** (518-872-1456), 1755 Township Road, Knox.

May: Tulip Festival, Pinksterfest, and Kinderkermis. These festivals are usually held over a long weekend in May and include outdoor crafts and food fairs, entertainment, the crowning of the Tulip Queen, and a dance. The celebrations are colorful and peopled with costumed performers. For information on the exact dates, call the Albany County Convention and Visitors Bureau (518-434-1217 or 1-800-258-3582).

Year-round: Other festivals held throughout the year include ethnic and arts celebrations, the New York State Chocolate Festival, and the fabulous First Night, which offers citywide New Year's Eve entertainment; call the visitors bureau for information.

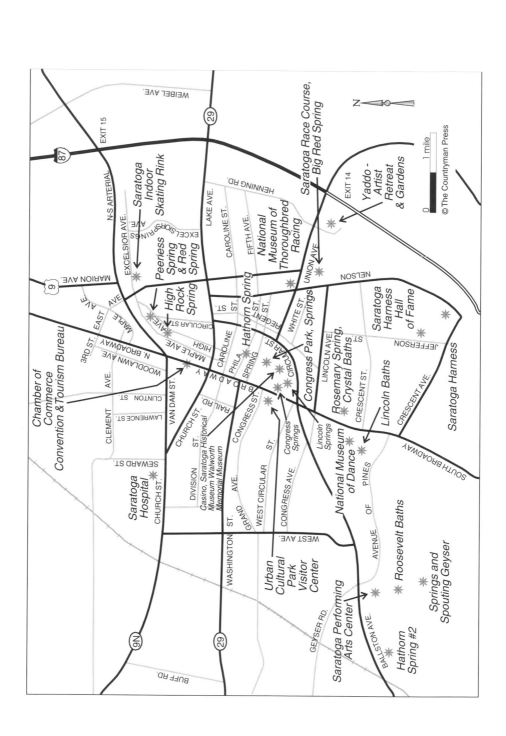

VIII. Saratoga Springs and Surrounding Area

It is nearly impossible to describe Saratoga Springs—*elegant, gracious, exciting, mysterious,* and *eccentric* are only a few of the words that come to mind. Since the 18th century, when natural medicinal springs were discovered in the region, Saratoga Springs has played host to visitors from around the world. There are modern spas in which to relax and plenty of outdoor activities to stretch the muscles. Classical music and dance enthusiasts can enjoy a picnic dinner while great orchestral selections and dances are performed under the stars. Lovers of Victorian architecture can stroll down a side street or two, where they will spot grand old mansions and exquisite gardens (some planted right in the middle of the road!). With all of this, Saratoga Springs also offers the best Thoroughbred horse racing in the world. Each July and August this quiet place pulses with the color, crowds, and excitement of the famed Saratoga Racetrack, where the best jockeys and horses vie for enormous winnings and fame. In addition, there are horse auctions, polo matches, and art exhibits, and the public is invited to just about everything. You can spend a month in Saratoga Springs and still not experience all it has to offer. The only thing you must not do is miss it.

GUIDANCE
Greater Saratoga Chamber of Commerce (518-584-3255), 28 Clinton Street, Saratoga Springs 12866; www.saratoga.org.

GETTING THERE
Saratoga Springs is located north of Albany on I-87 (Adirondack Northway), exits 13N through 15.

MEDICAL EMERGENCY
Saratoga Hospital (518-587-3222), 211 Church Street, Saratoga Springs.

TO SEE

✎ **Children's Museum at Saratoga** (518-584-5540), 36 Phila Street. Open year-round. Closed Monday, but call for hours and days; the schedule varies with the summer months. Admission fee. This unique museum

Daniel Chester French's statue, "The Spirit of Life," greets visitors to Congress Park in downtown Saratoga Springs

offers children ages 2–12 a chance to explore the world, from the local community to the international level. There are interactive exhibits that allow visitors to run a general store, make giant bubbles, even "freeze" their shadows. Special events have included art workshops and magic shows. This museum is so centrally located that a visit can be combined with shopping or stops at the Canfield Casino Museum and park.

Congress Park and **Canfield Casino** (518-584-6920), Broadway and Circular Street. The park is open daily year-round; the casino is open year-round, but hours vary widely, so call ahead. Admission charged for the casino. Part of the daily life of Saratoga Springs a century ago was "taking the waters," and Congress Park was a popular watering hole. The wealthy who came to Saratoga Springs each summer to escape the plagues and stink of the industrial cities would stay at the area's fine hotels and stroll along the park's pathways to various fountains (see *Springs*). Today the park has lovely plantings, places to sit and ponder the past, and some interesting decorative offerings. Daniel Chester French's statue *The Spirit of Life* greets visitors near the entrance (he also created the seated president's statue in the Lincoln Memorial), and two huge, lovely urns called "Day" and "Night" bloom with flowers each summer. Tucked in the back of the park is a small reflecting pool with the most popular of the park's denizens: a pair of Triton figurines that shoot out streams of water and are nicknamed Spit and Spat. Enjoy walking among the columns in the Italian Gardens. Also located in the park is the Canfield Casino, once one of the most famous gambling establishments in the country, today home to a museum and art gallery. The **Saratoga Historical Society** maintains a lovely series of rooms that offer vignettes of life in Saratoga Springs during the Gilded Age of the late 19th century, when Lillian Russell, Diamond Jim Brady, and a host of others sparkled each night over the gaming tables. Downstairs in the museum's art gallery there are changing exhibits of works by local and regional artists. The museum also hosts crafts shows each summer and fall (call for dates). (During the racing season the casino becomes the site of one of the most glamorous society events in the old style: philanthropist Mary Lou Whitney's "fantasy" parties, where guests may enjoy visiting Oz or watching Cinderella arrive in a real pumpkin coach. Of course, this is not a public event, but if you are in the area, you can watch the Saratoga glitterati arrive. A one-of-a-kind event, really.)

National Museum of Dance (518-584-2225), South Broadway. Open May through October; call for hours. Admission fee. This is the only museum in the country dedicated to preserving the history and art of dance in America, and it does a superb job. Changing exhibits feature costumes, artwork, personalities, and choreography of American dance. Videos help place various dances in their historical settings, and it is one of the few places where dance enthusiasts may get up close to the costumes and accessories of their favorite dance "characters." Special events include talks, films, and the Dance Flurry, a citywide event in which you can participate in dance workshops and shows of all types; call for a schedule of events.

National Museum of Thoroughbred Racing (518-584-0400), Union Avenue. Open year-round Monday through Saturday 10–5, Sunday noon–5; during racing season opens at 9; closed New Year's Day, Easter, Thanksgiving, and Christmas. Admission fee. This museum is one of the most modern sport exhibits in the world, and it is a must-see for anyone who ever enjoyed the sight of a racehorse blasting out of a starting gate. The film *Race America* is an introduction to the racetrack, and throughout the various galleries video and audio exhibits let visitors experience the sounds and sights of racing. Silks, fine paintings, furniture, and historic items all tell the story of the Thoroughbred in America; the museum covers nearly 300 years of history. Special exhibits held in smaller galleries feature art and photography from contemporary artists. Even if you've never placed a bet in your life, the gift shop here will turn you into a horse fan immediately. The museum also offers a virtual tour of its galleries, one of the few such web sites included in this book: www.racingmuseum.org. Harness racing fans will want to visit the **Saratoga Harness Racing Museum and Hall of Fame** (518-587-4210), 352 Jefferson Street, which is located at the Saratoga Harness Raceway and offers memorabilia and artwork depicting the history of harness racing (free).

Tang Teaching Museum and Art Gallery (518-580-8080), Skidmore College, 815 North Broadway, Saratoga Springs. Open Tuesday through Sunday, 11–5. The two-story building that houses this new museum (opened in 2000) was designed by Antoine Predock. Paid for by a gift from the Chinese-born American businessman Oscar Tang, whose daughter and wife both graduated from Skidmore, the museum covers post-war art, giving preference to visual work with an aural component. In addition to fine art, the Tang has a few peripheral exhibits (films, performances) in progress and some intriguing auditory treats, including collaborative exhibits with Skidmore's science and history departments.

HISTORIC SITE

Saratoga National Historic Park (518-664-9821), Routes 4 and 32, Stillwater. Open daily year-round 9–5; closed Thanksgiving, Christmas, and New Year's. The **Philip Schuyler House** is open daily Memorial Day through Labor Day. Admission fee. The battle of Saratoga turned the tide of the American Revolution, and history buffs will enjoy spending a day here. The British hoped to cut New York into sections with a three-pronged attack and destroy communications among the areas. At Saratoga the supposedly untrained, undisciplined American troops won the field, and history was changed. Your tour should begin at the battlefield visitors center, where dioramas, maps, and explanatory exhibits show how the battle was fought and won. Weapons, uniforms, and other items are on display, and because the battle was such a large one, it is necessary to read the material before you set out on the 10-mile self-guided driving tour. There are markers at each stop that explain what went on during the battle. At the Schuyler House memorabilia of Gen. Philip Schuyler and his wife show what life was like for

Visitors to the Saratoga National Historic Park in Stillwater will find cannons, like this reproduction of one used during the battle of Saratoga in 1777, scattered about the battlefield.

people who lived through the battle and the days after. There is even a monument to a leg on the field—Benedict Arnold was wounded in the leg during the battle and became a hero, until he turned traitor later. Special events, including military encampments, are held at the park throughout the year (call for a schedule).

SPRINGS

Saratoga is famous for its springs, many of which are still open. A spring tasting guide is available from the Urban Cultural Center (518-587-3241), 297 Broadway, opposite Congress Park. The center is open April through November and also has small exhibits on the history of Saratoga Springs and its commerce. The springs in Saratoga each have their own

Governor's Spring, one of the many springs in Saratoga, is a two-block walk from the downtown area.

chemical makeup and characteristics; there are explanatory signs at each spring and, usually, paper drinking cups. Just remember that too much of the springwater might not sit well with your digestive system; try no more than a sip or two to start. You can also find lots of bottled springwater at shops in Saratoga or at the spas.

High Rock Park (go north on Broadway, make a right onto Lake Avenue, then a left onto High Avenue). You can sample water from Old Red, the Peerless, and the Governor Springs here. These were the original public springs of Saratoga Springs, and each has its own taste; Old Red, so called because of its high iron content, was considered good for the complexion.

Congress Park, on Broadway, houses Congress Spring, located underneath an elaborate pavilion. Its waters were some of the first to be bottled and sold commercially in the early 19th century. Also in the park along the path are the Columbian Spring, Congress 3, and, in the northeast corner, Freshwater Spring. Across from the park, on Spring Street, the Hathorn No. 1 Spring is a popular stop on a hot summer's day; it has a small seating area, and lovely plantings surround it.

Saratoga Spa State Park (take Route 9 south to the Avenue of Pines and follow that into the park; the site is very well marked) has several springs and bathing facilities (see *Green Space*). Built in the 1930s, the

Roosevelt Baths and the Lincoln Park Baths still have mineral baths and massages. The Roosevelt (518-584-2011) is open all year; the Lincoln (518-583-2880) is open in the summer months only (call for reservations). Drinking springs throughout the park include Island Spouter (the only spouting geyser east of the Mississippi), Hayes Well (with an inhaling hole), Orenda Spring, Coesa, and Ferndale. There is a marked walking path to many of the springs—a lovely stroll on a warm summer's afternoon. There is no charge for tasting the springs.

WALKING TOUR

A walk through Saratoga Springs gives visitors a chance to see the great variety of architectural styles in vogue during the 19th and early 20th centuries, but it would be impossible to list all the houses that are worth looking at. A self-guided tour is usually available at the information booth near Congress Park or from the Greater Saratoga Chamber of Commerce (518-584-3255), 28 Clinton Street. Scores of homes offer a look at Italianate, Gothic Revival, Queen Anne, Romanesque, and other styles popular with the upper middle class and wealthy of the city. The **Batcheller House,** corner of Whitney and West Circular, is a fantasy of French Renaissance and Eastern influence; the **Jumel Mansion,** 129 Circular Street, was the summer home of the infamous Madame Jumel, onetime wife to Aaron Burr; the **Adelphi Hotel,** Broadway, recalls the hotels of the past, with tall columns and many arched windows. Several streets and areas you may want to enjoy for their architectural wealth include Broadway, Circular Street, Franklin Square, Clinton Street, Caroline Street, Lake Avenue, and Union Avenue. All the homes are private, but their beauty can easily be appreciated from the sidewalk.

Saratoga's main thoroughfare is Broadway, which has won numerous awards for its Main Street restoration. There are dozens of shops, galleries, and places of interest to check out—Irish specialty stores, rare books, clothing fashionable and funky, fine glass, needlework, and more. Don't forget to wander the side streets just off Broadway (Phila, Spring, and Caroline), where many other surprises await the intrepid walker.

TO DO

FARM STANDS AND PICK-YOUR-OWN FARMS

Among the many things Saratoga is famous for is melon; more specifically, Hand melons, named after the family that first grew them. The **Hand Melon Farm** (518-692-2376) is located 13 miles east of Saratoga Springs on Route 29; the melons are usually ready to go from late July through mid-August. They are sweet and resemble cantaloupes; you will see signs for them at many farm stands. A great deal of excellent produce is raised on local farms as well. At **Ariel's Vegetable Farm** (518-584-2189), 194 Northern Pines Road, 5 miles north of Saratoga Springs (open April through September), visitors can pick their own berries, buy fruit and vegetables off the stand, or take a tour of the farm.

Bowman Orchards (518-371-7432), Sugar Hill Road, Rexford (open September through November), has pick-your-own apples, as does **Bullards Farm Market** (518-695-3177), Route 29, Schuylerville (open August through February). Both also have well-stocked farm stands.

Riverview Orchards (518-371-2174), Riverview Road, Rexford, has pick-your-own apples, farm tours, lots of produce, and cross-country skiing in winter.

There is also a nice **farmer's market** at High Rock Park (take Broadway north to Grove and watch for signs) every Wednesday evening 3–6 and Saturday 9–1 from May through October. You can also sample more of the famous local waters.

HORSE RACING

Saratoga Equine Sports Center (518-584-2110), Nelson Avenue. Open March through November; simulcasts the rest of the year; post time 7:45 PM. Admission fee. Formerly a plain harness track, the Sports Center was often overshadowed by its sassier cousin, the Saratoga Racetrack. But it has expanded and now offers anyone who enjoys harness racing, polo, barrel, and rodeo events lots of excitement. Visitors can enjoy watching horses vie for purses on the world's fastest $1/2$-mile trotting and pacing track, which, unlike the "flats," is open 140 days a year. (The backstretch area contains the only pool in the state located on the grounds of a racetrack and reserved solely for the use of horses.) There are two polo fields and an outdoor arena with more than 200 acres and 1,100 stalls for the equine patrons. Special events include country music shows (Countryfest brings the platinum headliners to the area), carriage-driving competitions, and crafts fairs.

Saratoga Racetrack (518-584-6200; 718-641-4700 out of season), Union Avenue. Open during the July-August meeting only; call for specific dates. Closed Tuesday. Admission fee varies. Saratoga Racetrack is a hub of activity during the month of August, and it is busy from early in the morning until the late afternoon. Rub shoulders with celebrities, rail birds, and just plain people; dress in jeans and tees or elegant suits and hats; the choice is yours and the ghost of Damon Runyon hovers over all. You can begin with "Breakfast at Saratoga" (7–9:30 AM; get there early; free admission), a popular way for people to enjoy the horses and jockeys close up. There is an announcer to keep things lively as the horses and their riders breeze by. Handicapping seminars—very handy for novice bettors—are held at the track and are announced at breakfast; the seminar times are also posted throughout the track. Breakfast is also served daily in the clubhouse dining room, in an outdoor tent, and buffet style in the box seats; outside, a continental breakfast is served near the clubhouse. Visitors can enjoy a tour of the backstretch area as well, where the horses board during the racing season. The tour is escorted, and the area is viewed from an observation "train"; sign up for the tour early during breakfast.

The track opens to the racing crowd at 11 AM weekdays and 10:30 weekends. Although there is lots of parking and seating available, remember one thing: The crowds can be large and the track is smaller than many modern racetracks. Get there early for good viewing. You can park in an official track lot or at a private lot. The latter cost more, but the former fill up quickly; again, get there early so at least you have a selection. Bring your own chair, if possible, and remember that both restaurant food and snacks, though usually good, can be very expensive. You are allowed to bring coolers into the track. Both steeplechases and flat races are held throughout the season; check the daily racing forms to see exactly who is racing in what. Races begin (post time) at 1 PM weekdays, 12:30 weekends, rain or shine.

POLO

You can't play polo unless you have your own string of ponies, but you can watch weekly at Saratoga. The players come from all over the world and are the best in their sport. Matches are held Tuesday, Friday, and Sunday throughout August, but call for hours and a complete schedule (518-584-3255 or 584-8108). There is an admission charge. To get to the polo grounds, go north on Broadway, turn left onto Church Street, go approximately 0.5 mile, and make a right onto Seward Street. Go 1 mile to the railroad overpass and turn right; the polo field is on your left.

GREEN SPACE

Saratoga Spa State Park (518-584-2000), 1 mile south of Saratoga Springs on Route 9. Open year-round. The park is free; there is a small charge for swimming and the bathhouses. This 2,000-acre park is a gem: clean, wide open, full of activities to keep visitors busy—and located only minutes from Saratoga Springs. Listed on the National Register of Historic Places, the park is home to the Saratoga Performing Arts Center (see *Entertainment*) and the Gideon Putnam Hotel (see *Lodging*) as well as the Roosevelt Baths and the Lincoln Park Baths (see *Springs*). Recreation opportunities abound in Spa Park: Three pools, tennis courts, streamside trails for walking, and two golf courses (reservations required) are open in summer; in winter cross-country skiing, ice skating, and even a speed-skating oval are available. Special film evenings, nature walks, tours, and other special events are held throughout the year (call for a schedule).

Yaddo (518-584-0746 for garden information), Route 9P, Union Avenue. Open year-round, but the gardens are at their height from June through August. Free. The rose gardens here are superb, and visitors are welcome to walk among the paths and enjoy the fountains, roses, plantings, and quiet seating areas. Yaddo was once a private home but is now an

Yaddo Gardens, on the grounds of the renowned artists' retreat, just outside the downtown area of Saratoga Springs

artists' retreat used by both the famous and the someday-to-be-famous; the site offers a respite from the August frenzy of racing and society.

LODGING

A note on lodging and dining in Saratoga Springs: The Spa City is a wonderful place to visit and spend a day or a week. As in many other resort areas, prices range from moderate to expensive. But during the "season"—late July through August, when Thoroughbred racing is the main event—prices can go sky high, and accommodations may be difficult to obtain (some places are booked as early as May). Restaurants can be crowded, expensive, and difficult to get reservations for—that is, unless you know someone. We don't suggest you pass up the excitement that is Saratoga Springs during the summer—it's still the best time to visit—but be prepared to pay top price for lodging and dining. If you are going to visit the area, you may want to consider staying in Albany (see "City of Albany"), which is about 40 minutes away. Restaurant hours vary so widely during the different seasons that they have been noted only if they do not change. If you are in doubt, call before you go.
Note: All listings are in Saratoga Springs 12866, unless otherwise indicated.
Chestnut Tree Inn (518-587-8681), 9 Whitney Place. ($$$) Named after

the last remaining chestnut tree in Saratoga Springs, this inn offers country ambience within walking distance of the racetrack and other points of interest. Continental breakfast is served on the Victorian porch in summer, and the inn is furnished with antiques. Suites and nine rooms, all with private bath. Open May through November.

Eddy House (518-587-2340), Crescent and Nelson Avenues. ($$$) This B&B, one of the oldest in Saratoga Springs, sits on 1½ acres of well-tended lawns and gardens, and guests can play badminton or bocce, use the golf net, or just relax. Your hosts will go out of their way to make you feel at home. If you walk or jog in the morning, the location is perfect for a peaceful excursion on foot. In addition to the four private rooms sharing two baths, there are two living rooms, a library, and a screened-in porch for guests' use. A large gourmet breakfast is served daily and may include French toast, eggs, homemade muffins, and other baked goods. Open year-round.

Gideon Putnam Hotel (518-584-3000), Saratoga Spa State Park. ($$$) The hotel is set in the 2000-acre park, a few minutes' walk from the Saratoga Performing Arts Center (see *Entertainment*) and minutes away from the track and from downtown Saratoga Springs. In addition to double rooms, there are 18 parlor and porch suites available. The service is excellent, and guests may choose to have meals included in the rate. Open year-round.

The Inn at Saratoga (518-583-1890), 231 Broadway. ($$$) This establishment combines the modern comforts of a hotel and the charming touches of an inn. There are 38 rooms and suites, all decorated in Victorian style. A restaurant downstairs serves dinner daily, and the Sunday brunch features live jazz. Continental breakfast is served. Open year-round.

Lombardi Farm (518-587-2074), 34 Locust Grove. ($$) This bed & breakfast is only 1½ miles from downtown Saratoga Springs and is located in a restored 1850s farmhouse. Guests may enjoy a hot tub, air-conditioned rooms with private bath, and a large gourmet breakfast. There are four rooms with private bath, and a new recreation center with an exercise room. This is a nice, casual farm setting, a change from the rush of Saratoga Springs in August. Open year-round.

The Mansion (518-885-1607), Route 29, Rock City Falls 12863. ($$$) This inn, a dream come true for lovers of Victoriana, has been featured in several publications. The rooms are furnished with period furniture, and the service is elegant, with a full gourmet breakfast included. Guests may use the parlor, walk the grounds, visit the antiques shop, or laze on the porch. This is truly a special spot, and it is worth traveling the few miles outside of Saratoga to stay here. There is an old mill and a lovely stream across the street from the inn where visitors can take a stroll. All five rooms have private bath and air-conditioning; adults only. There is now a two-bedroom cottage as well. Open year-round.

Six Sisters Bed and Breakfast (518-583-1173), 149 Union Avenue. ($$$)

This charming establishment, named after the six sisters of one of the owners, is located on the flower-bedecked Union Avenue approach to the racetrack. At Six Sisters guests will enjoy a gourmet breakfast and their choice of four guest rooms or suites, all with private bath and air-conditioning. Only minutes from most of the goings-on in Saratoga Springs, this inn is a special place to enjoy a special weekend. Older children welcome. Open year-round.

✎ **Union Gables Bed & Breakfast** (518-584-1558 or 1-800-398-1558), 55 Union Avenue. ($$) This recently restored Queen Anne Victorian, circa 1901, is a family-owned and -occupied bed & breakfast. Each of the 10 guest rooms is exquisitely decorated to reflect the style of Old Saratoga. Every room has a modern bath, TV, telephone, and small refrigerator. The establishment is conveniently located near the downtown area and only one block from the Thoroughbred racetrack. Children are welcome. Open year-round.

Westchester House (518-587-7613), 102 Lincoln Avenue. ($$$) Built in high Gothic style—complete with towers, crenellations, and oddments—this charming inn is a fairy tale come true. There are seven rooms, all with private bath. The rooms offer luxury touches like ceiling fans (or air-conditioning) and fresh flowers from the surrounding gardens in summer. Downtown Saratoga Springs is a few minutes' walk away, and guests can enjoy sitting on the porch while looking forward to the morning's breakfast of home-baked goods and fresh gourmet coffee. Open year-round.

WHERE TO EAT

Note: All listings are in Saratoga Springs unless otherwise indicated.

DINING OUT

Adelphi Hotel (518-587-4688), 365 Broadway. ($$) Dessert and coffee are served in the evening year-round, and the pastries are excellent. The Victorian surroundings, which echo the old-time elegance of Saratoga Springs, should not be missed on a walk up Broadway.

Beverly's (518-583-2755), 47 Phila Street. ($$) Open for breakfast and lunch Sunday 8–3. This small café is tucked down a side street just off Broadway. The food is fresh and carefully prepared, and the baked goods are excellent. Beverly's is well known for thick slabs of French toast and will prepare gourmet take-out lunches for picnics trackside (or anywhere else).

The Brew Pub (518-583-3209), 14 Phila Street. ($$) Open daily 11:30 AM–midnight. Rustic, casual dining on two floors; the first floor is informal, the upstairs is reserved for elegant dining. Enjoy American cuisine featuring burgers of all kinds, salads, sandwiches, and steaks. There are four of the pub's own brews on tap as well as a wide variety of other beers. A microbrewery is on the premises—a must for beer lovers.

JOANNE MICHAELS

Union Gables Bed & Breakfast

Cafe Lena (518-583-0022), 47 Phila Street. ($$) Open Thursday through Sunday from 8 PM. Almost all major folk and folk-rock artists have appeared at this well-known coffeehouse and nightspot over the years. The food is secondary to the performances, although the coffee, including specialties like iced mocha java, is excellent. Worth a stop, no matter who is on the bill. Not recommended for children.

Chez Sophie Bistro (518-583-3538), 2853 Route 9, Malta Ridge. ($$$) Open daily, except Sunday and Monday, for dinner from 5:30. The French cuisine is first-rate in this elegant spot outside the city. The pâté and escargots are just two of the appetizers, and both the half duckling in apricot and green peppercorns and the Black Angus New York strip steak with peppercorns are excellent. Save room for the chocolate mousse.

Chianti's Ristorante (518-580-0025), 208 Broadway. ($$$) Open for dinner daily 5:30–10. Savor new trends in northern Italian cuisine in this upscale establishment. The chef suggests the cappellini with lobster and prawns or the penne pasta with cannellini beans and sausage. A few of the other entrées include stuffed quail, risotto, and salmon dishes. There are over 300 selections on the wine list. Make sure to leave room for dessert; the *tiramisu* and chocolate soufflé are first-rate.

Eartha's (518-583-0602), 60 Court Street. ($$$) Open for dinner Wednesday through Saturday from 6. A popular spot with diners in the know, this restaurant serves fresh dishes with a Continental flair, including mesquite-grilled seafood, duck, and steaks. There is a small sidewalk patio, and reservations are a must anytime. Not recommended for children.

✎ **43 Phila Bistro** (518-584-2720), 43 Phila Street. ($$) Open for dinner from

Gideon Putnam Hotel

5 daily except Sunday. This New American bistro features dishes from around the world. You can sample such tempting entrées as New Zealand lamb, Maryland crabcakes, and wild boar; there are a number of flavorful vegetarian dishes as well. All the pasta is homemade, and the pastry chef creates sensational desserts daily. Children welcome.

Gaffney's (518-587-7359), 16 Caroline Street. ($$) Open for lunch Monday through Friday 11:30–3, Saturday 10–4, Sunday brunch 9:30–3. Dinner served Monday through Saturday 5:30–10:30, Sunday 4:30–9:30. Casual dining featuring steaks, seafood, veal, chicken, pasta—classic American cooking. However, Cajun night is Tuesday and Mexican night is Wednesday for those looking for something a little different to spice up the week.

Gideon Putnam Hotel (518-584-3000), Saratoga Spa State Park. ($$) Open daily for breakfast 7–11; lunch noon–2; dinner 6–9. Set in the lovely Spa Park, this hotel is often packed in the evening before a concert or ballet. The Sunday brunch is outstanding and well worth the wait (seatings every half hour 11–2). Jackets are required for dinner, as are reservations.

Little India (518-583-4151), 423 Broadway. ($) Open daily for lunch 11:30–3; dinner 5–10. This Tandoori-style restaurant offers a variety of Indian specialties. The mixed grill is the most popular dish, and includes chicken, lamb, and beef. Vegetarians will enjoy the pureed spinach casserole with potato and cheese. A variety of curry entrées and different types of Indian breads are available as well.

Longfellow's (518-587-0108), 500 Union Avenue. ($$$) Open daily for dinner 5–10. Continental cuisine here features prime rib, seafood, and pasta. Try the bourbon-glazed salmon or the rack of lamb. The restaurant is unusual in that it has a waterfall and pond *inside*.

Maestro's (518-580-0312), 371 Broadway. ($$) Open Tuesday through Sunday for lunch 11:30–4; dinner 5–10. This establishment combines Italian and French cuisines, resulting in an eclectic menu. For lunch, try the baked ham and Brie sandwich, or the special vegetarian sandwich. For dinner, the roast rack of lamb or chicken novello (chicken with mushrooms in a cream sauce) are our favorites.

Panza's on the Lake (518-584-6882), 510 Route 9P, Saratoga Lake. ($$) Open Wednesday through Saturday 5–9, Sunday 1–9. Enjoy Italian American cuisine with a Continental flair and beautiful views of the lake. Known for his veal dishes, the chef suggests the veal martone (with shrimp, artichoke hearts, and mushrooms). The shrimp sorentino (shrimp topped with eggplant, prosciutto, and fresh mozzarella) is another popular entrée. All desserts are homemade on the premises.

✎ **Professor Moriarty's** (518-587-5981), 430 Broadway. ($$) Open daily for lunch and dinner 11:30–9:30. Victorian in feeling, this café is named after Sherlock Holmes's nemesis. A nice place for lunch, with very hearty sandwiches and homemade soups. Try Dr. Watson's filet mignon; there is no mystery about its popularity. Children welcome.

Siro's (518-584-4030), 168 Lincoln Avenue. ($$$) Open daily for dinner in August only. Call for hours, which vary. This is probably the most popular dinner spot with racegoers. Reservations are required, although the bar area is open (and crowded). The food here is Continental, with steak and seafood the specialties. Recommended if you want to continue enjoying the horsey atmosphere for the evening.

Sperry's (518-584-9618), 301/2 Caroline Street. ($$) Open daily for lunch 11:30–3:30; dinner 5:30–10. This American bistro–style restaurant offers grilled seafood and steak specials, fresh pasta, and softshell crabs in-season. The homemade pastries and desserts are first-rate: the crème caramel was featured in the *New York Times.* One of Saratoga's most reliable year-round gems.

Springwater Inn (518-584-6440), 139 Union Avenue. ($$) Open for dinner Tuesday through Sunday 5–10. The American cuisine ranges from veal, shrimp, and rack of lamb to salmon, vegetarian, and pasta dishes. There is something for everyone on this varied menu, which highlights traditional favorites.

✎ **The Waterfront Restaurant and Marina** (518-583-BOAT), 3 miles out of town; take Union Avenue to 628 Crescent Avenue, Saratoga Lake. ($$) Open daily from 11:30 for lunch and dinner. The glass-walled dining room and shoreline deck offer an uninterrupted view of Saratoga Lake and make this casual spot special. Steaks, seafood, pasta, and burgers are served in a relaxing atmosphere. Children welcome.

EATING OUT

Bruno's (518-583-3333), Union Avenue, opposite the Saratoga Racetrack. ($$) In summer open daily 11–11. Pizza lovers will want to stop by Bruno's and enjoy one from the wood-fired oven. During the August racing season the restaurant opens early for breakfast, with special egg, bacon, ham, and other creative start-your-day pizzas. Kids are welcome, and the atmosphere is funky '50s.

Country Corner Cafe (518-583-7889), 25 Church Street. ($) Open daily 6–2. The best breakfast in town is served until closing in this cozy café. Try the home-baked breads and muffins with preserves or the fresh fruit pancakes with maple syrup. The hearty soups and sandwiches make this a popular lunch spot with local residents.

Esperanto (518-587-4236), 612 Caroline Street. ($) Open Monday through Saturday, serving lunch and dinner from 11:30 AM until 11 PM. Closed Sunday. Authentic American cuisine using the freshest ingredients for soups, salads, and healthy sandwiches. There are always a few imaginative daily specials as well.

Hattie's Chicken Shack (518-584-4790), 45 Phila Street. ($) Open for dinner, Wednesday through Sunday from 6. During July and August open for breakfast, lunch, and dinner from 8 AM until 10 PM. This is the place for great fried foods: chicken, fish, potatoes. There are also nice pancake breakfasts, and biscuits with everything. For lovers of the lost art of the deep-fry. Children welcome.

Mrs. London's (518-581-1652), 464 Broadway, Saratoga Springs. ($$) The homemade soups, sandwiches, and wraps are first-rate and the baked goods are the best in the city. Don't miss this spot for an elegant lunch.

Old Bryan Inn (518-587-2990), 123 Maple Avenue. ($) Open daily at 11 AM. This unpretentious country inn is a nice stop for lunch and dinner. The burgers are hearty, the salads are fresh, and the steaks are grilled. Try the hot spinach salad or deep-fried cheese sticks with an unusual raspberry sauce. Children welcome.

One Caroline (518-587-2026), 1 Caroline Street. ($$) Open Tuesday through Saturday for lunch 11:30–3; dinner 6–10. This family-owned and -operated bistro-style restaurant has live music nightly. The cuisine is an international mix, featuring Cajun, Italian, and Asian dishes. The chef tells us that the jambalaya and filet mignon are among the most popular entrées—but adventurous diners won't want to miss the tasty Thai-style bouillabaisse.

The Parting Glass (518-583-1916), 40 Lake Avenue. ($) Open daily from 11 AM until the early-morning hours. An Irish pub–style restaurant. Try the Guinness and black bean soup for a hearty meal. There is entertainment on Wednesday and Saturday night, and the place is a favorite with the racetrack crowd. Great fun if you enjoy pubs; there's a vast selection of beers and even a serious dart shop. Not recommended for children.

PJ's Bar-b-q (518-583-CHIK), Route 9S, Broadway. ($) Open at noon for

Saratoga Performing Arts Center

lunch and dinner. Real, thick, smoky ribs and chicken. Spicy and satis-
fying for takeout or eat-in-the-parking-lot. Seasonal hours; call ahead.

Scallions (518-584-0192), 404 Broadway. ($) Open daily 11–9. A gourmet
eatery with a cheerful café atmosphere. Try the unique sandwich com-
binations, homemade soups, and specialty chicken and pasta dishes.
Desserts are first-rate: The carrot cake is the best around. A great place
to take out a meal for a picnic if you are heading to the Saratoga Performing Arts Center or the track.

ENTERTAINMENT

Saratoga Performing Arts Center (SPAC) (518-587-3330), Saratoga Spa
State Park, off Route 9, Saratoga Springs. Open from Mother's Day
through early September; schedules, performances, and ticket prices
vary. Each summer there are performances by the New York City Ballet, jazz, rock, and folk concerts, and more with matinee and evening
shows. You can bring a picnic, select foods from the gourmet food carts,
or stop at one of the restaurants in town and arrange for an elegant
take-along dinner. There is a covered, open-air seating area as well as
lawn seats under the stars, and plenty of parking. SPAC is but a few
minutes' drive from the center of town, but beware: A popular concert
can create bottlenecks, so plan to get there early. Lawn tickets can be
purchased the night of most performances, but it's a good idea to call
ahead and inquire about ticket availability.

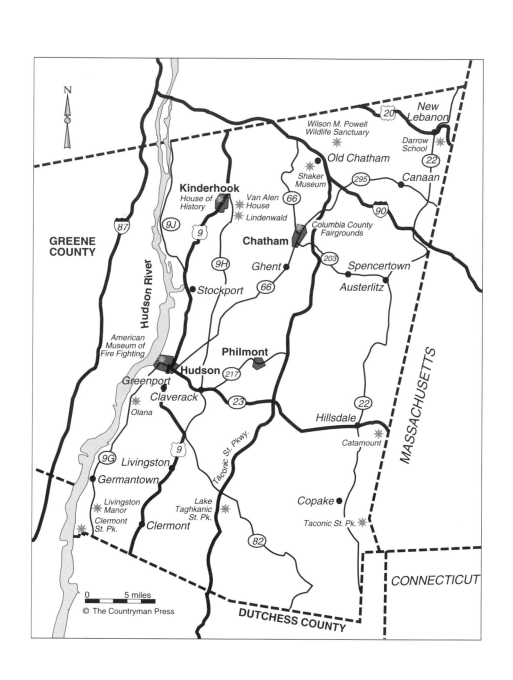

N

Wilson M. Powell
Wildlife Sanctuary

Old Chatham

New
Lebanon

20

Darrow
School

22

Canaan

Shaker
Museum

295

90

Kinderhook

House of
History

Van Alen
House

66

Lindenwald

87

**GREENE
COUNTY**

9J

9

Columbia County
Fairgrounds

Chatham

Hudson River

9H

Ghent

66

203

Spencertown

Austerlitz

Stockport

American
Museum of
Fire Fighting

Philmont

Hudson

217

Greenport

Claverack

23

Olana

Hillsdale

22

Catamount

9G

Livingston

9

Germantown

Taconic St. Pkwy.

Copake

Livingston
Manor

Lake
Taghkanic
St. Pk.

Taconic St. Pk.

Clermont
St. Pk.

Clermont

82

0   5 miles

© The Countryman Press

DUTCHESS COUNTY

MASSACHUSETTS

CONNECTICUT

IX. Columbia County

First the home of the Native Americans who greeted Henry Hudson, Columbia County later attracted Dutch, German, and New England settlers with its river and its fertile land. Whaling became a major industry, with the ships moving up the Hudson River and unloading their international cargo at Hudson in the 1830s. The city echoed with the noises of shipping, rope making, and trading. Fine homes resembling the wooden and brick extravaganzas of Maine and Massachusetts were built for men and women of substance and sophistication. The unusual is the rule here: a colorful museum filled with firemen's equipment, and a library that was once a lunatic asylum. The Shakers built settlements here and led their sober lives, which were also filled with song, dance, and fine craftsmanship. Across the county antiques glow in the windows of well-appointed shops, while the simplicity of Shaker furniture offers its own comment on life and living. Martin Van Buren lived in Columbia County (in fact, the term *OK* is thought to have originated from Van Buren's nickname, Old Kinderhook). Thoroughbred racehorses are bred, raised, and trained in Columbia County, and each year the state's oldest county fair brings together folks of all ages in celebration of the harvest's best.

GUIDANCE
Columbia County Tourism (518-828-3375 or 1-800-724-1846), 401 State Street, Hudson 12534; www.columbiacountyny.com.

GETTING THERE
Columbia County be reached from the Taconic State Parkway and by Routes 9 and 9H; the Massachusetts Turnpike also cuts directly across the county from west to east.

MEDICAL EMERGENCY
Columbia-Greene Medical Center (518-828-7601), 71 Prospect Avenue, Hudson.

TO SEE

✎ **American Museum of Fire Fighting** (518-828-7695), Harry Howard Avenue, Hudson. Open year-round, 9–4:30. Closed Easter, Thanksgiving, Christmas, and New Year's Day. Admission fee. Take a step back in

The American Museum of Fire Fighting in Hudson

time to the glory days of fire fighting at this fascinating museum located next door to the **Firemen's Home.** You will discover the oldest and broadest collection of fire-fighting gear and memorabilia in the United States. Scores of horse-drawn and steam- and gas-powered pieces of equipment are on display, some dating back to the 18th century. Greeting you as you enter the museum is a wooden statue of a volunteer fire chief dressed in patriotic red, white, and blue, complete with stars and golden trumpet. The museum is divided into two halls that house fire-fighting pumps, mobile apparatus, and engines, as well as paintings, clothing, banners, photographs, and other memorabilia. There is a Newsham engine, which was used to quench flames in Manhattan houses in 1731 and saw more than a century and a half of use. A delicate silver parade carriage from Kingston is topped by the figure of a fireman holding a rescued baby. Throughout the museum you will see lots of gleaming brass, bright red paint, and an oddity or two, like ornate firemen's parade trumpets, hand-grenade-style fire extinguishers, and brass fire markers, which indicated which fire company had the right to fight a particular fire. There are even modern fire clothes, which show the difference in fire-fighting techniques through the years. Several special events are held at the site, all involving displays of the firefighter's skills. Call for a schedule.

Louis Paul Jonas Studios (518-851-2211), Miller Road, Churchtown. By appointment only. Free. Discover dinosaurs lurking in Churchtown. This renowned workshop produced the dinosaurs that were displayed at the

1963 New York World's Fair (the great reptiles were floated down the Hudson River on a barge during their trip to Queens), and its craftspeople still make full-sized and smaller versions of the reptilian wonders, along with many other finely crafted wildlife sculptures. Jonas was one of the finest animal sculptors in history, with work at the American Museum of Natural History and dozens of other museums and gardens. Today the Jonas gallery resembles the Peaceable Kingdom with animal models from all eras and environments. Although not open to the general public, group tours may be welcome with advance notice. One of the least known treasures of the Hudson Valley.

The Shaker Museum and Library (518-794-9100), Shaker Museum Road, off County Route 13, Old Chatham. Open from late April through November, Thursday through Monday 10–5; the library is open by appointment at other times. Admission fee. Although there are several Shaker museums in the country, this one contains the foremost study collection of Shaker cultural materials, including journals, letters, and spirit drawings. In the late 18th century a group of Englishmen and -women immigrated to the colonies with the hope of being allowed to practice their communal religion. Called Shakers because they danced and moved during worship services, the group established settlements throughout their new country and became as well known for their fine crafts and innovations as for their unusual celibate lifestyle. Industry, thrift, and simplicity were their bywords. In their workshops chairs, seed packets, tin milk pails, and jams were made with equal skill and care, and today Shaker-made items are still valued for their beauty and grace. This museum is located in a restored barn and outbuilding; the collections were gathered by both Shakers and non-Shakers, with the goal of preserving a culture that is almost gone. All the major Shaker industries are represented at the museum—trip-hammer and washing machine manufacturing as well as clothing and broom making. The Shakers are credited with inventing the circular saw and the revolving bake oven, although they rarely took out a patent, preferring that the world benefit from their work. The museum also houses a fine collection of furniture and household items from the various settlements. Special events are held throughout the season, including crafts workshops, lectures, and concerts.

Columbia County Museum (518-758-9265), 5 Albany Avenue, Kinderhook. The museum, owned by the Columbia County Historical Society, is open May through September. The exhibits here include paintings, textiles, and other items that tell the story of Columbia County.

HISTORIC HOMES

Clermont (518-537-4240), located on Route 6 just off Route 9G, in Germantown. Open April 1 through October 31, then seasonal schedule; call for hours. The grounds are open year-round from 8:30 AM until sunset. Admission fee. Standing on land that was awarded to the

Lindenwald, home of President Martin Van Buren

Livingston family in 1686, this Georgian mansion remained in the family for nearly three centuries. The Livingstons' illustrious history—Judge Robert Livingston wrote the letter of protest to King George just before the Revolutionary War, and Chancellor Robert R. Livingston helped draft the Declaration of Independence—is evident throughout the house. Although Clermont itself was burned by the British during the war, it was later rebuilt around the old walls and foundation. Alterations and additions were made into the late 19th century, so the house today reflects changes wrought by several generations. Clermont's 35 rooms are furnished with family heirlooms and fine examples of period furniture and decorative accessories. A crystal chandelier brought from France in 1804 hangs above the drawing room, where you will also find a French balloon clock made to commemorate the first hydrogen balloon in Paris in 1783. Family portraits decorate the hallways and help visitors sort out the confusing Livingston family tree, and there are exquisite examples of cabinetmaking throughout the mansion.

But as lovely as Clermont is, the setting makes it more so. The views of the Catskill Mountains across the Hudson River are magnificent; the family purchased as much land as possible in order to preserve the setting. Tradition holds that the black locust trees flanking the house were planted by many generations of Livingstons. The roses in the English box garden transform the month of June into an enchanting time. There are a number of special events at Clermont, including a July Fourth celebration with costumed colonial soldiers, a Fall Fair, and Christmas open house.

Lindenwald (518-758-9689), Route 9H, Kinderhook. Open May through December, Wednesday through Sunday 9–4:30, but call for seasonal hours. Admission fee. Built in 1797, the house was renovated in 1849 as the retirement home of Martin Van Buren, eighth president of the United States. The resulting structure was a blend of Federal, Italianate, and Victorian styles. Van Buren was born in Kinderhook (Dutch for "children's corner"), the son of a tavern keeper. He studied law and from Kinderhook embarked on a 30-year political career. At Lindenwald visitors will see the house Van Buren returned to in order to look back upon three tumultuous decades of public service. Named after the trees on the property, the graceful building—complete with shutters, double chimneys, and arched windows—is today a National Historic Site; it was recently renovated in order to remove or lessen the impact of certain Victorian "improvements." The grounds offer an escape to the peace of rural 19th-century America, but it is inside that the recent renovations are more evident. A center stairway winds upward through the house, the hundreds of turned spindles polished so they gleam. The old wallpaper was stripped and replaced with paper appropriate to the era, and furniture and decorative objects finally look as if they belong to the home. The house contains a fine collection of Van Buren memorabilia, and a visit is an excellent way to become acquainted with the president known as the Little Magician, because of both his size and his political acumen.

Luykas Van Alen House (518-758-9625), Route 9H, Kinderhook. After visiting Lindenwald, you may want to stop at the Luykas Van Alen House, which is operated by the Columbia County Historical Society. This brick Dutch farmhouse of the early 18th century has been restored to reflect its heritage. The site contains the **Ichabod Crane School House**—a restored, one-room schoolhouse open to the public and named after the character in Washington Irving's tale. In fact, Irving based Crane on a local schoolteacher who worked in this schoolhouse.

Olana (518-828-0135), Route 9G, 1 mile south of Rip Van Winkle Bridge, Greenport. Open April through October daily except Monday and Tuesday. The house is viewed by guided tour only, and group size is limited; call to reserve tickets before you go. The grounds can be viewed without a guide. Admission fee. Frederic Edwin Church was one of America's foremost artists, a painter who captured the grandeur and mystery of the nation in the 19th century. Church first gained acclaim for his vision of Niagara Falls, a painting that won a medal at the 1867 Paris International Exposition. In 1870 Church and his wife, Isabel, returned from their travels in the Middle East and Europe to their farm in Hudson and began the planning and building of the Persian fantasy that would become known as Olana. Hand-painted tiles on the roof and turrets of the 37-room mansion, situated 460 feet above the river, add touches of pink and green to the sky. Church called his style "personal

Olana, a Persian-style mansion, was home to Hudson River School painter Frederick Church.

Persia," and inside you will discover hand-carved, room-sized screens, rich Persian rugs, delicate paintings, decorative pottery and china, and even a pair of gilded crane lamps that look as if they stepped out of an Egyptian wall painting. Olana is also rich in examples of Church's paintings, including *Autumn in North America* and *Sunset in Jamaica*. His studio is still set up as it was in his time. During the holiday season the house is decorated with elaborate greenery and Yuletide confections grace the tables. Visitors can hike year-round along the carriage paths and roadways that wind through the property, or take in the Hudson River views; just across the river was Cedar Grove, Thomas Cole's home (see *To See* in "Greene County") and the place where Church apprenticed as an artist. The house tour is not recommended for younger children.

James Vanderpoel House (518-758-9265), Board Street, Kinderhook. Open Memorial Day through Labor Day, Wednesday through Saturday 10:30–4:30, Sunday 1:30–4:30; call for additional seasonal hours. Admission fee. This site is also called the House of History, and indeed it does present some fine exhibits of life in Columbia County, especially the era when the area was a bustling industrial and whaling center. Built around 1819 for lawyer and politician James Vanderpoel, the Federal house is characterized by delicate ornamentation including plasterwork ceilings, graceful mantelpieces, and a wide staircase that seems to float to the second floor. The work of several New York cabinetmakers, who created in their work a blend of American pride and European style, is displayed throughout the rooms. A fine selection of paintings, including many by country artists, depicts Columbia County life. The Vanderpoel House holds several special events throughout the year, including a Christmas greens show and a coaching competition.

HISTORIC SITE

Mount Lebanon Shaker Village (518-794-9500), Route 20, New Lebanon. Open daily Memorial Day to Labor Day; weekends only Labor Day through October. Hours vary with the season, so call ahead. Admission fee. Located on the site of a former Shaker settlement and now part of the Darrow School, the village tour includes an introductory slide show about the Shakers and a walking tour through several buildings, including the stone dairy barn and meetinghouse.

SCENIC DRIVES

It is difficult to avoid taking a scenic drive in Columbia County—wherever you look, you can see rolling, bright green meadows, misty ponds, and quiet villages that look the same as they did a century ago. You may find yourself on a bluff overlooking the Hudson River or in a city that recalls the glory of the whaling industry. The roads are well maintained, and you can't get lost for very long.

For a sampling of the county's charms, Route 9 and Route 9H will take you through Hudson, Kinderhook, and Valatie, with plenty of museums, shops, and restorations to explore. Other routes worth a drive include Route 82, Route 7, and Route 22, all of which take you through the eastern part of the county. A road that has actually received an award for its scenic beauty—Route 11 between Routes 23 and 27, near Taghkanic—has been declared a National Beautiful Highway.

WALKING TOURS

The city of Hudson, located on Route 9G, is rich with the traditions and cultural heritage of its settlers: first the Dutch, then seafarers from Massachusetts and Rhode Island, and Quakers and whalers. Carefully designed in the 1780s as a shipping center, with straight streets and "gangway" alleys, ropewalks, wharves, and a warehouse, Hudson was the first city to receive a charter after the Declaration of Independence. Soon whaling and industry took over as the mainstays of the economy, and although Hudson has had its ups and downs since, the city is now in the full flower of a renaissance. On a walking tour of Hudson you'll see

JOSEPH PUGLISI

An example of the finely crafted furniture at the Shaker Village Museum

dozens of architectural styles and hundreds of commercial buildings and homes that have been maintained or restored to their earlier glory. A visitor to the city may want to stop in at the Chamber of Commerce, 729 Warren Street, and pick up a detailed walking guide. Columbia County Tourism (518-828-3375), at 401 State Street, may also be a source for the walking guide. But whether or not you follow a specific tour, a walk around several main streets will reveal the architectural heritage of the area. Visitors to Hudson who enjoy antiques will discover some of the best shopping on the East Coast. Many of the shops are located along Warren Street (see *Selective Shopping*), and range in selection from fine European furniture and 18th-century American examples to lamps, textiles, ephemera, glassware, and fine arts. Many are open by chance or appointment, although Friday through the weekend is a good bet for browsers.

From Route 9G follow Warren Street to Front Street and park. At Front Street you will see the Parade, an 18th-century park that was kept open for use by the city's inhabitants. From the park, also called Promenade Hill Park, you'll have a dazzling view of the Hudson River and the Catskill Mountains, and of the Hudson-Athens Lighthouse, built in 1874 and used to warn ships off the Hudson Middle Ground Flats. Inside the park you will find a statue of St. Winifred, donated to the city by a man who felt that Hudson needed a patron saint.

The easiest walk in Hudson is along Warren Street, the aforementioned antiques mecca. The architectural styles to be found here include Greek Revival, Federal, Queen Anne, and Victorian. At the **Curtiss House,** 32 Warren Street, look up at the widow's walk, which was built by the whaling owner in the 1830s to provide a sweeping view of the river. Some of the houses here sport "eyebrow" windows—narrow windows tucked under the eaves, which often appear at floor height from within the houses. The Adams-style house at 116 Warren Street is considered a rare remnant from the early 19th century and boasts an enclosed private garden.

The 1811 **Robert Jenkins House** (518-828-9764), 113 Warren Street, is open to the public in July and August, Sunday and Monday 1–3 or by appointment. The house serves as the headquarters of the local Daughters of the American Revolution chapter and was built by an early mayor of Hudson. The exhibits offer a look at the city over the past two centuries and contain material on whaling and genealogy, paintings by Hudson River School artists, and other historic items.

Another good walking area is around State Street. At the Hudson Area Library Association, 400 State Street, you will find an 1818 stone building guarded by stone lions. The structure has also served as an almshouse, a lunatic asylum, a young ladies' seminary, and a private home. If the building is open, stop in at the second-floor History Room, which has some local memorabilia, prints, and books.

You'll notice the *Register Star* newspaper building, with its tiny park, at 354 North Fourth Street. Like many other of the buildings here, it has served several purposes: It was a dance hall, an opera house, a county jail, and an assembly hall. Continue south down Warren Street and spend some time looking at the fine 18th- and 19th-century buildings, many of which are undergoing restoration.

Other walking areas include Union Street, Court Street, and East Allen Street.

TO DO

FARM STANDS AND PICK-YOUR-OWN FARMS

Not only are the lush, rolling farmlands of Columbia County a lovely place to visit, but you'll find a remarkably large variety of farm stands and pick-your-own farms here as well. Along with the traditional apple orchards and berry fields, discover the county's vineyards, melon patches, and cherry orchards, where the selection of the fruit is left up to you. If you go to a pick-your-own farm, bring along a container, a hat to shade you from the sun, and a long-sleeved shirt to protect you from insect bites, sunburn, and scratches. The delightful thing about the smaller farm stands, which sprout as fast as corn in the summer, is that many of them carry unusual or hard-to-find varieties of corn, apples, and tomatoes.

The **Berry Farm** (518-392-4609), Route 203, Chatham, is a haven for berry lovers, raising everything from gooseberries and currants to boysenberries, strawberries, and even kiwi fruit! Call the farm to find out when the crops are ready.

In Germantown **Wintje Farms** (518-537-6072), Route 9G, lets you buy or pick apples, cherries, melons, berries, squash, plums, and more.

A truly special farm is found in Ghent on Route 9H, north of Hudson: **Loveapple Farm** (518-828-5048), open July through November, lets you pick your apples, but you can also buy pears, prunes, cherries, and more than a dozen varieties of peaches at the roadside market. The pies and doughnuts are heavenly.

Kinderhook is home to **Samascott Orchard** (518-758-7224), Sunset Avenue (open June through November), which has more than a dozen pick-your-own harvests, including grapes, pears, plums, strawberries, and just as many varieties of apples.

Near Claverack you'll find **Hotalings** (518-851-9864), Route 9H, which lets you pick cherries, apples, and strawberries; **Philip Orchards** (518-851-6351), Route 9H, with pick-your-own apples and pears; **Holmquest Farm** (518-851-9629), 516 Spook Rock Road (County Route 29), has fruits and vegetables; and **Bryant Farms** (518-851-9061), Route 9H, which is strictly a roadside market but offers a huge selection of fruits, vegetables, and local products.

The region around the city of Hudson is filled with seasonal farm stands, including **Taconic Orchards** (518-851-7477), Route 82, where you can pick berries and buy everything else imaginable; **Kleins Kill Fruit Farm** (518-828-6082), Route 10, which has sweet, deep red cherries; and **Don Baker Farms** (518-828-5890), Route 14 (follow signs), with more than seven varieties of apples, both standard and heritage.

If you are in the Hudson area, don't miss the **Sunset Meadow Marketplace** (518-851-3000), 3521 Route 9, Hudson. There is an enormous array of fresh baked goods and local produce, as well as a terrific selection of gourmet food products from all over the Hudson Valley. You can also enjoy a cup of coffee and a pastry in the adjoining café after shopping. The couple who own this establishment moved north from Manhattan and truly enjoy sharing the bounty of the region with visitors.

Valatie is home to **Golden Harvest Farms** (518-758-7683), Route 9, with pick-your-own apples and a large roadside stand, and **Yonder Farms** (518-758-7011), Maple Lane, with pick-your-own apples, blueberries, raspberries, and strawberries.

There are two farmer's markets in the area. The **Hudson's Farmers Market** (518-828-3373), North Sixth Street and Columbia, operates April through October, Saturday 9–1. The **Kinderhook Farmers' Market** is held in the village square on Route 9 from late spring to October, Saturday 8–noon.

HIKING

Wilson M. Powell Wildlife Sanctuary off County Route 13 on Hunt Club Road, Old Chatham, is a small nature site and bird sanctuary with a lovely view of the mountains. A marked trail leads you on a ½-mile walk to the observation area. Open year-round.

Lake Taghkanic State Park (518-851-3631), Route 82 at Taconic Parkway, is open year-round and includes fitness trails and areas for hiking.

There are hiking trails and a nature center at **Taconic State Park** (518-329-3993), Route 344, off Route 22, Copake Falls, where you can enjoy the outdoors in all seasons.

WINTER SPORTS

CROSS-COUNTRY SKIING

Cross-country skiing in Columbia County is centered in the state parks, where well-marked trails are uncrowded—and free—and natural surroundings are breathtaking. You must bring your own equipment.

Lake Taghkanic State Park (518-851-3631), Route 82 at Taconic Parkway, 11 miles south of Hudson, has skiing and ice skating.

Clermont State Park (518-537-4240), Route 6 off Route 9G, has skiing, as does **Taconic State Park** (518-329-3993), east of Route 22 in Copake; **Rudd Pond** (518-789-3059), off Route 22 near Millerton; the **Harlem Valley Rail Trail,** Route 22, off Under Mountain Road in Ancram; and **Olana State Historic Site** (518-828-0135), in Hudson.

DOWNHILL SKIING

Catamount (518-325-3200), in Hillsdale, straddling the borders of New York and Massachusetts, is popular with downhill skiers of all ages, beginner to expert, and offers many services, including snowmaking, night skiing, dining, lessons, rentals, and even RV and camping facilities. In summer Catamount has grass skiing and mountain coasters, a sort of bobsled on tracks.

ICE FISHING

Ice fishing is allowed at **Lake Taghkanic State Park** (518-851-3631), Route 82 at Taconic Parkway, 11 miles south of Hudson, and at **Rudd Pond** (518-789-3059), off Route 22 near Millerton.

GREEN SPACE

Crailo Gardens (518-329-0601), Route 82, Ancram. Open May through September, Sunday afternoon or by appointment. Free. Fans of the world of horticulture should make a stop at this unusual site, which was founded in 1960 by Edwin R. Thomson. A member of the American Conifer Society, Thomson planted more than 450 varieties of rare and dwarf conifers throughout the exhibit gardens. Visitors can walk along the paths and enjoy discovering singular trees, all of which carry identifying markers. The owner also stocks a wide variety of plants for sale.

LODGING

The following establishments welcome visitors to the Columbia County area, but if you have special requirements or you just want to know more about bed & breakfasts in the region, contact American Country Collection of Bed and Breakfasts (518-439-7001), 4 Greenwood Lane, Delmar 12054.

Aubergine (518-325-3412), Routes 22 and 23, Hillsdale 12529. ($$$) An outstanding example of Dutch Colonial architecture, this inn was built in 1783 by an officer in the Revolutionary War. There are three Palladian windows, a museum-quality corner cupboard, and eight fireplaces with their original mantelpieces. Each of the four guest rooms is decorated differently, and the furniture includes many period pieces. A high continental breakfast is served 8:30–10, and the restaurant serves dinner Wednesday through Sunday (see *Dining Out*). Two rooms share a bath; two others have private bath. Open year-round, but closed last two weeks of March.

Inn at Blue Stores (518-537-4277), Route 9, Hudson 12534. ($$$) Built in 1908, this lovely, luxurious inn is one of the nicest in the region and is located on a working farm. Guests can enjoy the pool, take a nap on the veranda, or have a cozy chat in front of the fireplace. Decorative accents include stained glass, a clay-tile roof, and black oak woodwork throughout the house. Four rooms have king-sized beds and private or shared baths, and a full gourmet breakfast is included in the fee. Open year-round.

The Inn at Green River (518-325-7248), 9 Nobletown Road, Hillsdale 12529. ($$) Set on an acre of lawn and gardens above a meadow where Cranse Creek flows into the Green River, this 1830 Federal house is a beautiful place for a relaxing weekend. The Green River is a good spot to fish or cool off in summer. Tanglewood, in the Berkshires, is just 20 minutes away. A full breakfast is elegantly served in the dining room or on the screened porch. The lemon-ricotta pancakes and honey-spice French toast are house specialties. Two rooms have private bath; two share a bath. Open year-round.

JOSEPH PUGLISI

The Inn at Shaker Mill Farm is one of the oldest inns in the Hudson Valley

🐾❦ **Inn at Shaker Mill Farm** (518-794-9345), off Route 22, Canaan 12029. ($$)
This restored Shaker gristmill was built of fieldstone and sits alongside a
waterfall on a quiet country lane, a perfect romantic spot. Innkeeper Ingram
Paperny has been in the business for over 30 years, making this inn one of the
oldest in the Northeast, as well as in the Hudson Valley. The inn is
surrounded by woodland trails just right for walking. You can take breakfast
or the Modified American Plan (MAP) package. Dining is informal and
provides a way to meet other guests. Twenty rooms with private bath; two
suites. Pets as well as children are welcome. Open year-round.

❦♿ **The Inn at Silver Maple Farm** (518-781-3600), Route 295, Canaan 12029.

($$) This 10-room inn is located in a converted barn with wide-board pine floors and exposed beams. There are 10 acres of woodlands surrounding the inn, and all rooms have countryside views. The owners live in a house next door. An outdoor hot tub on the deck is in use year-round. Breakfast includes homemade breads, muffins, fresh fruit, and quiche. No smoking or pets. Children welcome. One room is accessible to the disabled; all have private bath. Open year-round.

Kinderhook Bed and Breakfast (518-758-1850), 67 Broad Street, Kinderhook 12106. ($$) This majestic, classical Greek Revival house is near all the historic homes in Kinderhook. If you have never slept in a feather bed, it is one pleasure of country living you may want to try here. All three guest rooms have private bath; two rooms have air-conditioning. There is a comfortable sitting room where you can socialize with other guests or just relax. A continental breakfast is served in the spacious country kitchen. Children are welcome. Open year-round.

St. Charles Hotel (518-822-9900), 16–18 Park Place, Hudson 12534. ($$) This 120-year-old hotel has been recently renovated and is the perfect place to stay if you enjoy strolling around a city that is locally renowned for its numerous fine antiques shops and galleries. The reasonable rates in the 34 comfortably appointed guest rooms (all with color TV and cable) include a continental breakfast. The taproom has a fireplace and antique bar, and two restaurants are on the premises. Bradley's Grill serves traditional American favorites like burgers, pasta, and seafood; Rebecca's serves Continental entrées like beef Wellington.

Wolfe's Inn (518-392-5218), RD 2, Ghent 12075. ($$) A white, 19th-century farmhouse with black trim and red doors, this inn is nestled on 10 acres and has a large fishing pond. A hearty breakfast is served. Three rooms are available, all with private bath, cable TV, and air-conditioning. Open all year except Christmas Day.

WHERE TO EAT

DINING OUT

Aubergine (518-325-3412), Routes 22 and 23, Hillsdale. ($$) Open Wednesday through Sunday from 5:30 for dinner only. French-inspired American country cooking is the style here, in a 1783 brick Dutch Colonial house. The restaurant's warmth and character are the result of meticulous refurbishing. Our favorite entrée is the Maine scallop cakes with shiitake mushrooms, scallions, and sprouts, followed by the classic chocolate soufflé for dessert.

Blue Plate (518-392-7711), Central Square, Chatham. ($$) Open Tuesday through Sunday for dinner from 5. Closed Monday. This American bistro housed in a Victorian building serves a variety of pastas, steaks, seafood, and salads. Notice the antique copper bar and wonderful murals. This spot has earned a fine reputation with both local residents and travelers.

Carolina House (518-758-1669), Route 9, Kinderhook. ($$) Open daily (except Tuesday) for dinner at 5. A log cabin restaurant with a large fieldstone hearth in the dining room. The cuisine is American southern, and specialties include ribs, Chesapeake crabcakes, blackened beefsteak, and crispy catfish. For those who enjoy warm biscuits and other traditional southern favorites, this is the place to go.

Charleston (518-828-4990), 517 Warren Street, Hudson. ($$) Open daily Thursday through Monday for lunch 11:30–2:30, dinner 5:30–9:30. The eclectic international menu emphasizes grilled entrées. The grilled shrimp with spicy Mexican sauce is popular, and the restaurant grows many of its own vegetables and herbs. Selections such as fall apple chicken as well as many game dishes (including venison and buffalo) are seasonal.

La Gonia's Fire Hill Inn (518-392-5510), Route 203, Austerlitz. ($$) Open Wednesday through Sunday at 4. Relax in a casual atmosphere in a dining room overlooking a lovely pond. Northern Italian cuisine is served, with several Continental dishes to choose from as well. The chef recommends the *zuppa de pesce* with either red or white sauce, a house favorite. All pasta is made on the premises; there is a live lobster tank where you can choose your own dinner!

Hillsdale House (518-325-7111), Anthony Street, Hillsdale. ($$) Open daily for lunch 11:30–2:30; dinner 5:30–10. Regional American cuisine is served here in an informal atmosphere. Mussels are a house specialty, and they are served several different ways. The pasta is made fresh daily. There is also a wood-fired oven for breads and pizza.

Paramount Grill (518-828-4548), 225 Warren Street, Hudson. ($$) Open Thursday through Monday 5–9. Closed Tuesday and Wednesday. The international cuisine here features an eclectic mix of dishes including Cajun shrimp and chicken fajitas. The restaurant is housed in a beautifully restored brick building in downtown Hudson. The ambience is casual yet elegant.

Swiss Hutte (518-325-3333), Route 23, Hillsdale. ($$) Open daily for lunch at noon; dinner Monday through Saturday at 5, Sunday at 5:30; hours vary slightly with the season. Overlooking the slopes at the Catamount ski area, the dining rooms here are wood paneled, and the three fireplaces make them warm and cozy. The Swiss chef-owner is both a master chef and a ski racer. The menu features French-Swiss dishes and home-baked pastries.

EATING OUT

Brandow's (518-822-8938), 340 Warren Street, Hudson. ($) Open Thursday through Tuesday 8–8. This café/marketplace/bakery offers a taste of SoHo in Hudson . . . at reasonable prices. The finest, freshest ingredients are used in a menu that changes daily. The pumpkin tortellini, carrot ginger soup, and prosciutto on a bagel with radicchio, balsamic herb mustard, and tomato are just a few of the treats to be sampled. The buttermilk and sour cream scones are excellent, and there's a fresh juice bar as well as espresso and cappuccino. The market features specialty and gourmet products, prepared foods, organic dairy products, and many gift items.

The Cascades (518-822-9146), 407 Warren Street, Hudson. ($) Open daily 8–4. This café/gourmet deli has just about every type of fresh bagel imaginable. It is a terrific stop for a simple, healthful breakfast or lunch and features homemade soups, salads, and sandwiches. The desserts are sumptuous (try the chocolate silk pie).

Chatham Bakery and Coffee Shoppe (518-392-3411), 1 Church Street, Chatham. ($) Open Monday through Thursday and Saturday 5 AM–6:30 PM; Friday until 8:30 PM; Sunday until noon. An institution in Chatham, this family-run restaurant is famous for its baked goods. Other specialties include Wallyburgers, served on homemade bread, and pumpkin doughnuts in the fall. The soups, sandwiches, and coffee are great. The perfect stop for breakfast or lunch, and great for children.

The Claverack Food Mart (518-851-9164), Route 9H, Claverack. ($) Open daily 8–8, Sunday until 2. The place to go for enormous sandwiches made with high-quality meats and salads.

The Columbia Diner (518-828-9083), 717 Warren Street, Hudson. ($) Open Monday through Thursday 6 AM–10 PM; Friday and Saturday 24 hours. Closed Sunday. For a taste of vanishing Americana—good diner food—stop here for breakfast or lunch.

The Cottage Restaurant (518-392-4170), Route 295, East Chatham. ($) Open daily, except Tuesday, at 8:30 AM. Enjoy the peaceful country atmosphere and friendly service at this restaurant where all soups, breads, and desserts are prepared fresh every day. Specials include stir-fried shrimp, Cottage chili, and pastrami surprise (hot pastrami, mushrooms, and cheese on rye). A good place for children.

Random Harvest (518-325-5103), Route 23, Craryville. ($$) Open daily. This charming combination of gourmet shop and country store is an oasis on Route 23. It's filled with fabulous cheeses, salads, breads, and all kinds of tempting baked goods—the perfect stop if you're planning a picnic. You can also browse through the fine selection of cookbooks and regional books.

The Red Barn (518-828-5821), Route 9H, West Ghent. ($) Open Thursday through Sunday 11:30–9. Closed November through March. They make their own ice cream and toppings here, which are worth a stop in themselves, but hungry diners will want to try the salads, homemade soups, and hearty sandwiches.

ENTERTAINMENT

In Columbia County there are several places to go for good summer stock and concerts. The **Mac-Haydn Theatre** (518-392-9292), Route 203, Chatham, specializes in musicals.

At **The Spencertown Academy** (518-392-3693), Route 203, Spencertown, built in 1847 as a private school, visitors will enjoy shows, concerts, and other cultural events.

Pleshakov Music Center (518-671-7171), 544 Warren Street, Hudson. Housed in a beautiful brick and marble columned building that is nearly a century old, this is a marvelous venue to listen to chamber music and piano concerts. They feature an annual Hudson Valley composer series, so make sure to call for a schedule.

A number of smaller cultural organizations sponsor many under-the-stars summer programs, play readings and special events; call the Columbia County Council on the Arts (518-392-3289) for a schedule.

SELECTIVE SHOPPING

ANTIQUES

When searching for antiques in Columbia County, expect to discover rare and lovely items at shops that are often as well stocked as many museums. You'll see everything from severe Shaker rockers to ornate English sideboards, from fine examples of American folk art to the just plain odd. Quality antiques and shops are located throughout the county, but you may have to look around for bargains; many of the dealers here carry only the best, with prices to match. This is not to say that an English hunt table isn't worth several thousand dollars; just don't expect to find a Shaker table at a yard sale, since sellers have become savvy about their goods. Shop hours vary widely and by season, so call before you go.

In the city of Hudson, a sort of antiques hub, Warren Street and nearby blocks are a popular antiques haunt, with dozens of shops located in a five-block area. Some of the shops have regular hours; others are open by chance or appointment. The best way to enjoy Hudson antiquing is to spend a day wandering and looking. **Alain Pioton/The Hudson Antiques Center** (518-828-9920), 536 Warren Street, carries fine furniture and decorative objects. **Townhouse Antiques** (518-828-7490), 307 Warren Street, housed in a Hudson Valley town house, has a funky selection of antiques and collectibles. **Botanicus Antiques** (518-828-0520), 446 Warren Street, features rare 18th- and 19th-century pieces for the garden and garden rooms. **Antiques at the Oasis** (518-828-0365), 510 Warren Street, offers fine linens. **Hudson Photographic Center** (518-828-2178), 611 Warren Street, carries antique photo equipment and vintage photographs.

While in Hudson, also stop in at the following Warren Street shops: **Antiques, Etc.** (518-828-8580), 426 Warren; **Hudson House American Antiques**, 415 Warren; **Doyle Antiques** (518-828-3929), 711 Warren; **Foxfire, Ltd.** (518-828-6281), 538 Warren; **Kendon Antiques and Collectibles** (518-822-8627), 549 Warren Street; **Hannah Williamson Antiques** (518-822-8512), 438½ Warren.

In the Chatham area **The Librarium** (518-392-5209), Route 295, is a book barn that stocks more than 20,000 used books at great bargains. **Richard and Betty Ann Rasso** (518-392-4501), Route 295, specialize in Shaker items and American folk art. **Mark Feder & Sons** (518-392-3738), 161 Hudson Avenue, Chatham Village, have sterling flatware and antique silver. On Main Street, above the theater, quilt lovers will want to stop in at **Sarris Quilts** (518-392-6323); **Spencertown Arts and Antiques** (518-392-4442), Route 203 (Spencertown Road), has art and Americana.

In Malden Bridge shoppers should look for **Willard Vine Clerk Antiques** (518-766-4650). West Taghkanic has the nicely named **Rural Provisioner, Ltd.** (518 851-6934), intersection of Routes 82 and 10, with china, linens, and country furniture.

SPECIAL EVENTS

June: The **Hudson River Shad Festival** is held annually in honor of this river fish so important to the area's early economy and diet. There is a shad bake, music, and entertainment at the Hudson Boat Launch. Call Columbia County Tourism (518-828-3375) for information.

July: **Winterhawk Bluegrass Festival** (1-888-946-8495 for ticket and festival information), Rothvoss Farm, Route 22, Ancramdale. Considered the best gathering of bluegrass musicians in the East, Winterhawk is a must-stop for anyone who loves banjo, fiddle, singing, or clogging tunes. Held in mid-July, the festival is packed with sets, workshops, pick-up sessions, children's classes, and more. There is camping on the site and lots of family and group activities, including movies, magic shows, and, of course, music. Bluegrass learning sessions take place for all ages and skill levels, and you can enjoy traditional, contemporary, and progressive bands for 4 days. If you plan to camp, the advice is to book early.

September: **Columbia County Fair** (518-828-4417), County Fairgrounds, Routes 66 and 203, Chatham. Held Labor Day weekend. Admission fee. The oldest continuously held fair in the country, the Columbia County Fair is still as lively as ever. This 5-day celebration is less raucous and somewhat smaller than some other county fairs, but just as much fun. Horses, sheep, cows, and other animals are all displayed proudly by 4-H members, while prizewinning vegetables and fruits are shown off in the grange buildings. Handmade quilts and needlecrafts make a colorful display. Sheep-to-shawl demonstrations and antique gas engines enliven the fairgrounds throughout the week; modern farm machinery has its place here also. But the fair is more than just exhibits—it's also entertainment in the best country tradition. Bluegrass bands, folksingers, and country and western stars entertain the crowds in the evening, and because the fairgrounds are also the training area for more than 100 trotters and pacers, you'll see some fine racing as well. Children should love this fair and all the rides.

X. Dutchess County

When Henry Hudson sailed up the river that bears his name, one of his crew described the region known today as Dutchess County as "as pleasant a land as one can tread upon." With an area of 800 square miles, Dutchess boasts more than 30 miles of Hudson River shoreline and thousands of acres of farms and fields. The generous forests, impressive mountains, and abundance of wildlife attracted the Dutch first, but the county was named for the duchess of York, later Queen Mary of England. Powerful families controlled local industries like farming, lumbering, and mining and built elegant stone and wood manors overlooking the river and mountains. Today much of the county's past is still visible in the grand homes overlooking the Hudson, the gracious villages, and the historic restorations that dot the region.

GUIDANCE

Dutchess County Tourism (845-463-4000; 1-800-445-3131), 3 Neptune Road, Poughkeepsie 12601; www.dutchesstourism.com.

Rhinebeck Chamber of Commerce, Route 9, P.O. Box 42, Rhinebeck 12572.

GETTING THERE

Dutchess County can be reached via I-84, the Taconic State Parkway, or Route 9.

MEDICAL EMERGENCY

St. Francis Hospital (845-431-8220), North Road, Poughkeepsie.

TO SEE

✎ **Center for the Performing Arts at Rhinebeck** (845-876-3080), Route 308, Rhinebeck 12572-0148. Open June through September; call for a performance schedule. Admission fee. This center offers music and drama in a new theater, with professional entertainers who offer everything from comedic poetry to puppets. There are children's shows, jazz under the stars, discussions with the artists, and other great events.

The Culinary Institute of America (845-452-9600), Route 9, Hyde Park. Open year-round except for vacation periods in July and December. No admission charged. Founded in 1946 as a place where returning veterans could learn useful culinary job skills, today the school is regarded as

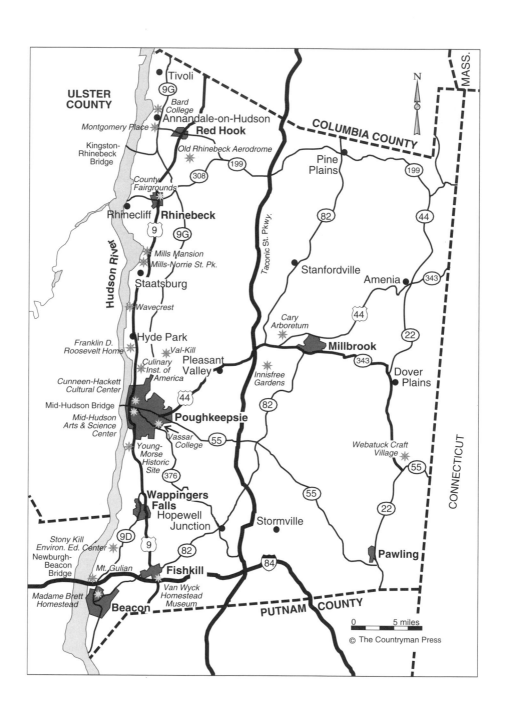

ULSTER COUNTY

Tivoli
9G
Bard College
Annandale-on-Hudson
Montgomery Place
Red Hook
Kingston-Rhinecliff Bridge
Old Rhinebeck Aerodrome
199
308
County Fairgrounds
Rhinecliff
Rhinebeck
9   9G
Mills Mansion
Mills-Norrie St. Pk.
Staatsburg
Hudson River
Wavecrest
Hyde Park
Franklin D. Roosevelt Home
Val-Kill
Culinary Inst. of America
Pleasant Valley
Cunneen-Hackett Cultural Center
Mid-Hudson Bridge
Mid-Hudson Arts & Science Center
44
Poughkeepsie
Young-Morse Historic Site
Vassar College
55
376
Wappingers Falls
Hopewell Junction
Stony Kill Environ. Ed. Center
9D
Newburgh-Beacon Bridge
9
82
Mt. Gulian
Fishkill
Madame Brett Homestead
Beacon
Van Wyck Homestead Museum

COLUMBIA COUNTY
N
MASS.

Pine Plains
199

199
82
44
Stanfordville
Amenia
343
Cary Arboretum
44
Millbrook
343
Dover Plains
22
Innisfree Gardens
82
Webatuck Craft Village
55
55
55
22
Stormville
Pawling
84
PUTNAM COUNTY
CONNECTICUT

Taconic St. Pkwy.

0   5 miles
© The Countryman Press

JOSEPH PUGLISI

The Poet's Walk

a premier training institute for those in the food-service and hospitality industries. Housed in a former Jesuit seminary, the grounds of the institute provide visitors with a sweeping view of the Hudson. Tours can be arranged only for prospective students or for groups (12 or more people) with reservations at one of the restaurants. Still, the courtyard has a fine display of carved pumpkins for Halloween and ice sculptures in winter; the bookstore is filled with culinary gifts, cookbooks, and a selection of baked goods and foods made by the students. Columbus Day weekend usually offers a chocolate festival that is to die for, as visitors can sample the wares and watch confectionary experts at work. (Also see *Dining Out*.)

Hyde Park Station (845 331-9233), at the foot of the hill that is formed by West Market Street and River Road (off Route 9), Hyde Park. Open mid-June through mid-September, Saturday and Sunday 11–5; open year-round Monday 7–10 PM. Other times by appointment. Free. This railroad station was built in 1914, although trains passed through the region during the 19th century. The building was nearly demolished in 1975, when the Hudson Valley Railroad Society acquired the station and set about restoring it. Nearly 30 years later, the station now houses exhibits that tell the story of the area's railroads and history. Model trains run throughout the building, and there are always ferro fans on board to answer your questions. A nice stop along historic Route 9.

The Mills Mansion

Old Rhinebeck Aerodrome (845-758-8610), Stone Church Road, off Route 9 in Rhinebeck (watch for signs). Open daily May 15 through October 31, 10–5. Tours Monday through Friday in July and August at 1; Saturday and Sunday air shows June 15 through October 15 at 2:30. Admission fee. Viewing stands for the air shows are outside; dress appropriately. One of the most unusual history museums around, the aerodrome is the site for air shows, displays, and demonstrations of aeronautic history. But the finely restored airplanes (or copies with original engines) are not earthbound—they are frequently taken for a spin over the Hudson Valley or used in a make-believe dogfight. Fokkers, Sopwiths, and Curtiss airplanes are found in the museum, which offers guided tours. On Saturday daring men and women reenact flights from the pioneer and Lindbergh eras; World War I battles are saved for Sunday, complete with nefarious villains, beautiful damsels, and brave fighter pilots.

Webatuck Craft Village (845-832-6601), Route 55 and Dogtail Corner Road, Wingdale. Open year-round, but the hours change with the seasons. Free, although admission is charged for some special festivals. Webatuck is a village of artists' studios and workshops that lies along the Ten Mile River. Visitors can watch craftspeople in action—there are glassblowers, weavers, furniture makers, and more at work. Special events include an Americana festival, a nature festival, and a medieval fair, which offer color and action on the site itself.

HISTORIC HOMES
Madame Brett Homestead (845-831-6533 for general information; 845-896-6897 to arrange tours, which are by appointment), 50 Van Nydeck

Avenue, Beacon. Open the first Sunday of each month, May through December, 1–4 and by appointment. Admission fee. When Catheryna and Roger Brett moved to the area now known as Beacon in 1708, they built a homestead of native stone graced with scalloped cedar shingles and sloped dormers. The house is one of the oldest in Dutchess County and was the center of a 28,000-acre estate. During the Revolutionary War the homestead was believed to have been a storage place for military supplies, as well as a stopping point for such luminaries as Washington, Lafayette, and the Baron von Steuben. The house remained in the family until 1954, when it was purchased by the Daughters of the American Revolution. Today it offers visitors a look back to the time when the home had lodgings for slaves and what is now the front door was the rear: As the town grew around the house, the main street formed at the back of the building, so the doors were switched for the convenience of callers. There was even a well accessible from inside the house—a major convenience in the 18th century. In summer the herb and formal gardens are lovely.

Mills Mansion (845-889-8851), Old Post Road, off Route 9, Staatsburg (watch for signs). Open April through October and again in December; hours vary with the season, so call ahead. Admission fee. One of the grand old Hudson River estates, the Mills Mansion has its origins in the 18th century, when Morgan and Gertrude Lewis built a home on the site. The house was destroyed by fire in 1832 and was rebuilt by Ruth Livingston Mills in 1896. Rooms were gilded and plastered, with ornamental balustrades, ceilings, and pilasters. The size of the rooms is still overwhelming, as are the furnishings: dining tables that take 20 leaves; carved, gilded, and floral furniture in the style of Louis XIV, XV, and XVI; and many fine paintings and elaborate tapestries. Ironically, the house was used primarily as an autumn retreat and then infrequently the remainder of the year. There is a new museum store on-site, and popular annual events include indoor summer theater, free outdoor concerts, an herb festival, a Celtic festival, and a Gilded Age Christmas.

Montgomery Place (845-758-5461), River Road, off Route 199 in Red Hook. Open April through October daily (except Tuesday) 10–5; weekends only November through mid-December. Admission fee. A magnificent, Federal-style mansion, Montgomery Place was once the home of Janet Livingston Montgomery, wife of the Revolutionary War general Richard Montgomery. Begun in 1802 and completed three years later, the mansion is the centerpiece of an estate that includes waterfalls (don't miss the Sawkill tumbling down to the Hudson River), footbridges, gardens, and Catskill Mountain views. The building was remodeled in the 1860s by the great architect Alexander Jackson Davis, and was home to the Livingstons until the 1980s. Purchased and restored by Historic Hudson Valley, the mansion reflects the family's history rather than one specific era. Gilbert Stuart portraits, Persian tile

The Vanderbilt Mansion in historic Hyde Park

chairs, Czechoslovakian chandeliers, family china, and rare books are only some of the treasures to be seen on a tour. Walking the grounds (all 434 acres), visitors may enjoy watching ships on the Hudson or imagine having tea in a "ballroom" of evergreen trees. Special events throughout the year include holiday tours, garden festivals, a wine and food festival, twilight harvest rides, and art shows. Visitors should not miss the selections at the Montgomery Place farm stand (Route 9, just south of the mansion), where heritage tomatoes, homemade jams and apples, grapes, and peaches are displayed in glorious, ripe color.

Mount Gulian Historic Site (845 831-8172), Sterling Street (take Route 9D north of I-84 for 0.3 mile, turn left into the Hudson View Park apartments, then make an immediate left onto Lamplight Street, which becomes Sterling Street; Mount Gulian is at the end of Sterling). Open mid-April through December, Wednesday and Sunday 1–5; call for summer hours or to make an appointment to view the site. Admission fee. This Dutch homestead was the family seat of the Verplancks, prominent Hudson Valley farmers, and offers a place to learn about domestic and agricultural life in the 18th and 19th centuries as it unfolded along the river. Mount Gulian was constructed between 1730 and 1740; during the American Revolution it was the headquarters of General von Steuben, who is credited with molding the colonial troops into a fighting force. The house was also where the Society of the Cincinnati was formed in 1783, a fraternal organization for officers that is still in existence. A visit to Mount Gulian includes a tour of the house and the English formal gardens, which are undergoing restoration; the gardens' history was recorded by James Brown, an escaped slave who worked in them from 1829 to 1868. Special events are held through the season—don't miss the scary Halloween storytelling in the barn or the colonial dinner.

Vanderbilt Mansion National Historic Site (845-229-9115), Route 9, Hyde Park. Open Wednesday through Sunday 9–5 year-round. Admission fee. This imposing Beaux Arts mansion was used by Frederick Vanderbilt and family as a spring and fall home. A fine example of Gilded Age living, the mansion was the focus of a large Hudson River estate and was built at a cost of $660,000. Lavish furnishings, fine art, and decorative items from around the world are on view throughout the spacious rooms (the living room is 30 feet by 50 feet); visitors can also stroll pathways, view the restored gardens, and take in the breathtaking river panorama.

Van Wyck Homestead (845-896-9560), at the intersection of Route 9 and I-84, 1 mile south of Fishkill. Open Memorial Day to Labor Day, Saturday and Sunday 1–5, or by appointment. Admission fee. Guides in period costume escort visitors through the Dutch Colonial house, built in 1732 by Cornelius Van Wyck and untouched by any changes after a 1757 addition. During the Revolution the house served as a depot and courtroom, and it is also believed to have been the inspiration for the setting of James Fenimore Cooper's *The Spy*. The homestead is furnished with 18th-century pieces, and visitors can examine artifacts recovered from surrounding archaeological sites or watch costumed colonial craftspeople at work.

Wilderstein (845-876-4818), Morton Road (off Route 9), Rhinebeck. Open May through October, Thursday through Sunday noon–4. Admission fee. The history of this country seat begins in 1852, when Thomas Suckley purchased this riverfront site and commissioned an architect to build an Italianate villa. He named the property Wilderstein (wild man's stone) in reference to an Native American petroglyph by a cove on the property. For over 125 years and three generations, Wilderstein was owned by the Suckley family. It is filled with their furniture, paintings, antiques, and other effects, which attest to the lively social history of the estate and the family's relationship to the Hudson Valley. The main-floor rooms were designed by J. B. Tiffany, and Calvert Vaux was responsible for the landscape art. There is an intricate network of drives, walks, and trails throughout the property, so make sure to explore a few of them when you visit. This National Historic Landmark is a gem and will intrigue both scholars and those interested in life in the region during the 19th century.

Wing's Castle (845-677-9085), Bangall Road, off Route 57 in Millbrook (call for detailed directions). Open May 31 through October 31, Wednesday through Sunday 10–5. Admission fee. A weird and intriguing site, the "castle" has been under construction for more than 25 years, and work is still in progress. Salvaged materials have gone into the towers, crenellations, cupolas, and arches—don't be surprised if a Victorian birdbath turns up as a sink or a cauldron as a bathtub. There are some special events throughout the summer, and children especially will enjoy a castle tour and owner Peter Wing.

Young-Morse Historic Site (845-454-4500), Route 9, Poughkeepsie. Open May 1 through November 24, daily 10–4; December, March, and April open daily 10–4 by appointment only. Grounds are open from 8 AM until dusk, weather permitting. Closed Thanksgiving and Christmas Day, and January and February. Admission fee. Situated along the old stagecoach route, this 150-acre site (known as Locust Grove) was the summer home of Samuel Morse. An artist and scientist who changed the way the world communicates, Morse purchased the country residence in 1847 and, under the tutelage of architect Alexander Jackson Davis, began to transform the house into an Italianate villa with extensive gardens. The octagonal house boasts a four-story tower, a skylighted billiard room, and a false stone exterior. Throughout the house decorative items (including the then elegant and new fabric known as denim), furniture, paintings by Morse and George Caitlin, and John James Audubon's *Birds of America* can be enjoyed. In the basement gallery there is a collection of telegraphs, Morse's most famous invention. The formal herb gardens, landscaping with giant floral urns, and a wildlife sanctuary offer a lovely setting in which to spend an afternoon. A new interpretive center presents visitors with a fascinating look at the contributions of Samuel Morse.

MUSEUMS

Bard College (845-758-6822), Route 9G, north of Rhinebeck in Annandale-on-Hudson. Open year-round. No admission charged to the campus, but there are fees for various programs. Founded in 1860 as a men's school, today Bard College is a coeducational institution known for its support and encouragement of the creative arts. Special programs open to the public include lecture series, art shows, performances, and concerts. There are several changing exhibits each year in the gallery of the **Edith C. Blum Art Institute;** the **Avery Center for the Arts** focuses on modern artists. The centerpieces of the campus are two Hudson River estate houses: Blithewood and Ward Manor. There are also gardens and a Victorian gatehouse nearby, which make the campus a nice stop in summer and fall.

Franklin Delano Roosevelt Home and Library (845-229-9115), Route 9, Hyde Park. Open year-round but call for hours, because the museum, library, and house hours vary. Admission fee. Springwood, a Victorian house embellished with Georgian touches, was the boyhood home of Franklin Delano Roosevelt. Here Eleanor and Franklin raised their family, entertained heads of state, and shaped world history. The site includes the house, the first presidential library, the rose garden, and the site of the Roosevelts' graves. In the house itself, once jokingly called the Summer White House by Roosevelt, family memorabilia, including photos, antiques, and the possessions of Franklin's iron-willed mother, Sara, are displayed. The museum has both permanent and changing exhibits that reflect the impact both Eleanor and Franklin had on their times and world events during the first half of the 20th century. The rose garden is exquisite in June.

Val-Kill (845-229-9115), Route 9G, Hyde Park. Call for hours. Admission fee. The only National Historic Site dedicated to the memory of a first lady, Val-Kill was a favorite spot for Roosevelt picnics; in 1924 FDR deeded the land to Eleanor for a personal retreat. A Dutch-style stone cottage was built (it now serves as a conference center), and an existing building was converted into a factory as part of Eleanor's efforts to encourage rural economic development. The factory was later remodeled into a house, which now holds the museum. Visitors can see a film about Mrs. Roosevelt, tour her home, and walk the grounds.

Vassar College and **Art Gallery** (845-437-7000), Raymond Avenue, Poughkeepsie, off Route 44/55. Hours vary; call for information or an appointment. When Matthew Vassar founded the college in 1861, he not only broke new ground by making it a women's college, but he also made it the first college to have an art gallery and museum. The gallery now owns more than 8,000 pieces, including Hudson River School landscapes, Whistler prints, and European coins, armor, and sculpture. Shows and exhibits change on a regular basis, and after enjoying the art, visitors can walk around the campus, with its lakes, gardens, amphitheater, and rare trees. Stop in at the chapel to see the Tiffany windows. Also on the campus is the **Warthin Geological Museum** (Ely Hall, open year-round; summer hours by appointment), which houses a large collection of mineral, gem, and fossil exhibits.

SCENIC DRIVES

In Dutchess County almost any drive is a scenic one. Even the Taconic Parkway, which is now over 50 years old, is more a country drive than a major highway here, and there are commanding views of distant mountains and lovely vistas along its length. The roads of Dutchess County are very well marked, both with direction and historic site signs, and Dutchess County Tourism publishes a series of detailed, self-guided tours that are keyed to roadside markers. Write to them at P.O. Box 2025, Hyde Park 12538, or call (845-463-4000 or 1-800-445-3131) for the free maps.

The following roads will take you through farmland and villages and along the river, but for detailed trips, we do suggest a map. Route 9 is the old stagecoach road that once was the main route to New York City; there are many restorations and historic sites along it. Route 9G (also known as River Road) takes you past old homes and gracious stone walls. Route 44/55 catches up with the Taconic, which is, despite being a parkway, a lovely road. Route 199 runs across the state toward Connecticut, and the views are more New England than New York.

Poughkeepsie has several historic districts that are fascinating to drive through. Garfield Place (go south off Montgomery Street) was a residential area in the 1850s and has been popular ever since. The houses boast turrets, towers, cupolas, and Hudson River bracketing, and they span several periods. Academy Street from Montgomery to Holmes Street is a gracious residential area with ornate Victorian houses, as is the Union Street Historic District (cross Market Street and continue down Union to Grand Street). In the 1760s Union was a path to the river, and later it was the German-Irish area of town. Notice the cast-iron details on the brick-and-clapboard buildings. Lower Mansion Avenue, off North Bridge Street, has fine examples of 19th-century architecture, although there are many modern buildings as well. **Clinton House,** on the corner of Main and North White Streets, is the headquarters of the Dutchess County Historical Society, where visitors can see exhibits of local history (open Monday through Friday 9–4); they also maintain the **Glebe House Historic Site.** At 185 Academy Street you will discover **Springside National Historical Site** (845-473-0108), which offers tours by appointment. Even if you don't take a tour, however, you can walk the 20-acre site, the work of America's first native-born landscape architect, Andrew Jackson Downing.

WALKING TOUR

Rhinebeck. The village of Rhinebeck is rich in architectural delights, and a walk through town can make the history of families like the Roosevelts, Livingstons, and Beekmans come alive. The Beekman Arms, in the center of town, is one of the oldest inns in the United States (see *Lodging*); across the street, the department store is housed in a Civil War–era building. The post office was reconstructed in 1938 under the direction of Franklin Delano Roosevelt; it is a replica of a 1700 Dutch house and contains murals by local artists. If you amble down Route 9 and along the side streets, you will discover Gothic Revival homes, Georgian-style churches, and homes with mansard roofs, arched windows, and Second Empire touches. For more information on tours of Rhinebeck, contact the chamber of commerce (845-876-4778).

WINERIES

A wine sampling is a nice way to spend an afternoon, and there are several wonderful places to choose from in Dutchess County. Two award-winning wineries welcome visitors with tours, demonstrations, and tastings. **Cascade Mountain** (845-373-9021), Flint Hill Road (off Route 82A, watch for signs), Amenia. Open daily year-round 10–5. This respected winery has won accolades from both wine lovers and diners. Visitors can take a tour of the winery and dine on regional foods indoors or outdoors in a country setting. **Clinton Vineyards** (845-266-5372), Schultzville Road, Clinton Corners, is open weekends 9–5 year-round. A small, family-run winery, it specializes in seyval blanc. You can take a tour, but please call before you go.

Millbrook Vineyards (845-677-8383), Wine Road, Millbrook (open daily, except holidays, noon–5), is the largest 100 percent vinifera vineyard in the Hudson River region. Production follows French techniques. Go for a tasting and a tour.

The **Dutchess County Wine Trail** brochure tells you about tours, tastings, and events at many of the wineries; call 845-266-5372 for a copy.

TO DO

BALLOONING

The main season for a hot-air balloon trip is April to November, but flights are available year-round, weather conditions permitting. **Blue Sky Balloons** (1-888-999-2461), 19 Teller Avenue, Beacon, organizes balloon festivals as well as flights and lessons. Flights are always within 2 hours after sunrise or 2 hours before sunset. This company uses only FAA-certified pilots and balloons and has 28 years of experience.

BICYCLING

Bicycle tours are popular in Dutchess County; try any of the roads listed in *Scenic Drives.* Or contact a club: **Mid-Hudson Bicycle Club,** P.O. Box 1727, Poughkeepsie 12601; **Dutchess and Beyond Bicycle Club,** 554 Creek Road, Pleasant Valley 12569. For maps, call the **Dutchess County Tourism Promotion Agency** (1-800-445-3131). Suggested rides average about 25 miles, although you can certainly enjoy a short trip and picnic just about anywhere.

BOAT CRUISES

Spend a day on the Hudson River sailing by elegant old estates, being dazzled by autumn's painted trees, and stopping at a riverside festival or two. There's a cruise for all budgets, from 1-hour introductory sails to daylong extravaganzas complete with champagne.

Riverboat Tours (845-473-5211), Rinaldi Boulevard Dock, Poughkeepsie, allows you to explore the Hudson on a motor launch with a decorative sternwheel. The *River Queen* is available for special tours, which can include trips to West Point for football games or to riverside festivals in Greene County.

One of the most famous of the ships plying the river is the sloop *Clearwater* (845-454-7673), 112 Market Street, Poughkeepsie. A fixture at festivals up and down the Hudson River, the *Clearwater* stops at many sites, and private tours and sailings can be arranged. The *Woody Guthrie* (845-297-7697) is operated by the Beacon Sloop Club and sails the Hudson on summer weeknights with up to a dozen guests. It is a sister ship to the *Clearwater* and allows volunteers to join the crew.

FARM STANDS AND PICK-YOUR-OWN FARMS

June's ripe strawberries, summer blueberries, and jewel-like raspberries are three of the most popular crops in Dutchess County. But the harvest doesn't end with the berries: There are asparagus, apples, and big-bellied orange pumpkins for the choosing. Farm stands sprout like corn along the back roads; many are homey little places where fresh cider and doughnuts lure you inside. Pick-your-own farms often have roadside signs indicating which crop is ready for harvest. For your own comfort, bring along a hat, sunscreen, and a container for the pickings (although you can usually buy buckets and boxes at the farms). Harvest times vary with the weather and the temperature, so please call before you go. Farmer's markets are also sponsored throughout the county, usually on weekends; call the **Cooperative Extension Service** (845-677-8223) for information.

Montgomery Place Orchards (845-758-6338), Back River Road, Annandale-on-Hudson. Here you can pick fruit in an orchard that has been operating for more than two centuries (see *To See—Historic Homes*).

Fishkill Farms (845-897-4377), East Hook Cross Road, Hopewell Junction, stocks its farm stand with luscious tomatoes, corn, plum beans, berries, and more. The apples are pick-your-own, and there are more than a dozen varieties to choose from. Freshly pressed cider can be sampled in fall, along with hot malt cider.

Kohlmaier Farm (845-226-5028), Route 376, Hopewell Junction, carries a broad selection of vegetables and fruits, including cherries, melons, and grapes from local growers. The farm also specializes in German yellow potatoes and offers tours by appointment.

Henry Dykeman's Farm (845-855-5166), Route 22, Pawling. Open May 1 through November 1. Pick your own strawberries in spring, and pumpkins in fall. Get some of the best fresh corn here.

Piggots Farm Market (845-297-3993), Spring Road, Poughkeepsie, stocks fruit and vegetables along with local maple syrup, eggs, and honey. Tours of the farm can be arranged with a phone call.

Adams Fairacre Farm (845-454-4330), 195 Dutchess Turnpike, Poughkeepsie, is a fantastic farm market with a gift shop.

Lewis Country Farms (845-452-7650), Overlook Road, Poughkeepsie, has fresh produce, homemade baked goods, and a large gift shop.

✎ **Greig Farm** (845-758-5762), Pitcher Lane, Red Hook (follow the signs), has acres of fields that are available for self-harvesting. Berries, beans, apples, pumpkins, and peaches are only some of the seasonal treats; you'll also find a greenhouse, farm market, and extensive herb and cut-your-own flower gardens on the site.

Oriole Orchards (845-758-9355), Route 9, Red Hook, specializes in pick-your-own plums, pears, and apples.

When in Rhinebeck, stop at **Wonderland Farm** (845-876-4981), Hilltop Road, which carries coveted springtime asparagus in addition to other harvests.

A specialty grower of strawberries, **Secor Strawberries, Inc.** (845-452-6883), Robinson Lane, Wappingers Falls, despite its name, has pumpkins in the fall and hayrides.

Blueberry Park (845-724-5776), County Route 21, Wingdale, lives up to its name—stocking only pick-your-own blueberries, in July and August. Farm tours are offered as well.

Those interested in "crop art" may wish to write to Dutchess County Tourism, 3 Neptune Road, Poughkeepsie 12601, for the locations of new works. Crop art is created by artist-farmers who plant, cut, and trim fields into acres of art; one "picture" of the American flag was created from more than 3,000 impatiens plants. Each year, new art flourishes and visitors can enjoy a unique agricultural event. A new event, corn mazes, lets you get lost in puzzling fields of cornstalks.

GOLF

There are several courses open to the public in Dutchess County. Since hours change with the seasons, courses may be more or less challenging, and there may be a waiting list; we suggest calling ahead. All charge use fees.

Beekman Country Club (845-226-7700), 11 Country Club Road, Hopewell Junction, has 27 holes and a clubhouse, restaurant, and lounge.

Dutcher Golf Course (845-855-9845), East Main Street, Pawling, is the oldest public course at the same location in the country.

Golfers should also try **Casperkill Country Club** (845-433-2222), 575 Route 9, Poughkeepsie; **College Hill Golf Course** (845-486-9112), North Clinton Street, Poughkeepsie; **Dinsmore Golf Course** (845-889-4751), Route 9, Staatsburg; **Vassar Golf Course** (845-473-1550), Vassar College, Poughkeepsie; and the **James Baird State Park Golf Course and Driving Range** (845-452-1489), Freedom Road, Pleasant Valley.

HIKING

The **Appalachian Trail** passes through several state parks in the southeastern portion of Dutchess County, and 30 miles of it is open to day hikers.

Edward R. Murrow Park (845-855-1131), Lakeside Drive, Pawling, has hiking trails, camping for Appalachian Trail hikers only, and picnic areas.

Pawling Nature Reserve (845-855-1569), Quaker Lake Road, Pawling, covers more than 1,000 acres and has several trails; guided nature walks are also offered.

Wilcox Park (845-758-6100), in Stanfordville, open year-round, has the amenities of a large park, along with marked hiking trails suitable for a family outing.

Mills-Norrie State Park (845-889-4100 or 889-4626), Route 9, near the Mills Mansion in Staatsburg (see *To See—Historic Homes*), has hiking trails, campgrounds, a well-marked fitness trail, playgrounds, picnic areas, and a golf course.

Stissing Mountain Fire Tower (845-398-5673) is reached by marked trails from the base of Stissing Mountain, Pine Plains. It offers incredible views coupled with an interesting piece of local history that has nearly disappeared in the Hudson Valley region.

Innisfree Gardens

JOSEPH PUGLISI

CROSS-COUNTRY SKIING

Dutchess County was made for cross-country skiing, with low hills that slope down toward the river, open meadows turned liquid silver by moonlight, and secret paths that cross streams and disappear into the pines. Many of the area's trails are maintained by towns and villages, and many are quiet even on a winter's day. Multiple-use sites dot the Dutchess countryside, offering camping and hiking in summer and skiing in winter, although you have to bring your own equipment. Be sure you know the area you are planning to ski, so you'll avoid being caught on private property.

Mills-Norrie State Park (845-889-4100 or 889-4646), Route 9, near the Mills Mansion in Staatsburg (see *To See—Historic Homes*), has several miles of well-marked trails, some of which have Hudson River views. The park also has picnic and sledding areas.

Wilcox Park (845-758-6100), Route 199, Stanfordville, offers more than 600 acres of land to explore; trails are not marked.

Bowdoin Park (845-758-6100), Sheafe Road, Poughkeepsie, is a 300-acre site that allows skiing and sledding throughout the winter.

James Baird Park (845-452-1489), Freedom Road, Pleasantville, is open all winter for outdoor fun, as are **Lafayetteville State Multiple Use Area** (845-677-8268), Route 199, Milan; **Roeliff Jansen Kill State Multiple Use Area** (845-677-8268), Route 44, Millbrook; **Stissing Mountain State Multiple Use Area** (845-677-8268), Hicks Hill Road, Stanford; and **Ferncliff Preserve,** Astor Road, Rhinebeck.

GREEN SPACE

Hudson River National Estuarine Research Preserve (845-758-5193), Tivoli Bay, Annandale. Located on the Bard College campus, this preserve has 1,700 acres that can be hiked (there are five trails) or enjoyed as part of the workshops and educational seminars that are offered annually. Call for information on classes, walks, and other events.

Hudson Valley Raptor Center (845-758-6957), South Road, Stanfordville. Call for a schedule. Fees for some events. This educational center offers guests a chance to discover the beauty and strength of eagles, hawks, and other raptors up close. There are flying demonstrations by the birds, some of which were wounded in the wild. The center also appears at many special events throughout the Hudson Valley and Catskills; check with the Dutchess County Tourism for a list of appearances.

Innisfree Gardens (845-677-8000), Tyrrell Road, 1 mile from Route 44, Millbrook. Open May through October, Saturday and Sunday 11–5, Wednesday through Friday 10–4; closed Monday and Tuesday. Free. Inspired by the Eastern cup garden, these individual "garden pictures" draw the attention to a particular object, setting it apart by establishing an enclosure around it. Following the tradition of Asian artists, garden founder Walter Beck used natural formations, as well as terraces, walls, and paths, to keep specific areas in "tension," believing that moving rocks or plants only an inch or so would destroy the effect. Visitors can stroll these public gardens and enjoy this visual laboratory and garden notebook.

Mary Flagler Cary Arboretum (845-677-5359), Route 44, Millbrook. Open May through September, Monday through Saturday 9–4, Sunday 1–4. Closed major holidays. Free, but stop at the visitors center for an access permit. There are more than 1,900 acres of nature trails and plant collections at this educational and research facility. Public ecology programs, perennial gardens, and a tropical greenhouse (where you'll find pineapples and banana trees) highlight a stop at these lovely grounds.

✍ **Stony Kill Environmental Education Center** (845-831-8780), Route 9D, Wappingers Falls. Open year-round; house hours vary. Part of a 17th-century estate owned by Gulian Verplanck, this nature center was later used as a farm. Today Stony Kill is fulfilling its mission to provide agricultural and natural history programs to the public. The trails are relatively short (the longest is 2 miles) and there are places to study pond life, deciduous forests, swamps, and fields. The bird observation area is a great place to view migrating and native birds, and special events and family-oriented workshops are held throughout the year.

✍ **Trevor Teaching Zoo** (845-677-3704), Millbrook School, Route 44, Millbrook. Open daily 9–5, but call ahead. Free. Started as a teaching zoo in 1936 with the hope that children would better appreciate wildlife if they were familiar with it, the zoo is now a 4-acre site accredited by the American Zoological Association that offers close-up looks at a more than 100 different types of animals, exotic and indigenous. Red-tailed hawks, coatis, otters, swans, and badgers are only some of the zoo's guests. There is a self-guided nature walk and a boardwalk that overlooks a lively marsh.

LODGING

A Cat in Your Lap (845-677-3051), Old Route 82 and The Monument, Millbrook 12545. ($$) All the rooms in this charming home have a private bath, and the village of Millbrook is within walking distance. There are also two barns with fireplaces and private baths; one has a king-sized bed. A hearty breakfast is served, and these elegant accommodations come at rock-bottom prices. Open year-round.

Beekman Arms (845-876-7077), 4 Mill Street, Rhinebeck 12572. ($$$) The oldest inn in America, the Arms is steeped in history and antiques. Located on the main road, it is within walking distance of many attractions and includes a courtyard annex. Private baths. If you want a quieter place, ask about the Delamater House, a gingerbread fantasy that dates to 1844. (See below.)

Belvedere Mansion (845-889-8000), P.O. Box 785, Route 9, Rhinebeck 12572. ($$$) *Belvedere* means "beautiful view," and there is a wonderful one from this restored Greek Revival mansion overlooking the Hudson River. In addition to the lavish accommodations, there are outside cottages within a separate building facing the mansion. All have individual entrances and private bath. Each cottage has a unique character and is decorated with antiques and American folk art. During the winter months a hearty country breakfast is served fireside in the main dining room. In warmer weather breakfast is served alfresco in a pavilion gazebo overlooking the fountain and pond. There is also an outdoor in-ground pool. Open year-round.

Bullis Hall (845-868-1665), P.O. Box 630, Hunns Lake Road, Bangall, NY 12506. ($$$) Some of the luxurious suites in this unusual establishment

Belvedere Mansion

have fireplaces and others have Jacuzzis, but all overlook the beautiful gardens. Staying here is like going away to a well-staffed private home. One guest told us there is nothing quite like this north of 93rd Street. We tend to agree. The room price includes breakfast and an open bar. Your host, Addison Berkey, is a former New York publisher.

Bykenhulle House (845-221-4182), Bykenhulle Road, Hopewell Junction 12533. ($$$) A Georgian Colonial, this house has five large bedrooms featuring poster beds and antiques, all with private bath. There are six fireplaces, a sun room, a flower garden, and a swimming pool. A full country breakfast is served on fine china. Open year-round.

Calico Quail Inn (845-677-6016), Route 44, Mabbettsville (near Millbrook) 12545. ($$) This classic 1830s farmhouse is set on a parklike property that has a Chinese bridge and a pond complete with boat. Service is the watchword here, and guests enjoy fresh flowers, antiques, homemade pastries, and breakfast in the Tavern Room. There are three rooms—two share a bath, and one has a private bath. No children. Open all year except February and March.

Castle Hill Bed and Breakfast (845-298-8000), Wappingers Falls 12590. ($$$) A tree-lined drive leads to this brick Victorian mansion, once the home of Henry Yates Satterlee, the designer of the National Cathedral in Washington. Four bedrooms and two suites are furnished with antiques; there are both shared and private baths. Continental breakfast. In summer the large outdoor pool is at the disposal of guests. Open April through November; children not permitted.

Le Chambord Inn (845-221-1941), Route 52 and Carpenter Road,

Hopewell Junction 12533. ($$$) A charming inn tucked away in the woods, Le Chambord offers elegance and relaxation with the convenience of a restaurant downstairs. The 25 rooms (with private bath) are furnished with antiques, and a continental breakfast is served by the fireplace. Children are welcome. Open year-round.

Chickadee Hill on the Lake (845-266-5619), Upton Lake Road, Clinton Corners 12514. ($$) This unusual custom-built home has cathedral ceilings and lots of skylights and glass. The two guest rooms each have private bath, canopied beds, and a deck overlooking Upton Lake. One room has air-conditioning and a fireplace.

Delamater House (845-876-7080), 44 Montgomery Street, Rhinebeck 12572. ($$) This romantic country inn is located in the heart of town. There are seven separate buildings, and four are historic structures. Walk to the restaurants and shops when staying in any of the 40 rooms, all with private bath, air-conditioning, phone, refrigerator, TV, and fireplace. There are five suites and five rooms with kitchenettes. Continental breakfast is served. Children are welcome.

Grand Dutchess Bed and Breakfast (845-758-5818), 50 North Broadway, Red Hook 12571. ($) This Victorian Italianate mansion is located on 1 acre and is centrally located within walking distance of shops and restaurants. There are six rooms; four have private bath, and two rooms share a bath. A full breakfast is served, and children over the age of 6 are welcome.

Hideaway Bed and Breakfast (845-266-5673), 36 Lake Drive, Rhinebeck 12572. ($$) Enjoy secluded elegance in the middle of a forest. The three suites and three guest rooms all have private bath, king-sized beds, air-conditioning, TV, and phone. Most rooms have a fireplace, Jacuzzi, wet bar, and deck. Located 1 mile from the Omega Institute.

Inn at the Falls (845-462-5770), 50 Red Oaks Mill Road, Poughkeepsie 12603. ($$$) This inn blends the luxury of a plush resort and the atmosphere of a country estate. Nestled next to a waterfall, the inn has rooms decorated in English, Oriental, and American country styles. A continental breakfast is delivered to your room. Twenty-four rooms and 12 suites have private bath, phone, and TV. Children welcome. Open year-round.

Journey Inn Bed & Breakfast (845-229-8972), One Sherwood Place, Hyde Park 12538. ($$) Situated directly across from the entrance to the Vanderbilt Mansion and grounds, this comfortable B&B is chock-full of fascinating memorabilia from the travels of the owners. There are two master suites, one with a king-sized bed, and three bedrooms (one with private bath, two with a shared bath). Open year-round.

Lakehouse Inn on Golden Pond (845-266-8093), Shelley Hill Road, Stanfordville 12581. ($$$) There are four separate buildings around a lovely lake on this 22-acre estate. The 10 guest rooms offer all the modern conveniences, including private bath and deck, color TV, and air-conditioning. Many rooms have Jacuzzis, and some have a fireplace. This is a wonderful spot to enjoy swimming and fishing in the summer months. Guests can take one of the rowboats out on the lake. A full gourmet breakfast is served. Open year-round.

Mansakenning Carriage House (845-876-3500), 29 Ackert Hook Road, Rhinebeck 12572. ($$$) This home is on the National Register and has five suites with private bath, air-conditioning, fireplace, and refrigerator. A six-course gourmet breakfast is included, and there are faxes and photocopy machines on hand for the executive. Open year-round.

Mill at Bloomvale Falls (845-266-4234), Route 82, Salt Point 12578. ($$) Located in the heart of hunt country, this house was once a stone cider mill. Guests can swim and splash under the nearby falls or hike the 24 acres surrounding the house. Inside, fireplaces and antiques greet guests; fountains, dining decks, and an antiques shop are on the site as well. There is a master suite and four guest rooms. Adults preferred. Open year-round.

Mulberry Street Guest House (845-876-5478), 25 Mulberry Street, Rhinebeck 12572. ($$) There are two rooms, both with private bath, air-conditioning, and cable TV, in this 1880s village Victorian. A full breakfast is served, and children over the age of 12 are welcome.

Old Drovers Inn (845-832-9311), Route 22, Dover Plains 12522. ($$$) This inn is coupled with a fine restaurant downstairs (see *Dining Out*). There are antiques in the four rooms (all have private bath); three rooms have fireplace. Breakfast is served in the Federal Room. Well-behaved children only. Open Thursday through Monday; closed part of December.

The Pines (518-398-7677), North Main, Pine Plains 12567. ($$$) This spacious Victorian mansion was built in 1878 and boasts walnut, cherry, and chestnut woodwork throughout. The rooms are decorated with period furniture. Breakfast consists of eggs, fresh fruit, and homemade bread. Five rooms have private bath; three others share a bath. Children not permitted. Open year-round.

✍ **Red Hook Inn** (845-758-8445), 31 South Broadway, Red Hook 12571. ($$) There are five rooms with private bath in this 156-year-old Federal-style house converted to a charming inn. A full breakfast is served on weekends only. Children are welcome. There is a restaurant and tavern on the premises (see *Dining Out*).

✍ **The Residence Inn** (845-896-5210), Route 9, Fishkill 12524. ($$$) Part of the Marriott hotel chain, this inn offers suites with fireplace, kitchen, and continental breakfast. A pool, a whirlpool, and a health club are all on-site. All 136 suites have private bath. Children welcome. Open year-round.

Rhinecliff Bed and Breakfast (845-876-3710), corner of William and Grinnell Streets, Rhinecliff. ($) This 1860 Victorian home on the banks of the Hudson River offers views of a different sunset every night. Located by the train station and only 2 miles from the town of Rhinebeck, the home offers three rooms (they share two baths). There is air-conditioning and cable TV. The front porch has a view of the river, and there is an in-ground swimming pool on the premises. The rates are among the least expensive in Dutchess County.

Roseland Ranch Resort (845-868-1350 or 1-800-431-8292), Hunns Lake Road, Stanfordville 12581. ($$$) Rates vary according to the season; a variety of family and midweek packages are available. A 2-night stay is required. The Fichera family has operated this 775-acre ranch for over 40 years. The rooms are basic motel style, and the hearty meals are served family style. Tennis, bingo, swimming, and many other indoor and outdoor activities are offered at a full resort. This is a great place to try horseback riding or to bring back memories of the fun-filled family getaways of your childhood. Open year-round.

Sepascot Farms Bed and Breakfast (845-876-5840), 301 Route 308, Rhinebeck. ($) Enjoy a gracious Victorian ambience in a farm setting. The spacious corner guest rooms offer views of grazing llamas. The rooms are furnished with fourth-generation family heirlooms. Two rooms share a bath. Farm-fresh continental breakfast, TV, air-conditioning. Children over the age of 10 are welcome.

  ♿ **Sheraton Civic Center Hotel** (845-485-5300), 40 Civic Center Plaza, Poughkeepsie 12601. ($$$) A full-service hotel, the Sheraton, which commands spectacular views of the Hudson, boasts 213 rooms and an on-site health club with sauna. Several suites have Jacuzzis. Guests will enjoy the fine restaurant on the premises, Cosimo's, featuring northern Italian cuisine. Open year-round.

 ★ **Simmon's Way Village Inn** (518-789-6235), Route 44, Millerton 12546. ($$$) Built in 1854, the Village Inn was remodeled in 1892 and now boasts nine rooms (all with private bath) filled with down pillows, fine linens, antiques, and canopied beds. Enjoy a continental breakfast in your suite, in the dining room, or on the front porch. There is an excellent restaurant on the premises as well. Eleven rooms with private bath. Children are welcome. Open year-round.

Troutbeck (845-373-9681), Leedsville Road, Amenia 12501. ($$$) This English country estate on 422 acres is an executive retreat during the week, but on weekends it's a relaxed getaway. Fronted by sycamores and a brook, the slate-roofed estate has leaded-glass windows, walled gardens, antiques, and an outdoor pool and tennis courts. Forty-two bedrooms and six suites, all with private bath, nine with fireplace. Not recommended for children. Open year-round, weekends only.

Veranda House Bed & Breakfast (845-876-4133), 6487 Montgomery Street, Rhinebeck 12572. ($$) This charming Federal house built in 1845 was once a farmhouse, and for almost a century served as a church parsonage. Located in the Rhinebeck Village Historic District, three blocks from the center of town, it features five cozy rooms, all with private bath. The Rose Room, with its queen-sized four-poster bed and lacy canopy, is our favorite. Guests are invited to enjoy the library, TV, VCR, and living room with fireplace. The terrace overlooks the garden and is a nice place to relax in the warm-weather months. Open year-round.

Whistlewood Farm (845-876-6838), 11 Pells Road, Rhinebeck 12572. ($$) This distinctive B&B is also a working horse farm, and animals abound. The living room has a stone fireplace and a view of the paddock area, and there are antiques, including a player piano, throughout the house. A hearty farm breakfast with home-baked muffins, breads, and jams and jellies is served daily. Four bedrooms with private bath; two cottages with fireplace, one with a hot tub. Children and pets are welcome. Open year-round.

WHERE TO EAT

DINING OUT

Dining in Dutchess means country settings and the finest food. Since many of the restaurants have hours that change with the day or the season, we recommend calling and checking on times and reservation requirements.

Allyn's Restaurant & Cafe (845-677-5888), Route 44, Millbrook. ($$) Open daily (closed Tuesday) for lunch 11:30–3, dinner from 5:30; Sunday brunch 11:30–3. Regional specialties and Continental favorites are served in two dining rooms—one elegant, the other informal. The restaurant tends to get crowded on weekends, so you may want to make a reservation.

Beech Tree Grill (845-471-7279), 3 Collegeview Avenue, Poughkeepsie. ($$) Open daily, except Monday, 11:30–11:30. The publike atmosphere makes for casual dining with both a light-fare menu (pasta with artichoke hearts, tomatoes, and capers in roasted garlic oil; Caesar salad with chicken breast) and more elaborate dinner selections like duck confit and grilled salmon with caramelized ginger and mustard chive sauce. There is a full bar with 10 draft beers and a number of wines available by the glass.

Beekman Arms (845-876-7077), 4 Mill Street, Rhinebeck. ($$) Open daily for breakfast, lunch, and dinner; Sunday brunch 10–3. This Hudson Valley institution is housed in the oldest inn in America (see *Lodging*) and dates back to 1766. Hearty breakfasts and weekend brunch are particularly good. Owner-chef Larry Forgione, formerly of An American Place, gives a modern lift to traditional food.

The Blue Fountain Restaurant (845-226-3570), 940 Route 376, Hopewell Junction. ($$) Open for lunch Tuesday through Friday, 11–3; dinner served daily 4–10. The Italian-American cuisine here includes the standard steaks, seafood, chicken, and veal dishes. Our favorite dish is the steak au poivre. The dining room tables all have a view of a huge fountain. The family who operate this establishment owned a restaurant in the Bronx for many years. There is a good-sized children's menu and families are welcome.

Brass Anchor (845-452-3232), 31 River Point Road, Poughkeepsie. ($$)

Open for lunch and dinner daily from 11:30. Seafood is the specialty here. In the warm-weather months enjoy dining outdoors overlooking a marina and the Hudson River.

Caesar's Ristorante (845-471-4857), 2 Delafield Street, Poughkeepsie. ($$) Open daily 5–11. Located in a historic district of the city, this first-rate Italian restaurant has art deco decor and a piano bar. Specialties include homemade pasta, veal, and Caesar salad. Not recommended for children.

China Rose (845-876-7442), 100 Shatzell Avenue, Rhinecliff. ($) Open every day except Tuesday 5–10; until 11 on weekends. Enjoy patio dining with a view of the Hudson during the warm-weather months in this Chinese bistro. The cuisine is exceptional, and may include the house special noodle soup or pork with eggplant. The ice cream here comes in flavors like almond cookie, which comes from Chinatown. The tangerine sherbet is also delicious.

Coppola's Restaurant (845-452-3040), 825 Main Street, Poughkeepsie. ($$) Serving Italian cuisine for lunch and dinner, Tuesday through Sunday 11–9.

Cripple Creek Restaurant (845-876-4355), 22 Garden Street, Rhinebeck. ($$$) Open for lunch and dinner daily, except Tuesday, from 11:30. The eclectic American cuisine in this fine establishment includes mouth-watering entrées like marinated grilled lamb on risotto with roasted garlic rosemary sauce and seared sea scallops on spinach and truffle-crushed potatoes with red wine sauce. Make sure to save room for the signature dessert, warm chocolate mousse cake.

Culinary Institute of America (845-471-6608), Route 9, Hyde Park. ($–$$$) Hours vary; call for reservations. There are five first-rate restaurants at this world-famous culinary institution, where the food is prepared and served by the students under the guidance of world-class chefs. Except for weekdays at St. Andrew's Cafe, reservations are essential and should be made several weeks in advance; the wait is well worth it. **American Bounty Restaurant** offers the best in the way of American regional cuisine: smoked turkey with black pepper pasta and cream, then a Mississippi riverboat for dessert. **Caterina d'Medici Restaurant** specializes in northern Italian food, like tricolor pasta diamonds with prosciutto or chestnut soup. **Escoffier Restaurant** has classical haute cuisine, such as pheasant with morels and fillet of sole with lobster mousse. **St. Andrew's Cafe** is informal and has healthful dishes that are delicious as well, like grilled salmon fillet with tomato-horseradish sauce or chocolate bread pudding soufflé. They will also provide diners with a computer printout of the food's nutritional analysis. **Apple Pie Bakery Cafe** (845-905-4500), open Monday through Friday 8–6:30, is a great place to stop for lunch or a midday snack. The cakes, pies, and breads are first-rate.

La Fonda Del Sol (845-297-5044), Old Route 9, Wappingers Falls. ($$)

Open daily for dinner 3–10; lunch served daily 11:30–3. The menu here is extensive, and the Mexican cuisine is excellent. Downstairs, **La Cantina** offers nightly entertainment, and the food includes Mexican specialties and paella.

Greenbaum & Gilhooley's (845-297-9700), Route 9, Wappingers Falls. ($$) Open daily for dinner 4–10. Lavish portions of traditional favorites are served at this popular steakhouse, including aged New York sirloin, prime rib, and jumbo lobster. Try the mud pie for dessert.

Guidetti's (845-832-6721), Pleasant Ridge Road, Wingdale. ($$) Open Thursday through Sunday for dinner 5–10. This restaurant serves fine northern Italian cuisine.

Harrald's (845-878-6595), Route 52, Stormville. ($$$) Open Wednesday through Saturday for dinner from 6. The dining here is prix fixe and five star. Set in a 200-year-old, Tudor-style house, this restaurant offers candlelight atmosphere and specials like Maryland jumbo lump crabmeat cakes and trout meunière. Children must be well behaved.

Hudson's Ribs and Fish (845-297-5002), Route 9, Fishkill. ($$) Open daily for dinner from 4. Moderately priced steaks and seafood dishes with an excellent selection of specials daily.

The Haymaker (845-486-9454), 718 Dutchess Turnpike, Poughkeepsie. ($$) Open for lunch, Monday through Friday, 11 AM–2:30 PM; dinner daily 5–9; until 10 on Friday and Saturday. This new establishment serves American regional cuisine prepared with the freshest local ingredients. The service is first-rate and the portions are generous. We can't recommend this highly enough for both lunch and dinner.

The Inn at Osborne Hill (845-897-3055), 150 Osborne Hill Road, Fishkill. ($$) Open for lunch Monday and Friday 11:30–2:30; for dinner Monday through Saturday at 5. *Connoisseur* magazine raved about this restaurant; the creative husband-wife team that runs it both graduated from the Culinary Institute of America. The American regional cuisine is particularly imaginative and includes such selections as breast of pheasant with cranberries and green peppercorns, as well as linguine with rock shrimp, scallions, mushrooms, and tomatoes in lobster cream sauce. The wine cellar is extensive, with many difficult-to-find selections.

Max's Memphis Barbecue (845-758-6297), Route 9, Red Hook. ($$) Open Tuesday through Sunday 5–10. Max's southern regional cooking is based on family recipes and includes traditional barbecue dishes like Memphis Jon's barbecue pulled pork plate and Big Mike's famous slow-smoked pork ribs. There are crabcakes, smoked brook trout, barbe-cued chicken, and a veggie sampler from a menu sure to appeal to just about everyone.

McKinney and Doyle's Fine Foods Cafe (845-855-3875), 10 Charles Colman Boulevard, Pawling. ($$) Open for lunch Wednesday through Friday 11:30–3; for dinner Wednesday through Saturday 6–9:30, for dinner Sunday 5–9; Saturday and Sunday brunch 9–3. This old-fashioned, high-ceilinged storefront café has exposed brick walls, a mix of booths and tables, and lots of local memorabilia in the decor. The eclectic cuisine includes such unusual treats as grilled shrimp with Thai peanut sauce over angelhair pasta, and breast of duck with peppercorns and applejack-soaked figs. An excellent bakery operates out of the café, so don't skip dessert. Sour cream apple pie and raspberry linzer torte are just a couple of the tempting creations. There is an Oktoberfest beer-tasting dinner, and wine tastings as well.

Mughal Raj (845-876-4696), 110 Route 9 south, Rhinebeck. ($$) Open noon–10 daily. This Indian restaurant specializes in Tandoori (clay-oven) and Balti cookery. Enjoy a large selection of fresh shrimp, fish, vegetable, saffron rice, and curry dishes. Many dishes are mild, and vegetarians will find a variety of choices. The clay oven is used to barbecue chicken, lamb, and beef as well as bake the bread. There is a fixed-price Wednesday dinner buffet and a Sunday brunch buffet.

Old Drovers Inn (845-832-9311), Route 22, Dover Plains. ($$$) Open daily for dinner 5–10; closed Tuesday and Wednesday. Lunch is served Friday through Sunday noon–3. Long ago this former tavern catered to the drovers who transported cattle to New York for sale. Today the more-than-240-year-old building is home to an appealing restaurant that serves dishes such as cheddar cheese soup, breast of pheasant in champagne sauce, and chocolate truffle cake. Well-behaved children are welcome.

Osaka, 18 Garden Street, Rhinebeck (845-876-7338 or 876-7278), and 74 Broadway, Tivoli (845-757-5055). ($$) Open for lunch Monday through Friday 11:30–2:30; dinner served daily at 5. Eat in or take out from this first-rate, informal Japanese restaurant. The sushi is some of the best to be had anywhere. The grilled fish daily special and chicken teriyaki are excellent. There is also the chef's special lunch box of the day for those considering picnic fare.

O'Sho (845-297-0540), 763 South Road, Poughkeepsie. ($$) Open for lunch Monday through Friday 11:30–2:30; dinner served daily from 5. Hibachi-style chicken and steak are the specialty, but the sushi is also very good. Dine in an elegant Japanese-style steakhouse. Delightful atmosphere.

Le Pavillon (845-473-2525), 230 Salt Point Turnpike (Route 115), Poughkeepsie. ($$) Open for dinner Monday through Saturday 5:30–10; reservations required. Closed Sunday. This over-200-year-old brick farmhouse provides an elegant dining setting. Serving French country cuisine, the specialties are game, fish, and seasonal dishes. Not for children.

Le Petit Bistro (845-876-7400), 8 East Market Street, Rhinebeck. ($$) Informal dining with a French touch, and a nice place to stop for dinner (5–10). Closed Tuesday and Wednesday.

Portofino (845-889-4711), 57 Old Post Road, Staatsburg. ($$) Dinner is served daily from 4 in this fine, moderately priced restaurant featuring northern Italian and Continental specialties. The town of Staatsburg is a quiet hamlet tucked away from the bustle of Route 9, and this restaurant is definitely worth a stop when passing through the area. A popular spot with local residents.

Red Hook Inn (845-758-8445), 31 South Broadway, Red Hook. ($$) Open Tuesday through Sunday for dinner 5–10. Enjoy American and Continental favorites in this Federal-style, 156-year-old building that houses the restaurant as well as an inn (see *Lodging*). Pan-fried trout with pecans and lemon and grilled pork chop with garlic mashed potatoes and greens are a couple of the mouthwatering entrées. For dessert, try the chocolate soufflé cake or espresso crème caramel. Espresso and cappuccino are served along with a selection of teas.

✐ **Rolling Rock Cafe** (845-876-ROCK or 876-ROLL), Route 9, Rhinebeck. ($$) Open daily 11:30 AM–2 AM. This American bistro serves hearty portions at reasonable prices. The Cajun chicken salad and blackened Delmonico steak are both excellent. There is a huge selection, with pizza, pasta, and a great children's menu.

Santa Fe (845-757-4100), 52 Broadway, Tivoli. ($) Dinner daily (except Monday) 5–10. Enjoy traditional Mexican favorites like tacos and enchiladas in a festive atmosphere. The goat cheese in the enchiladas is locally made.

Spanky's (845-485-2294), 85 Main Street, Poughkeepsie. ($) Open for lunch Monday through Friday 11:30–2:30; dinner is served daily from 5. The Cajun cuisine is a refreshing change from the usual light fare. A casual yet warm atmosphere and spicy selections make this spot one of the most appealing places to dine in the downtown area.

Stage Stop (845-868-1042), Hunns Lake Road, Bangall. ($$) Open Tuesday through Sunday for dinner from 5. American cuisine here features steaks, seafood, and chicken dishes as well as a fresh raw bar with clams, oysters, and shrimp. The country inn decor creates a relaxed atmosphere. For dessert, be sure to try the chocolate pecan caramel pie, a specialty of the house. The cheesecake is also superb.

Stoney Creek (845-757-4117), 76 Broadway, Tivoli. ($$) Open daily for dinner from 5. This lovely restaurant features Continental favorites in an elegant atmosphere.

EATING OUT

Bagel Shoppe (845-758-2001), 11 Old Farm Road, Route 9 South, Red Hook. ($) Open Monday through Friday 6 AM–4 PM; Saturday 7 AM–4 PM; Sunday 7 AM–2 PM. Take out or sit down for a bite at this delightful eatery featuring authentic New York water bagels. A few of the imaginative selections include the Gobbler, the Godfather, and the Grand Slammer. There is an array of gourmet coffee, tea, and hot chocolate, as well as omelets, bagelwiches, rugelach, biscotti, low-fat water rolls, and rice pudding.

Bread Alone Bakery & Cafe (845-876-3108), 45 East Market Street,

Rhinebeck. ($) Open daily 7–7. The homemade soups, hearty sandwiches, and salads offered here make this informal eatery a renowned stop among locals for breakfast, lunch, or takeout.

Cafe Pongo (845-757-4403), 69 Broadway, Tivoli. ($) Open daily (closed Monday) 8–6. Excellent baked goods, and a large selection of hearty soups and sandwiches made on their renowned freshly baked breads.

Calico Restaurant & Patisserie (845-876-2749), 9 Mill Street, Rhinebeck. ($$) Open Wednesday through Sunday 11:30–6. This establishment is great for takeout or for an elegant lunch. We recommend the smoked salmon with capers and the chicken salad sandwich. The pastries are first-rate.

The Cornerstone Restaurant (845-896-8050), Route 9 at Route 52, Fishkill. ($$) Open daily for lunch at 11:30, dinner 5–9. Traditional German food in a greenhouse setting, with many daily specials.

Foster's Coach House Tavern (845-876-8052), 22 Montgomery Street, Rhinebeck. ($) Open daily, except Monday, for lunch and dinner 11–11. Decorated with lots of horse collectibles, this is a great place to stop for a hamburger and homemade fries.

Lia's Mountain View (518-398-7311), Route 82, Pine Plains. ($) Open daily, except Monday, for lunch and dinner 11:30–10. Italian home cooking combined with a lovely view of the mountains. Try spidini, white pizza, calzones, and excellent desserts.

Luna 61 (845-758-0061), 61 East Market Street, Red Hook. ($) Open Wednesday through Sunday 5–9; until 10 weekends. The organic vegetarian cuisine includes an eclectic mix of flavors using the freshest ingredients. The salads, sandwiches, and veggie burgers are wonderful. There is a café atmosphere that makes this a wonderful stop for anyone seeking healthful cuisine that also tastes great.

Marco Polo's Ristorante (845-876-3228), 37 Montgomery Street, Rhinebeck. ($$) Open daily for lunch and dinner noon–10. Italian cuisine, including fine pasta and pizza from a wood-fired oven.

Mill House Panda Restaurant (845-876-2399), 21 West Market Street, Rhinebeck. Open Monday through Friday for lunch 11:30–3:30; dinner served Monday through Saturday 3:30–10, Sunday 1:30–9:30. This Cantonese Chinese restaurant elegantly prepares every dish to order. The Peking duck and walnut shrimp are excellent. The tofu vegetable soup is among the best we've had anywhere.

Northern Port Tea & Spice (845-876-6389), 59R East Market Street, Red Hook. Proprietor Kevin Rheden, chef and lecturer, is touted as the Hudson Valley's leading authority on tea. This tea salon has been set up for the convenience and comfort of his customers. Hours are by appointment or Fridays and Saturdays from 12–4. Tea sampling is encouraged.

The Palace Diner (845-473-1576), 294 Washington Street, Poughkeepsie. ($) This well-established gathering place near Marist College has become a mainstay of the community. It's a popular place for lunch among local

Foster's Coach House Tavern and owner, Bob Kirwood, in Rhinebeck

attorneys and politicians. In addition to the usual diner fare, there are Greek and international dishes, as well as daily specials. The portions are generous and the desserts should not be missed.

River Station Restaurant (845-452-9207), 25 Main Street, Poughkeepsie. ($$) Open for lunch and dinner daily. Enjoy American and Continental cuisine overlooking the Hudson River. There is a light menu featuring burgers, tacos, and pizza; the full dinner menu includes fresh fish, steaks, pasta, and salads.

Samuel's (845-876-5312), 42 East Market Street, Rhinebeck. ($) Open daily 9 AM–6 PM. This small confectionary and coffee shop is the perfect place to enjoy a cup of coffee, tea, or hot chocolate after browsing the stores in town. Children will be delighted by the attractively displayed penny candy and gourmet jelly beans. There is also a variety of truffles, hand-dipped chocolates, and sugar-free chocolate, sweetened with maltitol.

Schemmy's Ltd. (845-876-6215), 19 East Market Street, Rhinebeck. ($) Serving breakfast and lunch daily, this old-fashioned ice cream parlor features homemade soups and salads.

Town Crier Cafe (845-855-1300), Route 22, Pawling. ($) Open Thursday through Monday for dinner; call for hours. Hear top-name folk, jazz, and blues performers while you enjoy southwestern and Creole food.

Village Diner (845-758-6232), 39 North Broadway, Red Hook. ($) Open daily for breakfast, lunch, and dinner 6 AM–midnight. The only diner in the state on the National Historic Register, this art deco structure was built in 1927 and is family owned and operated. They serve hearty home-cooked meals and are known for their breakfasts, doughnuts, soups, and egg creams.

Vineyard Grill (845-677-8383), Winery Road, Millbrook. ($$) Open weekends only for winery guests to sample Millbrook wines and local produce and spices. The à la carte menu features items like gazpacho madrileño and grilled portobello mushrooms, asparagus, mozzarella, and roasted red peppers.

Yet Another Roadside Attraction (845-758-0535), Route 199, 1 mile west of the Taconic Parkway, Milan. ($) Open for breakfast and lunch Tuesday through Sunday 7–3; closed Monday. This kitschy eatery will delight dinerphiles and is an interesting oasis in the country. Ten different types of pancakes are offered, along with special soups, hamburgers, and sandwiches.

ENTERTAINMENT

Bardavon Opera House (845-471-5288), 35 Market Street, Poughkeepsie. Built in 1869, this opera house is one of the oldest theaters in the country and has hosted the likes of Mark Twain, Sarah Bernhardt, John Phillip Sousa, and Frank Sinatra. The building stands on the site of former lumber- and coal yards and was remodeled in 1921 in response to the public's desire for a grand movie palace. Today it is a major center for the performing arts, with many jazz, classical, and pop artists visiting on tour.

Mid-Hudson Civic Center/McCann Ice Arena (845-454-9800), 14 Civic Center Plaza, Poughkeepsie. This multipurpose recreation and entertainment center also hosts a number of conventions. There is ice skat-

Petting zoo at the Dutchess County Fair

ing year-round (call for hours), and a variety of programs including rock and pop concerts, consumer and trade shows, and cultural events.

Hudson Valley Film Festival (845-473-0318), 40 Garden Street, Poughkeepsie 12601. This growing festival is held in early June and offers many screenings, readings, and special film-related events throughout the county, including a chance to see distinguished denizens of the cinema. There is also the **Kaatsbaan International Dance Center** (845-757-8392), Tivoli, which is located on an estate and offers dance companies in all disciplines in concert.

Also see the **Center for the Performing Arts at Rhinebeck** under *To See*.

ART GALLERIES

Albert Shahinian Fine Art (845-454-0522), 198 Main Street, Poughkeepsie. Open Friday 4–7; Saturday 11–6; Sunday noon–5. At other times, by appointment. Contemporary regional, West Coast, and Hudson River art, with exhibits changing monthly.

Bard College Center for Curatorial Studies (845-758-7598), Route 9G, Annandale-on-Hudson. Open Wednesday through Sunday, 1–5, and by appointment. An impressive collection of 20th-century art housed in a wonderful contemporary museum.

Barrett House (845-471-2550), 55 Noxon Street, Poughkeepsie, exhibits distinguished Hudson River School and other American artists.

The Chocolate Factory (845-758-9244), 98 Elizabeth Street, Red Hook. Open weekends, call for hours other times. This artists' collective features a wide array of painters, sculptors, and artisans.

Cunneen-Hackett Cultural Center (845-471-1221), Vassar Street, Poughkeepsie, has theater, dance, and art shows on its schedule. The center is housed in restored Victorian buildings, and regional art and artists are usually featured.

Howland Center (845-831-4988), 477 Main Street, Beacon, sponsors exhibits, concerts, and workshops year-round.

John Lane Gallery (845-471-2770), 31 Collegeview Avenue, Poughkeepsie, stocks magnificent prints and original art by American artists; the shop is as much a tiny gem of a museum as it is a gallery.

Lorraine Kessler Gallery (845-452-7040), 196 Main Street, Poughkeepsie. Open Tuesday through Saturday, noon–5 and by appointment. Contemporary and modern art with exhibits changing monthly.

Marist College Art Gallery (845-575-3000, x2903), North Road, Poughkeepsie. Open Monday through Friday, noon–5; Saturday, noon–4. The college has a wonderful collection of work by local artists as well as other treasures.

Mill Street Loft (845-471-7477), 20 Maple Street, Poughkeepsie, is a multi-arts center that sponsors shows, workshops, and a unique art camp.

Vassar College Art Gallery (845-437-5632), 124 Raymond Avenue, Poughkeepsie. Open Tuesday through Saturday, 10–5; Sunday 1–5. There is an excellent permanent collection as well as special changing exhibits.

SELECTIVE SHOPPING

J. B. Peel, Inc. (845-758-1792), 55 North Broadway, Red Hook, has one of the best coffee selections available in the country. The aroma in the store is fantastic, and so is the coffeemaking equipment.

ANTIQUES AND AUCTIONS

Lovers of antiques and collectibles will have a field day in Dutchess County, where it seems that every village and hamlet boasts a selection of fine antiques shops. Clocks, vintage clothing, fine china, Hudson River School paintings, and rare jewels are all waiting for a home, and it's easy to spend an afternoon looking for that one-of-a-kind treasure. The search is made even easier at antiques centers that offer a cluster of dealers under one roof and regular hours year-round. You can call 845-868-2263 for a copy of the Dutchess County antiques map and guide.

The Annex Antiques and Accessories (845-758-2843), 9 South Broadway, Red Hook, is filled with Victorian and country furniture, jewelry, collectibles, and Americana.

Beekman Arms Antique Market (845-876-3477), Route 9, is behind the Beekman Arms Inn (see *Lodging*).

Hammertown Barn (845-398-7075), Route 199, Pine Plains, has country wares, folk art, and primitives.

Country Fare Antique and Arts Center (845-868-7107), Route 82, Stanfordville, offers a large collection of books, records, and miniatures.

At **The Hyde Park Antiques Center** (845-229-8200), Route 9, Hyde Park, there are more than 50 dealers and a very large range of specialty collectibles and antiques.

At the **Millbrook Antique Mall** (845-677-9311), Franklin Avenue, Millbrook, there are many 18th-century-furniture dealers, and the **Millbrook Antiques Center** (845-677-3921), 789 Franklin Avenue, has nearly 50 different "mini shops." Don't miss Millbrook's **Village Antiques Center** (845-677-5160), 388 Franklin Avenue, with dozens of quality dealers and offerings in categories as diverse as decorative items and sporting collectibles.

There are 28 dealers at **The Antique Center** (845-855-3611), Route 22. If you like auctions, call the **Pleasant Valley Auction Hall** (845-635-3169), South Avenue, for an auction schedule.

Rock City Relics (845-758-8603), Route 199, Rock City, has country collectibles and old finds.

At **The Village Antique Center at Hyde Park** (845-229-6600), 69 Albany Post Road, Route 9, Hyde Park, dealers stock pine and oak furniture, silver, glassware, books, and more.

SPECIAL EVENTS

August: **Dutchess County Fair** (845-876-4001), County Fairgrounds, Route 9, Rhinebeck. Last week in August; open daily. Admission fee. For the biggest—and some say the best—county fair in the Hudson Valley, a stop at the Dutchess County Fair is in order. The fairgrounds include large display buildings, show arenas, a racetrack, food stands, and even an "old-fashioned village" where kids can play. Plenty of livestock is displayed, and name entertainment is offered. The colorful, noisy midway attracts all ages, and the rides will please the adventurous and the not-so-adventurous. The fairgrounds are also home to the New York State Wool Festival, held in October. This is an outstanding exhibit and great fun for all ages, especially if you like sheep, llamas, and alpacas.

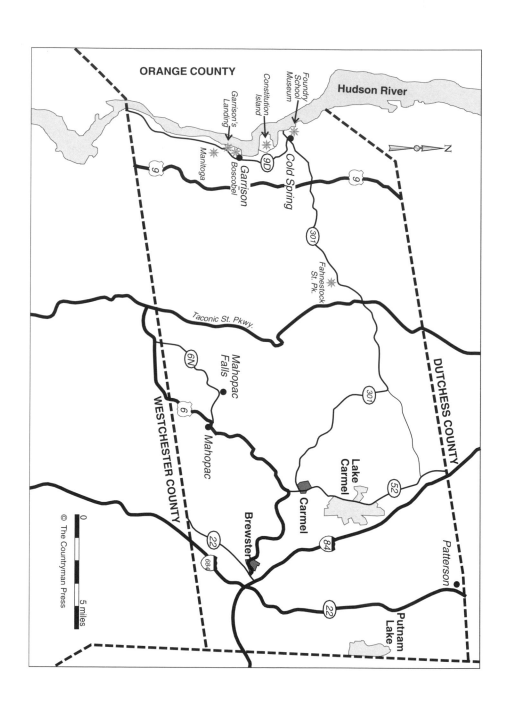

XI. Putnam County

One of the gateways to the Hudson Highlands, Putnam County offers splendid river views, lots of outdoor entertainment, and a chance to see small-town America before it disappears. In Cold Spring the tiny shops and riverside gazebo are charming reminders of a more leisurely past. Up north, the Federal mansion called Boscobel (which came within hours of being demolished) has been restored to its former elegance. A walk through the gardens there offers thousands of flowers in full color, blooming with scent. There are also thousands of acres of wetlands, lakes, forests, and meadows in Putnam beckoning the hiker, walker, and nature lover. A very different outdoor environment was created at Manitoga, where industrial designer Russell Wright constructed Dragon House, a unique home built into the wall of a quarry. In Putnam you can drive along rustic roads, smell apple blossoms, see houses that date back to before the Revolution, stop at an art gallery, or just laze away an afternoon watching the Hudson. Route 9D from the Bear Mountain Bridge goes past many historic areas. Route 9 is the old Albany Post Road and has been in constant use for more than two centuries. Just an hour from New York City, Putnam County can seem a century away, with a pace and a grace all its own.

GUIDANCE

Putnam County Visitors Bureau (845-225-0381 or 1-800-470-4854), 110 Old Route 6, Building 3, Carmel 10512; www.visitputnam.org.

GETTING THERE

Putnam County can be reached via I-84, the Taconic State Parkway, or Route 9.

MEDICAL EMERGENCY

Putnam Hospital Center (845-279-5711), Stoneleigh Avenue, Carmel.

VILLAGES

Cold Spring. This lovely river town was founded in the 18th century and, according to local folklore, got its name from George Washington's comment on the water found at a local spring. Cold Spring received an economic boost in the 19th century, when it became the site of one of the largest iron foundries in the United States. The town's West Point Foundry produced everything from weapons to some rather unusual furniture, some of which can be seen at the Tarrytown home of Washington Irving in Westchester County.

On Main Street you can visit **"antiques row,"** where many dealers own or share shops that specialize in everything from rare books to vintage clothing to brass beds. If you continue down Main Street to the railroad tracks, you will find a plaque commemorating Washington's visit. The bandstand here was constructed for riverside concerts—now it provides a wonderful place to look across the river to Storm King Mountain, which, true to its name, is the center of many storms. At the corner of Main and West Streets, follow West Street south to Market to see the **Chapel of Our Lady** (845-265-2781). This one-room Greek Revival chapel was built in 1834 for workers at the foundry; it is the oldest Roman Catholic church in the region and was one of the most popular subjects for painters and artists of the Hudson River School. The chapel looks across the river, but you may have to wait to get in on weekends, because it's popular for weddings.

Garrison. The Landing, which overlooks the Hudson River at the railroad station, is the town's hub. Walk down to the riverside gazebo, which was used as the set for the filming of *Hello, Dolly!* The Landing is also home to the **Garrison Art Center** (845-424-3960), which holds exhibits, auctions, workshops, and special events, including an art fair, throughout the year.

TO SEE

Chuang Yen Monastery (845-225-1819), 2020 Route 301, Carmel 10512. Open year-round 9:30 AM–dusk. The monastery houses the largest Buddhist statue in the Western Hemisphere as well as many other unique shrines, statues, and pieces of art. The library has over 70,000 books, the majority of them Buddhist texts. A morning meditation session and book discussion is held every Sunday, followed by a vegetarian lunch. Visitors are welcome.

Foundry School Museum of the Putnam Historical Society (845-265-4010), 63 Chestnut Street, Cold Spring. Open March through December, Tuesday and Wednesday 10–4, Thursday 1–4, Saturday and Sunday 2–5. Free. The original Foundry School served the children of Irish immigrants and apprentices who were employed at the West Point Foundry; today the 1820 building is a small museum. The exhibits offer a look at local history, including the Civil War artillery weapons (the Parrott gun was developed by a West Point officer) that were constructed here, and there are also small collections of paintings and furniture. There is even a horse-drawn cutter, once owned by Julia Butterfield, who is said to have received the sleigh from the tsarina of Russia.

Mahopac Farm Museum (845-628-9298), Route 6, Baldwin Place,

Mahopac. Open daily 10–5 April through November. Admission fee; admission to country store is free. This is a fun stop if you are traveling with children: There are antique cars, automatic musical instruments, costumes, bone-shaker bicycles, and other items of everyday 19th-century life. You'll also find a petting zoo, pony rides, and hayrides in this jumble of collections. The small country store has an ice cream parlor.

Putnam Art Council Art Center (845-628-3664), 255 Kennicut Hill Road, Mahopac. Open year-round Tuesday through Friday 9–3, Sunday 1–4. Fee charged for workshops. This cultural organization has a gallery with annual and changing exhibits, as well as workshops in visual and performaing arts for children and adults. There are concerts, lectures, and special events offered throughout the season.

Southeast Museum (845-279-7500), 67 Main Street, Brewster. Open April through December, Tuesday, Wednesday, and Saturday 10–4, Friday 12–5. Suggested donation. This Victorian-style building houses a small museum with an eclectic local collection. There are permanent exhibits on the Borden Dairy Condensory (condensed milk was developed by a Putnam County citizen), the construction of the Croton Water System (a project remarkable for engineering innovations), the American circus, Harlem Line Railroad, and a large collection of minerals from local mines. Local history is also a focus of this museum.

HISTORIC HOME

Boscobel Restoration (845-265-3638), Route 9D, Garrison-on-Hudson. Open April through October, Wednesday through Monday 9:30–4:30; March, November, and December, Wednesday through Monday 9:30–3:30. Admission fee. Standing on a bluff overlooking the Hudson River, the country mansion known as Boscobel looks as if it had spent all of its nearly 200 years in peace and prosperity. But appearances can be deceiving. States Morris Dyckman, a Loyalist of Dutch ancestry, began building the mansion in 1805, but he died before it was completed; his wife, Elizabeth Corne Dyckman, lived there with their family. Designed in the Federal style, Boscobel was furnished with elegant carpets, fine porcelain, and furniture from the best workshops in New York. The house remained in the family until 1888; from then on it had various owners, including the federal government. In 1955 the government decided it no longer needed Boscobel and the house was sold for $35 to a contractor, who stripped it of many of its architectural details and sold them off. Local people were so incensed that they tracked down the sections that had been sold, salvaged and stored the other parts of the house, and, finally, purchased land on which to re-erect the building. Today visitors to Boscobel will see the house as it was, complete with elegant staircase, fine decorative objects, and period furniture made by New York craftspeople. (It is requested that visitors wear broad-heeled walking shoes to tour the house; it helps to preserve the floors and rugs.) Boscobel's grounds are enchanting as well. At the Gate House you can

The guest chamber at Boscobel Restoration, decorated for the Christmas season.

see the home of a middle-class family of the era and explore the Orangerie, a 19th-century greenhouse. In spring and summer the gardens at Boscobel blaze with thousands of flowers, including tulips, daffodils, roses, pansies, and wildflowers. Special events are held all season, including a rose festival, concerts, candlelight holiday tours, and workshops in horticultural and American crafts.

HISTORIC SITES

Old Southeast Church (845-279-7429), Route 22 (Old Croton Turnpike), Brewster. Open June to Labor Day, Sunday 2–5. Free. Founded in 1735 by Elisha Kent, this is the church that most of the tenant farmers attended in the 18th century; the present building was built in 1794. Guides in period dress take visitors through the structure in summer.

Town of Carmel Historical Society (845-628-5300), 40 McAlpine Street. Open April through November, Sunday 2–4 and by appointment. Free. An interesting stop for history buffs, the center was donated by a general of the Civil War. Displays include a general store, an exhibit on local history, and decorative accessories of the period.

TO DO

FARM STANDS AND PICK-YOUR-OWN FARMS

Green Chimneys Farmstand (845-279-2995), Putnam Lake Road, Brewster, is open June through September, Wednesday through Saturday 3–6, and offers organically grown vegetables raised by the students of the Green Chimneys School.

Maple Lawn Farm Market (845-424-4093), Route 9, Garrison, is open daily March through December and stocks seasonal produce, baked goods, cider, and Christmas trees.

Christmas trees and flowers are found at **Philipstown Farm Market** (845-265-2151), Route 9, Cold Spring, along with fruit, vegetables, and imported foods; open daily March through December, 8–7.

Ryder Farm (845-279-3984), Starr Ridge Road, Brewster, has 125 acres of organically grown raspberries on its pick-your-own family farm, in operation for 200 years.

For a wide selection of local fruit and vegetables, stop in at **Salinger's Orchards** (845-279-3521), Guinea Road, Brewster, where a cider mill and bakery offer seasonal treats to visitors. Open daily June 1 to August, 9–6.

GOLF

The lush greens of Putnam County golf courses lure golfers from novice to expert. You may want to call before you go, since some of the courses are semiprivate and may have special events scheduled. All charge fees for use and cart rentals.

Centennial Golf Club (845-225-5700), Simpson Road, Carmel. Open daily April through November. Enjoy a 27-hole Larry Nelson–designed course, practice facilities, and world-class services.

Garrison Golf Club (845-424-3604), Route 9, Garrison, is open daily 8–7 April through November.

Highlands Country Club (845-424-3727), Route 9D, Garrison, is open daily April through December.

Putnam Country Club at Lake MacGregor (845-628-3451), Hill Street, Mahopac, has 18 holes and is 6,750 yards in length; open daily April through November.

Vails Grove Golf Course (845-669-5721), Route 121, Brewster, has nine holes. It's open to the public weekdays and weekends after 2, April through November.

GREEN SPACE

Thousands of acres of Putnam County are dedicated to public use and outdoor education. Most parks are free, but some charge use fees for special events, camping, and swimming; activities include nature studies, birding, hiking, walking, ski touring, and boating.

Constitution Marsh Wildlife Preserve (845-265-3119), access off Route 9D, 0.25 mile south of Boscobel. Open May through November. Visitors must make reservations for a tour. A National Audubon Society haven for nature lovers who enjoy birding along the river and spotting rare wildflowers in spring. There is a boardwalk to make viewing easier and a self-guided nature tour.

Taconic Outdoor Education Center (845-265-3773), Clarence Fahnestock Memorial State Park, 775 Mountain Laurel Road, Cold Spring. Free.

The tulip garden at Boscobel Restoration

This state-run center is situated on 500 acres and holds classes and workshops year-round. Boat, swim, fish, or just stay overnight in one of the park's cabins and enjoy the fellowship at **Highland Lodge** (reservations for camping required).

Other parks include **Hudson Highlands State Park** (845-225-7207), Route 9D, Cold Spring; **Pudding Street Multiple Use Area** (845-831-3109), Pudding Street, Putnam Valley; **California Hill Multiple Use Area** (845-831-3109), Gordon Road, Kent; **White Pond Multiple Use Area** (845-831-3109), White Pond Road, Kent; **Big Buck Mountain Multiple Use Area** (845-831-3109), Farmers Mills and Ressique Road, Kent; **Ninham Mountain Multiple Use Area** (845-831-3109), Gypsy Trail and Mount Ninham Roads, Kent; and **Cranberry Mountain Wildlife Management Area** (845-255-5453), Stagecoach Road, Patterson.

🚲👤 **Clarence Fahnestock Memorial State Park** (845-225-7207), Route 301, east of the Taconic Parkway, Carmel. Open year-round. Free. This 12,000-acre park consists of swamp, lake, forest, and meadow and was assembled through donations of land from private and state organizations. Several hiking trails, including part of the Appalachian Trail, weave in and out of the park; there are also fishing ponds, Canopus Beach, boat rentals, ice-skating areas, and cross-country ski trails. Fees are charged for boats and for swimming, and you must bring your own equipment for winter sports and for fishing and hiking. The park also sponsors performing arts programs and has provisions for camping, although you must call ahead to make reservations. The park's 1½-mile Pelton Pond Nature

Trail is a marked trail that follows the perimeter of a pond formed when an old mine shaft was dammed. You can picnic in this area or watch the woods from a small pavilion. Hikers will want to look for the 8-mile stretch of Appalachian Trail that crosses the park; the Three Lakes Trail, with its varied wildflowers and views; and Catfish Loop Trail, which cuts through the abandoned settlement once known as Dennytown. Since many of these trails cross one another, you should look for signs and trail blazes along the main park roads, which include Route 301, Dennytown Road, and Sunk Mine Road. If you plan to go fishing in the park, you will need a state license. When you visit, be sure to stop at the park headquarters first, where you can pick up a list of special events (some nice programs for children are offered in summer) and free maps and fishing guides. Some facilities are accessible to the disabled.

Graymoor (845-424-3671), Route 9, near Route 403, Garrison. Open daily 10–5 year-round. Free. Founded by the Episcopal Church in 1898, this historic site is home of the Franciscan Friars of the Atonement. Today the site is an ecumenical retreat center, with nature trails and access to the Appalachian Trail.

Manitoga, Man with Nature Center (845-424-3812), Old Manitou Road and Route 9D, Garrison. Open year-round, but hours vary. Admission fee. The name of this center is taken from the Algonquian word for "place of the spirit," and the philosophy of Manitoga lives up to its name. Here people and nature are meant to interact, and visitors are encouraged to experience the harmony of their environment. The center was designed by Russell Wright, who created a 5-mile system of trails that focus on specific aspects of nature. The Morning Trail is especially beautiful early in the day, the Spring Trail introduces the hiker to wildflowers, and the Blue Trail wanders over a brook and through a dramatic evergreen forest (the trail system hooks up with the Appalachian Trail). You will find a full-sized reproduction of a Native American wigwam, which was constructed with traditional methods and tools. The site is used as an environmental learning center, and many special programs are offered here. There are workshops in art, poetry, photography, and botany, along with guided nature walks and concerts of music and dance. You can even visit Dragon Rock, the glass-walled cliff house built by Wright. Manitoga is a place where human design and the natural world reflect and inspire each other.

LODGING

Unless otherwise noted, all of the following inns are in the $$$ range, although some of them offer special packages; call for reservations and rate information.

The Bird and Bottle Inn (845-424-3000), Route 9, Garrison 10524. For history buffs, this is a great place to stay. Constructed in 1761, the building has had a romantic and colorful past. Each room has a fireplace and period furnishings that include a canopied or four-poster bed. A full breakfast is served to guests in the restaurant dining room downstairs (see *Dining Out*). Two double rooms have private bath; there is also one suite and one cottage. Children not permitted. Open year-round, except part of January.

The Country House Inn (845-228-5838). 1457 Peekskill Hollow Road, Kent Cliffs, Carmel 10512. ($$) Open year-round. Here you will find charming antiques-filled bedrooms in a beautiful setting.

Heidi's Inn (845-279-8011). Route 22, Brewster 10509. ($$) Open year-round. This quiet, comfortable inn has 40 rooms, all with private bath. There is an excellent Italian restaurant on the premises, **LaGinestra,** which serves hearty lunches and dinners.

Hudson House Inn (845-265-9355), 2 Main Street, Cold Spring 10516. The second oldest continuously operating inn in New York State, Hudson House is completely restored and filled with antiques. In addition to quaint bedrooms, there's a cozy lounge, river views, and an exquisite garden. Twelve rooms with private bath; one suite. A full breakfast is served. Children over the age of 12 are welcome. Open year-round, except January.

Mallard Manor (845-628-3595). 345 Lakeview Drive, Mahopac 10541. ($) Open year-round. Two bedrooms share a bath in this 25-year-old Colonial with Old World charm. The history of Mahopac is depicted in paintings in the stairwell and foyer. Guests may enjoy a hearty breakfast with views of the flowering gardens in-season.

Pig Hill Inn (845-265-9247), 73 Main Street, Cold Spring 10516. This Georgian brick town house is a most unusual place to stay. Each guest room is furnished in a different style and all have a fireplace—and if you fall in love with the rocking chair or anything else in your room, you can buy it. All breads and cakes are homemade. Breakfast in bed is offered, as is a morning meal in the dining room. You can even make reservations for a picnic lunch. Four rooms with private bath; four others share two baths. Open year-round.

Plumbush Inn (845-265-3904), Route 9D, Cold Spring 10516. Now you can stay at this famous restaurant on an 1867 estate. Period furnishings fill the rooms, and, of course, the food is superb (see *Dining Out*). Three rooms with private bath. Open year-round; closed Monday and Tuesday.

WHERE TO EAT

DINING OUT

The Arch (845-279-5011), Route 22, Brewster. ($$$) Open for lunch Wednesday through Friday and Sunday, noon–2:30; dinner Wednesday through Sunday 6–10; Sunday lunch and brunch served noon–2:30. An elegant, intimate spot filled with antiques and separated into three small dining rooms with fireplaces and lots of airy windows. The chef specializes in Continental cuisine with a French touch. The menu changes seasonally; game is the specialty in fall. Reservations and jackets for men are required. Not recommended for children.

The Bird and Bottle Inn (845-424-3000), Route 9, Garrison. ($$) Open Wednesday through Sunday 6–9; Sunday brunch noon–2. Established in 1761 and originally known as Warren's Tavern, this restaurant was a major stagecoach stop between New York and Albany. The inn still retains a colonial ambience with wood-burning fireplaces, beamed ceilings, wide-plank floors, and authentic antiques. Brunch and dinner are both prix fixe; the dinner specialties include salmon and, for dessert, a crème brûlée. Reservations suggested; jackets required for men. Not recommended for children.

Capriccio (845-279-2873), Route 22, Brewster. ($$$) Open daily for lunch noon–2:30; dinner 5:30–9:30. Enjoy a lake and countryside view from this fine restaurant, which is housed in a large, white-clapboard house. Northern Italian specialties include pasta, shrimp, and lamb. Reservations are required on weekends; men must wear jackets. Not recommended for children.

Heidi's Brauhaus (845-628-9795), 241 Route 6 North, Mahopac. ($$) Open Wednesday and Thursday 5–9; Friday and Saturday 4–10; Sunday brunch 11:30–2:30, dinner 3–9. Reasonably priced German specialties, including sauerbraten and Jaegerschnitzel, in a comfortable setting.

✎ **Hudson House Restaurant** (845-265-9355), 2 Main Street, Cold Spring. ($$) Open for lunch Thursday through Monday noon–3; dinner Wednesday through Saturday 5:30–9; Sunday noon–7. Country touches fill this charming 1832 landmark building, and the dining rooms have Hudson River views. Specialties include Maryland-style crabcakes, Long Island duckling, and New Zealand lamb. Desserts are superb. Children welcome.

Northgate at Dockside Harbor (845-265-5555), 1 North Street, Cold Spring. ($$) Open Wednesday through Sunday for lunch 11:30–3; dinner 5–10. The emphasis here is on American regional cuisine, and there are steaks and seafood as well as pasta dishes. This is a great stop in summer; most tables have a magnificent view of the Hudson River. There is outdoor dining, weather permitting.

Plumbush Inn (845-265-3904), Route 9D, Cold Spring. ($$) Open for dinner Wednesday through Sunday 5:30–10. Closed Monday and Tuesday. A restored Victorian home, complete with antiques and cozy paneled rooms. Both dining rooms have fireplaces and candlelight. During the summer dine on the spacious porch overlooking the grounds. There is a live-trout tank and lots of attention to service. Jackets for men required on weekends. Not recommended for children.

Riverview Restaurant (845-265-4778), 45 Fair Street, Cold Spring. ($$) Open daily (closed Monday) for lunch noon–3; open daily for dinner

5:30–10; Sunday brunch from noon. The Italian cuisine here is hearty and the place is popular with locals. The wood-fired brick-oven pizza is the specialty; Wednesday night is pizza night and everything on the menu is reduced in price. Enjoy the river view while dining on the terrace, weather permitting.

Xaviar's Restaurant (845-424-4228), Route 9D, Garrison, at the Highland Country Club. ($$$) Open for dinner Friday and Saturday 6–9; brunch served Sunday noon–3. A prix fixe six-course meal is offered at Xaviar's, one of the finest restaurants in the region. Tables are set with flowers, crystal, and silver, and the menu, which changes continually, features such entrées as grilled quail on pasta and medallions of rabbit with grapes and mustard. Jackets recommended for men. Reservations required. Not recommended for children.

EATING OUT

Cold Spring Depot Restaurant (845-265-2305), 1 Railroad Avenue, Cold Spring. ($) Open daily for lunch 11:30–4:30; dinner 4:30–10. A casual restaurant housed in a restored train station where, to the delight of rail fans, trains still pass by. Burgers and fries are hearty, and there is an antique ice cream and soda fountain.

Dolci (845-265-6332) 63 Main Street, Cold Spring. ($) Open Monday through Friday 6 AM–9 PM; Saturday and Sunday 9 AM–10 PM. The pies, breads, muffins, cakes, and Italian pastries here are first-rate. Espresso, cappuccino, imported gelati, soups, and sandwiches are available, with outdoor dining on the patio in-season. A touch of Italy in downtown Cold Spring.

Flannigan's (845-628-9394), 156 East Lake Boulevard, Mahopac. ($$) Open daily 11–10. Local residents flock here for the best burgers around. There is also a variety of salads and sandwiches. Enjoy outdoor dining in the warm-weather months.

Foundry Cafe (845-265-4504), 55 Main Street, Cold Spring. ($) Open Monday through Friday 6–5; Saturday and Sunday 8–5. Naturally healthy foods (low fat, whole grain, and tasty) are the specialty here, prepared in the spirit of regional America. Home-baked goods and hearty, fresh soups are prepared daily.

Lombardi's Dugout Restaurant (845-628-6600), 466 Route 6, Mahopac. ($$) Open noon–10 daily except Monday. This casual neighborhood restaurant has been under the same ownership for more than 50 years and features a wide variety of Italian specialties as well as steaks, chops, and seafood.

Papa John's Pizzeria and Restaurant (845-265-3344), Route 9, Garrison. ($) Open daily 11–10. This family restaurant featuring pizza, pasta, sandwiches, and fantastic calzones is patronized by local residents who enjoy hearty Italian food at reasonable prices.

Texas Taco (845-878-9665), Route 22, Patterson. ($) Open daily 11:30–9:30. In business for more than 25 years, this unique Tex-Mex restaurant has a talking parrot and a monkey that lives out back. Owner Rosemary Jamison is from Texas and started out with a pushcart in front of New York's Plaza Hotel. The chili dogs, franks and chips, and burritos are delicious.

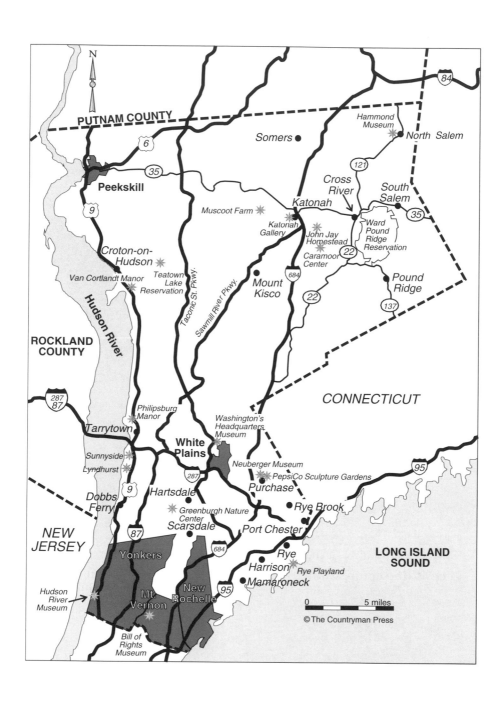

N

PUTNAM COUNTY

84

6

Somers

Hammond Museum

North Salem

35

121

Peekskill

Cross River

South Salem

9

Muscoot Farm

Katonah

35

Katonah Gallery

Ward Pound Ridge Reservation

Croton-on-Hudson

John Jay Homestead

22

Van Cortlandt Manor

Teatown Lake Reservation

684

Caramoor Center

Mount Kisco

Pound Ridge

22

137

ROCKLAND COUNTY

Hudson River

Taconic St. Pkwy.

Sawmill River Pkwy.

CONNECTICUT

287
87

Philipsburg Manor

Washington's Headquarters Museum

Tarrytown

White Plains

95

Sunnyside

287

Neuberger Museum

Lyndhurst

PepsiCo Sculpture Gardens

Dobbs Ferry

9

Hartsdale

Purchase

Rye Brook

NEW JERSEY

87

Greenburgh Nature Center

Scarsdale

Port Chester

LONG ISLAND SOUND

684

Rye

Yonkers

Harrison

Rye Playland

Mamaroneck

Hudson River Museum

Mt. Vernon

New Rochelle

95

0   5 miles

© The Countryman Press

Bill of Rights Museum

XII. Westchester County

Home of the unexpected, Westchester—which calls itself the Golden Apple—can be a nature preserve, a riverfront mansion, a 17th-century Dutch house tucked just off the old Post Road, or a bustling shopping district. The county has made extraordinary attempts to preserve both its history and its natural environment. Although Westchester borders urban New York, it is an area replete with parks and nature preserves that offer an enormous selection of children's activities and special events for visitors. Washington Irving described the enchantment of Westchester in his short stories, immortalizing Tarrytown and the Headless Horseman. On historic Route 9 visitors will be awed by the Gothic castle called Lyndhurst and the working Dutch mill at Philipsburg Manor. From the Pinkster Festival in spring to December's candlelight tours of historic homes, Westchester is fun to visit year-round.

GUIDANCE
Westchester County Visitors Bureau (1-800-833-WCVB); www.westchesterny.com.

GETTING THERE
Westchester is accessible from I-87, I-95, Route 684, and Route 9.

MEDICAL EMERGENCY
White Plains Hospital Medical Center (914-681-0600), Davis Avenue at East Post Road, White Plains; **Peekskill Community Hospital** (914-737-9013), 1980 Crompond Avenue, Peekskill.

TO SEE

ART AND SCULPTURE
PepsiCo Sculpture Gardens (914-253-2000), Anderson Hill Road, Purchase. Open daily 9–5 year-round. Free. Located at the world headquarters of PepsiCo, this site is properly called the Donald M. Kendall Sculpture Gardens. Here, on more than 100 acres, visitors will see more than 40 large sculptures by Rodin, Giacometti, Nevelson, Moore, and Noguchi. Carefully landscaped with paths, reflecting pools, and fountains, the gardens, a sight in themselves, bloom from early spring until fall. Picnicking is permitted.

Reader's Digest Tour (914-241-5125), Route 117, Pleasantville. Tours are offered Monday through Friday; reservations are required. Not many

The PepsiCo Sculpture Gardens in Purchase

people know that the headquarters of *Reader's Digest* also houses an outstanding collection of impressionist and postimpressionist artworks. Paintings by Monet, Renoir, Chagall, and others and sculpture by masters like Modigliani and Brancusi are on view throughout the building. This is a special stop for an art lover, but not recommended for children.

HISTORIC HOMES

Caramoor Center for Music and the Arts (914-232-5035), Girdle Ridge Road, off Route 22 in Katonah. Open year-round, but hours vary; call for a schedule. Admission fee. Built in the 1930s by lawyer and banker Walter Tower Rosen, this 117-acre estate was meant to be the setting for Rosen's magnificent collection of fine art from Europe and the Orient. The house itself was created by combining entire rooms (55 in all) from European villas with an American "shell"; the result is a unique, magical building that provides an architectural tour of the world in a few hours. Rosen's bedroom, for example, was taken from an Alpine cottage; in his wife's room is a headboard made for Pope Urban VIII; the music room is from a 16th-century Italian villa; portions of the outdoor theater are from the south of France. Throughout the house are thousands of breathtaking pieces of priceless needlework, tapestries, porcelain, furniture, and art, some of which date from the Middle Ages and China's golden age. Tours are offered, and lectures are given by art historians who illustrate their talks with pieces from the collections. Don't miss the exquisite gardens at Caramoor, where fine statuary is set among evergreens and flowers. Caramoor is also the site of a world-renowned music festival, which is presented each summer. The **Venetian Theater** is a showcase in itself and was built around 15th-century Venetian columns; operas and concerts take center stage on warm evenings, while chamber concerts are offered in the **Spanish Courtyard.** Concertgoers are allowed to picnic on the grounds before the shows. Special events are also held throughout the year, including Renaissance Day, crafts and antiques shows, and holiday tours.

Jasper F. Cropsey Home and Studio (914-478-1372), 49 Washington Avenue, Hastings. Open weekdays by appointment only. Free. Although you have to make an appointment to view this site, it is well worth the extra time. Cropsey was a member of the Hudson River School of painters as well as an architect (he designed part of the New York City railroad system), and his Gothic home has about 100 of his works, including paintings, sketches, and studies. The furniture spans those styles that appealed to the Victorian taste, and the artist's studio is part of the tour. Maintained by a private foundation, the site also offers visitors a short film about the life and times of Cropsey.

John Jay Homestead (914-232-5651), Route 22, north of Bedford Village. Open mid-April through October, Wednesday through Sunday. Hours vary, so call ahead. Admission fee. This 18th-century farmhouse was home to five generations of Jays. As president of the Continental Congress, first chief justice of the Supreme Court, minister to Spain, and Foreign Affairs Secretary, John Jay—the most famous member of the family—held some of the most influential appointments in the new country's government. He retired to this homestead in 1801, and the house reflects the changes wrought by his descendants. Family portraits grace the walls, and the kitchen has an impressive beehive oven along with the hearth. Various styles of furniture and decorative items can be viewed, and the tour adds an interesting dimension to America's early years. The homestead also hosts special events, including candlelight tours during the winter holidays.

Kykuit (914-631-9491), Route 9, North Tarrytown. Tours begin from Philipsburg Manor. Open mid-April through November, except Tuesday; call for details. Admission fee. Tours are 2 hours, and not recommended for children under 12. John D. Rockefeller, the founder of Standard Oil, delegated the task of building Kykuit, his home, to his son John D. Rockefeller Jr. The neo-Classical country house and its gardens were completed in 1913, and Kykuit remains one of the finest and best-preserved Beaux Arts homes in America. Gov. Nelson Rockefeller lived here from 1960 to 1979. The gardens contain masterpieces by Henry Moore, Alexander Calder, and Louise Nevelson, and there are special tours that focus on the landscapes around the estate.

Kykuit, the home of John D. Rockefeller, is one of the best preserved Beaux Arts homes in America.

Lyndhurst (914-631-0046), Route 9, Tarrytown. Open March through October, Tuesday through Sunday 10–4:15; November and December, Saturday and Sunday 10–3:30; closed Thanksgiving and Christmas. Admission fee. The term *Gothic Revival* may bring to mind castles, turrets, and crenellations, but it won't prepare a visitor for the wealth and magnificence of Lyndhurst. Built in 1838 for William Paulding, a former New York City mayor, the house and grounds were enlarged by the Merritt family. Lyndhurst was later owned by the notoriously wealthy Jay Gould. Much of the furniture, paintings, and decorative accessories are original to the mansion, which was owned by the Goulds until 1961, when it was given to the National Trust. The rooms are sumptuous, and many are decorated in "faux" material—a substance made to resemble something else. Ironically, in the case of marble, to imitate it with wood and paint often cost more than real marble would have (some of the mineral "marble" was actually limestone quarried at Sing Sing Prison). Each room is filled with rare furniture, paintings, and decorative accessories; Tiffany glass and windows are outstanding highlights. Outside in the gardens there are magnificent roses, a children's playhouse, a conservatory with brick paths, and nature paths among the dozens of different trees, ferns, and plantings.

Sunnyside (914-631-8200), Route 9, at Tarrytown-Irvington line. Open daily, except Tuesday, April through December, 10–5; March, weekends only 10–4; closed Thanksgiving and Christmas. Admission fee. Washington Irving once referred to it as being "as full of angles and corners as an old cocked hat," and indeed the charming, wisteria-draped home of the author of *The Legend of Sleepy Hollow* and *Rip Van Winkle* is an original.

Irving purchased the small estate in 1835 and soon began to remodel it, adding weather vanes, gables, and even an Oriental-style tower. There is much locally made furniture, and some furnishings from Irving's time, including his desk and many of his books, remain. The kitchen was considered a modern wonder; a large hot-water heater was fed from the nearby pond by a gravity-run system. Every year Sunnyside is lovingly decorated for the holiday season and candlelight tours are held, recalling Irving's pleasure at seeing his home bustling with relatives and guests. The grounds are carefully attended and overlook the Hudson and the railroad tracks; Irving made a deal with the railroad, allowing it to pass through his land if trains would stop to pick him up for the trip to New York. Visitors can also stroll the paths, picnic near the Little Mediterranean (a pond) and watch the swans, and see the icehouse, root cellar, and "necessary." (Note that boat trips leave from New Jersey and Manhattan spring, summer, and fall to visit Sunnyside and Philipsburg Manor. Call 1-800-53-FERRY for a schedule.)

✍ **Van Cortlandt Manor** (914-631-8200), Route 9, Croton-on-Hudson. Open daily 10–5, although winter hours vary; closed Thanksgiving, Christmas, and New Year's Day. Admission fee. This manor originally consisted of 86,000 acres of land. The main floors of the present manor house were built in 1748 and remained in the Van Cortlandt family until the middle of this century. As supporters of the American Revolution, the Van Cortlandts were hosts to such luminaries as Washington, Franklin, and Lafayette. Inside the house there is a blend of styles and periods, reflecting the history of the family. One of the most impressive items is the fowling gun, a huge firearm that was fired into a flock of birds and reduced hunting time considerably! Outside, the gardens beckon the flower lover, and the Long Walk—a brick path that leads to the **Ferry House,** a nearby inn and tavern—wanders by well-maintained flower beds and herb gardens. Special events are held throughout the year, with Autumn Market Days, candlelight tours, and colonial crafts workshops among the most popular. The Ferry House has been restored and furnished with Hudson Valley pieces and offers a rare look into the social life of the colonial period. Notice the familiar white clay pipes that were for rent; the ends were broken off for each new smoker. The Ferry House is open for tours as well.

HISTORIC SITES

✍ **Muscoot Farm** (914-232-7118), Route 100, Somers. Open 10–4 daily year-round except Thanksgiving, Christmas, and New Year's Day. Free, but certain workshops charge a fee. A showplace for the farming techniques of the 19th century, this 700-acre farm is now run by the county. Built in 1885 by a pharmacist, Muscoot's (it means "something swampy" in a local Native American language) farmhouse and outbuildings were once—and fortunately still are—the heart of a well-run, progressive agricultural enterprise. Such events as cooking demonstrations are held in the Main

Sunnyside, the home of Washington Irving, in Tarrytown

House, while the farm is a great place to tour. The huge dairy barn was a model of innovative construction in its day, with its hay chutes and natural insulation, and the corn crib kept the feed clean and (almost) rodent-free. Out in the carriage shed, exhibits show what it was like to depend on horses to get from the farm to town. The duck pond still fills with ducklings in the spring, and the herb and vegetable gardens are still stocked with heirloom varieties. Children will love to meet the farm animals up close, and the horses, sheep, and cows are good-natured. Special programs may involve a blacksmith or pony rides or even a beekeeper. Muscoot also has a series of trails that wind through ferns and wildflowers, along which animals and an amazing number of birds make their homes; there are ponds, wetlands, and meadows to explore as well.

Old Dutch Church (914-631-1123), Route 9 near Philipsburg Manor, Tarrytown. The cemetery is open year-round, but the church has infrequent tours; call for hours. Free. One of the oldest churches in New York State, this stout stone building was erected in the late 17th century and is still used, albeit infrequently, for services. Surrounding the church is the fascinating Sleepy Hollow Cemetery, where visitors can read old Dutch and English tombstones. Washington Irving is buried here (his grave site is a National Historic Landmark), and the cemetery was reputed to be the spot where a headless Hessian ghost resided, giving rise to *The Legend of Sleepy Hollow*.

Old Marble School (914-793-1900), 388 California Road, Eastchester. Open by appointment. Admission fee. Although you have to make arrangements with the Eastchester Historical Society to visit this site, if you are interested in seeing a school of the past, by all means go. The school, built of locally quarried "marble" (actually limestone), is furnished in the style of the 19th century, with many antique toys and games still available for playtime. A good collection of children's books from the past is also contained in the society's archives.

Philipsburg Manor and the Upper Mills (914-631-8200), Route 9, north of Tarrytown. Open April through December daily, except Tuesday, 10–5; March, weekends only 10–4; closed January and February, as well as Thanksgiving and Christmas. Admission fee. Once the center of a 17th-century estate of more than 50,000 acres, Philipsburg Manor was founded by Frederick Philipse, an immigrant Dutch carpenter. The manor was in the middle of a bustling commercial empire, which included milling and trading concerns. For almost a century the Philipses were respected colonists; then the family fled to England as Loyalists during the Revolution, and their landholdings were broken up. Today tours of the manor begin with a short film that traces its history; visitors then cross the wooden footbridge that spans the Pocantico River and walk to the main site. At the two-story stone house and office building the rooms have been restored to their earlier simplicity. The house was not the main residence of the family, so it was not furnished lavishly, but there are several bedrooms, a kitchen, and the counting office to explore. The next stop is the mill, still run by waterpower, still grinding meal for the kitchen (you can purchase the flour in the gift shop). The resident miller explains the intricacies of a millwright's job, how waterpower turns corn into flour, all the while working the dusty, noisy machinery. Then it's outside again to the barn and the outbuildings, where costumed guides go about the business of working a small farm. Special events are held throughout the year, including sheep shearing and spinning demonstrations (call for a schedule).

Union Church of Pocantico Hills (914-631-8200), Route 9 to Route 448 (River Road), Pocantico Hills. Call for tour hours. Admission fee. Art lovers may wish to schedule a stop here; there are church windows by Henri Matisse and Marc Chagall (the only complete set of his windows in the United States), which are exquisite on a sunny day. Chamber concerts are given during the year.

MUSEUMS

Bill of Rights Museum (914-667-4116), St. Paul's Church, South Columbus Avenue, Mount Vernon. Open Tuesday through Saturday year-round. Hours and holidays vary, so call ahead. Free. Few people realize that the 18th-century libel trial of John Peter Zenger led directly to the establishment of the Bill of Rights in 1791; fewer still know that this all took place in Mount Vernon, and that an unusual museum preserves the story. Begin your visit with a tour of St. Paul's Church, which was founded in 1665 (the present building dates from 1763). The church has a highly carved bishop's chair from 1639 as well as one of the oldest working church organs in the country. You will also see the Freedom Bell, sister of Philadelphia's Liberty Bell, which was cast at the same time in the same

London foundry. At one time the church was used as a courthouse during the week, and lawyers, including Aaron Burr, presented their cases here. The Bill of Rights Museum is located in the former carriage house and has exhibits that recall young America's drive to guarantee essential freedoms. Displays include historic dioramas and panels, a working printing press, and papers and prints that describe America's historic dedication to individual rights. There are self-guided sections of the museums; guided tours are available as well. Special events include holiday tours and printing demonstrations.

Hudson River Museum (914-963-4550), 511 Warburton Avenue, Yonkers. Open year-round Wednesday through Sunday, but call for hours, since the galleries, mansion, gift shop, planetarium, and café differ slightly; some tours are by appointment only. Admission fee. When financier John Bond Trevor built a 19th-century mansion called Glenview on a rise overlooking the Hudson River, he probably never envisioned it becoming a museum; but when the house was purchased by the city of Yonkers, that is what happened. And a lucky thing, too. Period artwork, clothing, furniture, and decorative accessories are displayed throughout the mansion; the museum is located in a separate wing and contains science and art exhibit areas. The **Red Grooms bookstore** is a favorite stop with visitors, and the **Andrus Space Planetarium** (the only public planetarium in the area and one of the few in the Northeast) can take you on a journey through the universe with its Zeiss star machine. There are special events at this site all year, so it is best to call ahead for a schedule. You can even plan a birthday party for young people in the planetarium; call for reservations.

Katonah Museum of Art (914-232-9555), Route 22 at Jay Street, Katonah. Open Tuesday through Friday 1–5, Saturday 10–5, Sunday 1–5. Free. This lively teaching museum was founded in 1953 to display the best art of the past and present and to foster arts education. There are exhibits by museum members, an annual local studio tour, and changing displays, which might range from a look at the creations of fashion designers to Navajo rugs or modern art. Special events and shows are held year-round at this museum, which is well worth a stop.

Neuberger Museum (914-251-6133 or 251-6100), SUNY Purchase Campus, Anderson Hill Road, Purchase. Open Tuesday through Friday 10–4, Saturday and Sunday 11–5; closed Monday, along with Thanksgiving, Christmas, and New Year's. Children welcome. Masterpieces of modern art by Avery, Hopper, O'Keeffe, and others are displayed in several galleries at this extraordinary teaching museum. There is also an important collection of African art, and selections from Nelson Rockefeller's collection of ancient art are exhibited. Special shows and events are held all year; call for a schedule.

Peekskill Museum (914-737-6130), 124 Union Avenue, Peekskill. Open Saturday and Sunday year-round 2–4; an appointment may be necessary during the winter months. Free. This local history museum is

Philipsburg Manor looks very much as it did 100 years ago.

housed in a Victorian home that offers visitors a look at how well-to-do New Yorkers lived in "the country." Exhibits focus on Peekskill's religious, social, and Native American history, and locally made cast-iron items, including some Revolutionary War cannon, are on display.

Somers Circus Museum (914-277-4977), junction of Routes 100 and 202 in Somers. Open Friday 2–4 and by appointment. This unusual museum is located in the historic Elephant Hotel, probably the only hotel in the world built in memory of an elephant. Recalling the birth of the American circus in the 18th century, the hotel was erected by showman Hachaliah Bailey (a distant relation of the Bailey of Barnum & Bailey), who imported the first elephant to America in 1796. Called Old Bet, the elephant journeyed with Bailey up and down the eastern seaboard as part of a traveling menagerie, until it was shot by a suspicious farmer in Maine. Today the former hotel houses a museum full of circus memorabilia, posters, photographs, a miniature big top, and exhibits of local history.

Square House Museum (914-967-7588), 1 Purchase Street, Rye. Open year-round Tuesday and Saturday 12:30–4:30; Wednesday, Thursday, Friday, and Sunday 2:30–4:30. Closed Monday. Admission fee. This 1760 Federal farmhouse and tavern once hosted George Washington, and today the restored rooms offer a fascinating look at 18th-century life. In the tavern room visitors learn that the term *bar and grill* derives from the fact that barkeepers secured a wooden covering over the bar at night in order to avoid having the liquor stolen. In the kitchen a beehive oven (the interior was shaped like an old-fashioned bee skep) and open hearth are still used by museum staff. There was also an early medical office in the building, and you'll discover that the barber, who was also the doctor, would wrap bloody cloths around a stick to indicate that he was open for business: the origin of the striped pole still used by barbers today.

✎ **Town of Yorktown Museum** (914-962-2970), 1974 Commerce Road, Yorktown Heights. Open year-round Monday through Friday 9:30–4:30, Saturday and Sunday 1–4. Free, but donations accepted. A unique collection of dollhouses and miniature landscapes depicting Victorian homes, street scenes, and stores is on display, as are exhibits of Native American life, railroad memorabilia, and local history. Antiques shows and special events are held throughout the year.

✎ **Washington's Headquarters Museum** (914-949-1236), Virginia Road, North White Plains. Open Wednesday through Sunday 10–4. Free. Take the self-guided tours of this small farmhouse museum and visit the rooms where Washington planned the strategy for the battle of White Plains. On display here are unusual items such as one of the great general's boots (or at least his reputed boot), which appears very large until you discover that insulation was tucked inside to keep his feet warm. There's a rifle pellet still embedded in a piece of furniture (a remnant of the Revolutionary War), an early washing machine that was "child and stick" powered, and uneven floors that have been raised by the roots of a 300-year-old sycamore tree. This is an old-fashioned, fun museum, with many special events throughout the year.

WINERY

North Salem Vineyard (914-669-5518), Hardscrabble Road, North Salem (watch for signs). Open year-round Saturday and Sunday 1–5. Free. This small, privately owned vineyard produces several wines and welcomes guests to sample its products. There is a short tour and a wine- and snack shop on site. A picnic area is available.

TO DO

BICYCLING

If bicycling is your sport, plan to take part in **Bicycle Sundays** (May through September except holiday weekends, 10–2), when the Bronx River Parkway is closed to vehicular traffic. Call 914-285-PARK and request trail maps for the Bronx River Pathway, North County Trailway, and

Briarcliff-Peekskill Trailway, which have free bike paths that are open year-round. In-line skates are also welcome in some of the areas.

CRUISES

Take a sail aboard the *Half Moon,* the only ship that offers daily scheduled cruises from the east bank of the Hudson River (914-736-0500), King Marine, Sixth Street, Verplanck (the dock is located at end of Sixth Street). Open daily June through October. Visitors can enjoy a sightseeing cruise, theme nights, brunches, and more on the river or splurge and charter the ship for a private trip.

FARM STANDS AND PICK-YOUR-OWN-FARMS

Even though Westchester is more built up than many other Hudson River counties, farm stands provide fresh local produce during the summer and fall harvest seasons. Farmers' markets are held in many towns, including Hartsdale, Hastings-on-Hudson, Peekskill, Pleasantville, and White Plains. Call the visitors bureau for a detailed map and schedule.

Egg Farm Dairy (914-734-7343), 2 John Walsh Boulevard, Peekskill. Open Monday through Saturday 9–5. Try to stop by this establishment where cheese and butter are made the old-fashioned way. Once the well-kept secrets of America's great chefs, these fine cheeses are available for sale. It's a perfect place to stock up before going on a picnic.

Outhouse Orchards (914-277-3188), Hardscrabble Road, Croton Falls, offers tours; you can pick apples in the fall or shop at the stand year-round.

Schultz's Cider Mill (914-273-3521), 103 Old Route 22, Armonk, open daily 8–5:30, closed Tuesday. Doughnuts, cider, apples, and fruits and vegetables in-season.

Stuart's Fruit Farm (914-245-2784), Granite Springs Road, Granite Springs, is open year-round.

Titicus Farm Produce (914-669-5421), Keeler Lane, North Salem, open June through November, carries seasonal fruits and vegetables, plus eggs, honey, and flowers.

Westchester Farms (914-592-4610), 701 Dobbs Ferry Road, White Plains, open April through December, has tours and organic produce, maple syrup, and honey.

Wilkens Fruit Farm (914-245-5111), 1313 White Hill Road, Yorktown, has a farm stand and pick-your-own apples and peaches in-season.

FOR FAMILIES

Playland (914-925-2701), Playland Parkway, off I-95, Rye. Different sections of the park are open year-round, although the rides end around Labor Day; hours vary widely, so call for a schedule. Free. A true old-fashioned amusement park, Rye's Playland is an architectural gem. Built in 1928, Playland was the first amusement park constructed according to a complete plan, where recreational family fun was the focus. Fortunately, the park's family atmosphere and art deco style are still here to be enjoyed. Set on the beaches of Long Island Sound, Playland offers a famous 1,200-foot boardwalk, a swimming pool, gardens, a saltwater

JOSEPH PUCLISI

Playland in Rye with its renowned 1,200-foot-long boardwalk

boating pond (paddleboats can be rented), a beach, and, of course, the rides and amusement area. There are seven original rides still in use; among them are the carousel (with a rare carousel organ and painted horses), the Dragon Coaster (a rare wooden roller coaster), and the Derby Racer (horses zip around a track). Fireworks and special entertainment like musical revues, along with an amusement area, are active all summer; in winter the ice-skating rinks at Rye are open to the public.

GOLF

Westchester is famous for some of the professional golf tourneys hosted in the county, but there are also five county-owned courses that are open to the public (other courses are sometimes for members only): **Dunwoodie** (914-476-5151), Wasylenko Lane, Yonkers; **Maple Moor** (914-949-6752), North Street, White Plains; **Mohansic** (914-962-4065), Baldwin Road, Yorktown Heights; **Saxon Woods** (914-723-0949), Mamaroneck Road, Scarsdale; and **Sprain Lake** (914-779-5180), Grassy Sprain Road, Yonkers. For general information about green fees, tournaments, and special events, call 914-428-0760.

HIKING

   ᕫ **Franklin Roosevelt State Park** (914-245-4434), Route 202 and the Taconic Parkway, has hiking and cross-country ski trails and a huge outdoor pool that is also accessible to the disabled.

Indian Brook Assemblage (914-232-9431), Mount Holly Road, Lewisboro, is really a "collection" of smaller parks and preserves maintained by The Nature Conservancy. Lakes, waterfalls, ponds, and trails form a perfect getaway for the outdoors lover, and the hiking ranges from a leisurely walk to a challenging outing.

Marshlands Conservancy (914-835-4466), Route 1, Rye. Marked trails take the hiker through fields and woods and along the seashore. This is a great spot for birders, and a small nature center has exhibits on the natural history of Long Island Sound.

More hiking is found at the **Mianus River Gorge** (203-322-9148 for a guided Saturday hike), Mianus River Road, Bedford, and along the **Old Croton Aqueduct** (914-271-2196), Route 129, to the Croton Dam Plaza. The latter hike is a total of 30 miles, but both hikers and bicyclers can follow as much or as little of the trail as they want. Stop at the plaza spillway, which was considered an engineering marvel in its day.

HORSEBACK RIDING

Horseback riders can rent horses and use the trails at **Rudan Stables** (914-636-9371), 960 California Avenue, Eastchester. This county-run facility is open daily, except Monday, year-round.

SWIMMING

Those who want to go to the beach can enjoy the one at Playland in Rye (see *For Families*).

Blue Mountain Reservation Beach (914-737-2194), Welcher Avenue, Peekskill, has beaches, a pool, and extensive recreation areas.

Croton Point Beach and Park (914-271-6858), Croton-on-Hudson, overlooks the Hudson River and has special events all summer.

ICE SKATING

There are indoor rinks at Rye's Playland (see *For Families*), and at the **Hommocks Park Ice Rink** (914-834-1069), Boston Post Road,

Larchmont. Call for hours. Skaters should be aware that many parks offer lake and pond skating; call the individual site to check on conditions and rentals (see *Green Space*).

GREEN SPACE

Westchester may be a bustling region for big business, but you'll also find dozens of lovely public parks and outdoor facilities throughout the county.

Blue Mountain Reservation (914-737-2194), Welcher Avenue, Peekskill. Open year-round. Situated in the northwest part of the county, this recreation area has a large lake for swimming in summer and ice skating during the winter. There are facilities for hiking, fishing, and picnicking. Camping is available in the Trail Lodge, which has a dining hall with a fireplace.

Cranberry Lake Preserve (914-428-1005), Old Orchard Street (off Route 22), North White Plains. Open year-round. This lovely preserve consists of 135 acres of unspoiled wetlands and hardwood forests. The park has a 10-acre pond with trails and boardwalks so visitors can observe life in an aquatic habitat. You'll find fishing, cross-country ski trails, and hiking. A small lodge offers interpretive programs and seasonal exhibits.

Croton Point Park (914-271-3293), Croton Avenue (off Route 9), Croton. Open year-round. This park is located along the banks of the Hudson River and features a pool, canoe-launching area, recreation hall, and ball fields. The location is ideal for fishing, hiking, and picnicking. There are also cabins, lean-tos, and facilities for tents and trailers available.

Greenburgh Nature Center (914-723-3470), Dromore Road, off Central Avenue in Scarsdale. Open daily year-round. Situated on 32 acres, this innovative nature center offers visitors a chance to explore several environments, including woodlands, a vineyard, orchards, and cultivated gardens. There are more than 30 different species of trees in the preserve, along with wildflowers, ferns, and a host of songbirds. At the center's museum, Nunataks, an Inuit word meaning "hill of stone," there are animal exhibits and descriptive displays that explain some of the area's natural history. You can also pick up maps here to use on the self-guided nature walks. Many special events are held at the nature center, from concerts on the lawn to art exhibits; there is even a Honey Harvest Brunch (the museum has a glass beehive!).

Hammond Museum and Oriental Stroll Gardens (914-669-5135), Deveau Road, off Old Route 124 in North Salem. Open weekends May through October, 11–5; call for other times. Admission fee. A chance to step back into the Edo period of Japanese history. Created by Natalie Hays Hammond in memory of her parents, these gardens are actually 15 small landscapes, including waterfall, Zen, azalea, and fruit gardens.

Each section is lovely and has a symbolic meaning: In the reflecting pool, for example, five water lilies, beautiful on their own, represent humanity, justice, courtesy, wisdom, and fidelity. There is also a small museum here, with a mix of art, antiques, and collectibles, but it is the gardens that must not be missed. Reservations are necessary for lunch at the small restaurant on the site.

Marshlands Conservancy (914-835-4466), Route 1, Rye. Open year-round. There is an environmental education center with changing exhibitions and four saltwater aquaria at this 137-acre wildlife sanctuary. The unique character of the conservancy lies in the diversity of habitats preserved within its boundaries, including woods, fields, freshwater ponds, a salt marsh, and shore. There are paths throughout to these points of interest.

✐ **Rye Nature Center** (914-967-1549), 873 Boston Post Road, Rye. Open daily 9–5 year-round. A "small" nature center (under 50 acres), this is a nice stop if you are traveling with children. A small museum has exhibits of local animals and plants, and there are several mini exhibits about nature. Take the 2½-mile nature walk, which is described in guidebooks you can pick up at the museum. There is a picnic area.

Teatown Lake Reservation (914-762-2912), Spring Valley Road, Croton. Take exit 134 off the Taconic, then take Grant's Lane to Spring Valley Road. Open daily year-round; museum open Tuesday through Saturday 9–5. Free. This 400-acre reservation has marked nature walks and hiking trails, a museum, and outdoor exhibits. Wildflowers are abundant here in the spring, and there is an unusual selection of fences. Visitors can enjoy viewing waterfowl and other animals at a large lake; inside the museum there are live exhibits of local animals and plants.

✐ **Ward Pound Ridge Reservation** (914-763-3493), Routes 35 and 121, Cross River. Open year-round. Ward Pound Ridge is the largest park in Westchester County, covering more than 4,700 acres. There are miles of trails for cross-country skiing, sledding, snowmobiling, hiking, and horseback riding. There are also several places to go fishing and to picnic. You can easily spend a day here. On weekends there are often nature programs for families and children.

✐ **Westmoreland Sanctuary** (914-666-8448), Chestnut Ridge Road, Mount Kisco. Open year-round 9–5 Monday through Saturday, Sunday 10:30–5. Free, but fees are charged for some workshops and special events. The sanctuary is an active site, with more than 15 miles of walking and hiking trails, wildlife displays, and exhibits of local natural history. There are workshops, lectures, and events all year, including "Building Bathhouses," seasonal hikes, birdsong identification walks, Earth Day celebrations, even a search for the first ferns of spring! An excellent site for a family visit.

Also see PepsiCo Sculpture Gardens under *To See*.

LODGING

Westchester County is home to many conference centers and four-star hotels, which offer visitors everything from saunas to fine dining. Visitors who prefer B&B establishments (and these can range from mountaintop estates to cozy town houses) must make their reservations through the **Westchester Bed & Breakfast Association,** 92 Old Post Road South, Croton-on-Hudson 10520 (914-271-4663). Unless otherwise noted, the establishments in this section are open year-round.

Crabtree's Kittle House (914-666-8044), Route 117, Mount Kisco 10549. ($$$) This more-than-200-year-old building has been an inn since the 1930s, when it attracted film stars like Henry Fonda and Tallulah Bankhead. One of the few inns in Westchester, the Kittle House is moderately priced for the area. Continental breakfast is served, and children are welcome. There are 12 rooms with private bath, telephone, and cable TV, and a fine restaurant on the premises (see *Dining Out*).

Alexander Hamilton House (914-271-6737), 49 Van Wyck Street, Croton-on-Hudson 10520. ($$$) This Victorian house dates back to 1889 and has 10 luxurious rooms; three have Jacuzzis and seven have fireplaces. The bridal chamber is on the third floor and has a king-sized bed, skylights, and a pink marble fireplace. All rooms have private bath, TV, and telephone. There's also an in-ground pool. A full breakfast is served.

HOTELS AND CONFERENCE CENTERS

The following full-service hotels and conference centers welcome individual guests as well as groups.

The Castle at Tarrytown (914-631-1980), 400 Benedict Avenue, Tarrytown 10591. ($$$) Only 25 miles north of Manhattan, perched in splendor on 10 hilltop acres overlooking the majestic Hudson River, is this establishment—an authentic castle and one of the oldest and grandest historic landmarks in the region. The main tower rises 75 feet, the highest point in Westchester County. Built between 1897 and 1910 by the son of a Civil War general, the Castle has changed little in the last 100 years. Much of the hewn-oak girders, beams, and woodwork and some of the furniture were brought over from Europe. The innkeepers are Swiss and a stay here is like a European mini-vacation. The service is excellent. Today a luxury inn, gourmet restaurant (the Equus; see *Dining Out*), and special-events facility, this is one of the most magical, romantic spots anywhere. The accommodations include five enormous suites that range from 750 to 900 square feet. For a special occasion, ask for the tower suite—it is magnificent and has fantastic views of the river and mountains. Spacious living rooms, working fireplaces, and luxurious bathrooms are standard. Each suite includes color cable TV, in-room fax, and mini bar, and most have a fireplace. All guest rooms are nonsmoking; open year-round.

ℐ **Doral Arrowwood** (914-939-5500), Anderson Hill Road, Rye Brook 10573. ($$$) This full-facility resort of 272 rooms is located on 114 wooded acres. You'll find a nine-hole golf course, indoor-outdoor pools, tennis, and squash, along with a sauna and Universal gym. The atrium dining room is a multilevel restaurant that overlooks the grounds and gardens and serves excellent food. Weekend packages are available during the spring and summer. Children are welcome.

Hampton Inn (914-592-5680), 200 Tarrytown Road, Elmsford 10523. ($$) There are 156 rooms in this moderately priced hotel. A fitness room and outdoor pool are available to guests, and a deluxe continental breakfast is served 6–10. All local calls are free of charge. Open year-round.

&. **Holiday Inn Crowne Plaza** (914-682-0050), 66 Hale Avenue, White Plains 10601. ($$$) This hotel has 400 guest rooms and an indoor pool, whirlpool, sauna, and exercise room. The Fenimore Bistro offers breakfast, lunch, and dinner daily.

ℐ&. **The Renaissance Westchester Hotel** (914-694-5400), 80 West Red Oak Lane, White Plains 10601. ($$$) A 364-room, full-service hotel with an indoor pool, sun deck, sauna, exercise room, tennis courts, and volleyball courts. There are excellent dining facilities in **The Woodlands Restaurant** and 24-hour room service; transportation within a 5-mile radius of the hotel is provided. Special weekend rates. Children welcome.

&. **Residence Inn Marriott** (914-761-7700), 5 Barker Avenue, White Plains 10601. ($$$) This all-suite hotel has 120 guest suites, a fitness room, and a lounge.

Royal Regency Hotel (1-800-215-3858), 165 Tuckahoe Road, Yonkers 10710. ($$) This hotel is located in a convenient spot (exit 6W off the NYS Thruway). The 92 elegantly appointed rooms include luxurious Jacuzzi suites. The **Crystal Manor Restaurant and Cocktail Lounge** serves dinner daily.

The Rye Town Hilton Inn (914-939-6300), Westchester Avenue, Port Chester 10573. ($$$) This hotel has 440 guest rooms, indoor and outdoor pools, saunas, a whirlpool, tennis courts, and an exercise room. There are two restaurants: **Tulip Tree** serves casual, inexpensive fare; Penfield's serves gourmet American cuisine (see *Dining Out*).

The Tarrytown Courtyard (914-631-1122), 475 White Plains Road, Tarrytown 10591. ($$) A relatively small (139 rooms), moderately priced hotel, where guests can enjoy relaxing in the Jacuzzi and pool or simply enjoying the scenic courtyard. The **Courtyard Cafe** is on the premises, open for breakfast daily and dinner Monday through Thursday. Special weekend rates are available in the winter months.

&. **The Tarrytown Hilton** (914-631-5700), 455 South Broadway, Tarrytown 10591. ($$) Guests have a choice of 236 rooms and the use of indoor and outdoor pools, exercise rooms, tennis courts, and jogging trails. Fine Continental cuisine is served in the Pennybridge restaurant.

 ᕕ   **Westchester Marriott** (914-631-2200), 670 White Plains Road, Tarrytown 10591. ($$$) The Marriott has 444 guest rooms, an indoor pool, saunas, and a fitness center. Allie's Restaurant serves Continental cuisine; Ruth's Steakhouse serves fine food in an elegant atmosphere every evening from 5. There is also a nightclub, Gambit's, and a sports bar, The Pub, on the premises.

WHERE TO EAT

DINING OUT

Westchester is lucky enough to have hundreds of restaurants, in all price ranges and for all tastes. The following were selected from personal experience and are only a few of the fine choices available to the visitor. Don't be afraid to try the broad range of restaurants, from Jamaican to Continental, that you will find on just about every street and back road in the county.

Abhilash India Cuisine (914-235-8390), 30 Division Street, New Rochelle. ($$) Open daily for lunch (11:30–2:30) and dinner (5–10). Authentic Indian cuisine is served in an atmosphere of Indian decor and music. The menu features such Tandoori specialties as chicken *dhaka-sag* and vegetable fritters and exotic desserts like frozen milk with cashews, raisins, and saffron.

Abis (914-698-8777), 406 Mamaroneck Avenue, Mamaroneck. ($$) Open for lunch Monday through Saturday 11:30–2:30; dinner served 5:30–10. This lovely Japanese restaurant serves teriyaki dishes as well as sushi and sashimi.

Auberge Argenteuil (914-948-0597), 42 Healy Avenue, Hartsdale. ($$$) Open daily, except Monday, for lunch (11:30–2:30) and dinner (5–9:30). Set in a building that was a speakeasy in the 1920s, this restaurant is hidden high up in a wooded area above Central Avenue. Specialties include lobster bisque, veal with wild mushrooms, and a superb ice cream bombe. Not recommended for children.

Auberge Maxime (914-669-5450), Route 116, North Salem. ($$$) Open daily, except Wednesday, for lunch at noon and dinner at 6. Enjoy classical French cuisine with a nouvelle touch in this lovely country inn. Comfortable chairs and beautifully appointed tables grace the dining room, and the six-course prix fixe dinner includes such treats as duck with pear or fresh ginger sauce and hot and cold soufflés.

Bayou Restaurant (914-668-2634), 580 Gramatan Avenue, Mount Vernon. ($$) Open daily for lunch and dinner 11:30–11. The Cajun Creole cuisine includes stuffed pork chops, jambalaya, gumbo, and mudbugs (boiled crawfish.) For those who prefer less adventurous fare, steak, sandwiches, and burgers are offered as well.

Buffet de la Gare (914-478-1671), 155 Southside Avenue, Hastings-on-Hudson. ($$$) Open for lunch Thursday and Friday from noon; dinner

Tuesday through Saturday from 6. Enjoy classical French cuisine in a relaxing ambience. Everything here is prepared to order and the desserts should not be passed up. The fine reputation of this establishment, long a favorite with local residents, has spread throughout the country.

❧ **La Camelia** (914-666-2466), 234 North Bedford Road, Mount Kisco. ($$) Open daily, except Monday, for lunch at noon and dinner at 6. One of the best Spanish restaurants you will find anywhere, La Camelia is located in a landmark, more-than-140-year-old building. Northern Spanish cuisine is the specialty and includes gazpacho, shrimp Catalan, squid with angelhair pasta, and homemade desserts. Children welcome.

❧ **Central Square Cafe** (914-472-7828), 870 Central Park Avenue, Scarsdale. ($$) Open daily 8 AM–midnight; Sunday until 10. Sunday brunch is served. You will find just about every American culinary favorite served with an Italian influence. The filet mignon and fresh seafood are both first-rate. There is a variety of pizzas, and the pasta is made fresh on the premises daily. Our favorite is the tortellini.

❧ **Chart House Restaurant** (914-693-4130), High Street, Dobbs Ferry. ($$) Open for dinner Monday through Saturday at 5, Sunday noon–9. This contemporary restaurant has a magnificent view of the Palisades, the Tappan Zee Bridge, and the New York City skyline. Specialties include prime rib, thick steaks, and an enormous selection of seafood dishes. The mud pie here is famous throughout the area. Children are welcome.

Le Chateau Restaurant (914-533-6631), Route 35, South Salem. ($$) Open daily, except Monday, for dinner at 6. This French restaurant with Old World charm is situated on 32 wooded acres and offers magnificent sunset views and lavishly decorated dining rooms. House specialties include wild mushroom soup, salmon in parchment, and quail in raspberry sauce. An assortment of mousses set in crème anglaise are served for dessert.

Crabtree's Kittle House (914-666-8044), Route 117, Mount Kisco. ($$$) Open for lunch Monday through Friday noon–2:30; dinner served daily 6–10; Sunday champagne brunch noon–2:30. The American and Continental cuisine here has Italian, French, and Asian influences. The menu changes daily, but the excellent cherrywood-smoked Norwegian salmon is always available. Other house specialties are venison and sweetbreads of milk-fed Hudson Valley veal. The pastry chef suggests the Alsatian cheesecake—one of his favorites. Live jazz Friday and Saturday night.

Dudley's (914-941-8674), 6 Rockledge Avenue, Ossining. ($$) Open for lunch Monday through Friday noon–2:30; dinner served daily 6–9:30, Sunday 5:30–8:30. The American cuisine includes grilled breast of duck, sea scallops, swordfish, and grilled baby pheasant. The sirloin steak is also a popular entrée.

Equus Restaurant at the Castle at Tarrytown (914-631-3646), 400

Benedict Avenue, Tarrytown. ($$$) Open daily for lunch and dinner and Sunday brunch. This is one of the most romantic spots in the Hudson Valley, a castle constructed almost 100 years ago. The restaurant has several elegantly appointed rooms as well as an enclosed veranda with magnificent views of the Hudson River and the New York City skyline. The Oak Room is constructed with wood brought from Germany. The smoked filet of Black Angus beef with sweet potato tamale, corn truffles, and chipotle bordelaise is phenomenal. You might also try medallions of venison with warm mango and green peppercorn sauce, or a root vegetable stew *en papillote*. Save room for the beautifully presented and mouthwatering desserts.

L'Europe (914-533-2570), Route 123, South Salem. ($$$) Lunch (noon–2:30) and dinner (6–9:30) served daily, except Monday. This attractive dining establishment reminiscent of an English club serves outstandingly good Continental cuisine. Specialties include fillet of sole stuffed with seafood mousse, fettuccine with prosciutto and smoked salmon, and galantine of halibut and salmon, as well as such tempting desserts as lemon and orange torte and délice (layers of chocolate and buttercream in a meringue). Not recommended for children. Dinner reservations suggested.

Hudson Café (914-591-9850), 63 Main Street, Irvington-on-Hudson. ($$) Open daily for lunch 11:30–4, dinner 5–11; closed Monday. The emphasis in all the cooking here is on fresh ingredients and healthful preparation. The cuisine is American and the atmosphere is intimate and informal. There is a beautiful antique bar, a tin ceiling, and many other lovely, old-fashioned architectural details. The fresh fish and pasta dishes are highly recommended.

India House (914-736-0005), 199 Albany Post Road, Montrose. ($$) Open daily for lunch 11:30–2:30 and dinner 5–10. Lots of greenery surrounds this attractive restaurant. The dining rooms are decorated to resemble a colorful, handmade tent, with walls hung with antique tapestries. Tandoori lamb, chicken, and shrimp dishes are the specialty. The vegetarian entrées are excellent, and everything can be prepared from mild to very hot and spicy. Children welcome.

Inn at Pound Ridge (914-764-5779), 258 Westchester Avenue, Pound Ridge. ($$$) Open Tuesday through Friday for lunch noon–2:30; dinner daily at 6; Sunday brunch noon–3. Closed Monday. The American cuisine here includes rack of lamb, sautéed pork chops, and grilled tuna. The menu is contemporary yet familiar, and all breads and desserts are made fresh daily on the premises. The proprietor enjoys the crème brûlée and the Bavarian chocolate cake—only two of the tempting selections offered.

Lussardi's (914-834-5555), 1885 Palmer Avenue, Larchmont. ($$) Open daily for lunch and dinner 11:30–10:30. The northern Italian cuisine is served in an informal atmosphere. Enjoy veal Martini, homemade pasta stuffed with spinach and porcini mushrooms, or artichoke salad with arugula, Parmesan cheese, and diced cherry tomatoes.

Main Street Café (914-524-9770), 24 Main Street, Tarrytown. ($$) Open for lunch Tuesday through Saturday noon–3; dinner 5–10; Sunday brunch noon–3 and dinner 3–9. A casual stop for bistro food and jazzy entertainment, this restaurant features American cuisine including a wide variety of pasta entrées, steaks, fresh seafood, and an extensive wine list.

Mamaroneck Harbor Grille (914-698-1011), 136 Mamaroneck Avenue, Mamaroneck. ($$) Open Tuesday through Sunday from 11:30. Sunday brunch is served. This American bistro offers an array of grilled seafood and pasta dishes, organic salads, and vegetarian entrées. The atmosphere is casual, and there is patio dining in summer.

Maxime's (914-248-7200), Old Tomahawk Street, Granite Springs. ($$$) Open Thursday through Sunday for lunch noon–4; dinner Wednesday through Sunday 6–10:30. Fine French cuisine is featured here, along with an excellent wine list. There is a fireplace in the charming dining room, and the selections include unusual dishes like baby quail eggs, mousse of duck liver in pastry, medallions of venison, and excellent desserts like chocolate terrine. Not recommended for children.

Monteverde (914-739-5000), Bear Mountain Bridge Road, Peekskill. ($$) Open Monday, Wednesday, Thursday, and Friday for lunch noon–2:30; dinner 5:30–9:30; open Saturday 5:30–9:30 and Sunday noon–8:30. Closed Tuesday. This 18th-century stone mansion was built by the Van Cortlandt family and is now an outstanding restaurant. Great views of the river and a rural setting make this stop a treat in summer for fine Continental cuisine.

La Panetiere Restaurant (914-967-8140), 530 Milton Road, Rye. ($$) Open for lunch Tuesday through Friday noon–2:30; dinner Tuesday through Saturday 6–9:30; Sunday 1–8:30. The building dates back to the 1800s and the Provençal interior features exposed beams, stucco walls, and a huge grandfather clock. Appetizer specials include warm oysters with leeks, duck terrine with truffles and pistachios, and fresh foie gras; entrées include squab, venison, and Dover sole filled with puree of artichokes. Six-course prix fixe menu.

Penfield's Restaurant (914-939-6300), 699 Westchester Avenue, Rye Brook. ($$$) Open for dinner daily, except Sunday, 6–10. This restaurant, located in the Rye Town Hilton Inn, features upscale American cuisine. Try the rack of lamb or fresh fillet of Dover sole. Save room for dessert.

Provare Restaurant (914-939-5500), Anderson Hill Road, Rye Brook. ($$) Lunch Tuesday through Friday 11:30–2; dinner Tuesday through Thursday 5:30–9:30, Friday and Saturday night until 11, Sunday 4–9. A cheerful trattoria-style restaurant, Provare is decorated in black and yellow from the wallpaper to the tile floors. The gourmet pizzas are baked in a wood-fired brick oven; the smoked pheasant pizza and the barbecued chicken pizza are two unusual varieties. The menu is extensive, and vegetarian lasagne and linguine with mussels are both recommended.

Ray's Cafe (914-833-2551), 1995 Palmer Avenue, Larchmont. ($$) Open for lunch Monday through Friday noon–3; dinner 3–10; Saturday 3–10; Sunday 4:30–9:30. This Chinese restaurant serves Shanghai-style cuisine. The crispy shrimp with honey walnuts is excellent, as is the sesame chicken. You can also order crispy or steamed whole fish, prepared to order any way you like.

Rustico (914-472-4005), 753 Central Park Avenue, Scarsdale. ($$) Open Monday through Saturday 11:30–10; Sunday 4–10. Northern Italian cuisine with a French influence is the style of cooking here. There are standard favorites like veal scaloppine as well as an array of pasta dishes (all pasta is homemade on the premises). The gnocci and fettuccine are excellent.

Santa Fe Restaurant (914-332-4452), 5 Main Street, Tarrytown. ($$) Open daily for lunch and dinner 11:30–10. You can get steak, chicken, shrimp, and even shark fajitas at this colorful Mexican dining spot. For taco lovers, there is a make-your-own taco basket: Diners are served chicken or beef, beans, rice, peppers, and other fixings from which they can create their own meal. One of the most unusual and delicious dishes is the shrimp and crab enchiladas with blue corn tortillas.

Zephs' (914-736-2159), 638 Central Avenue, Peekskill. ($$$) Open Wednesday through Sunday at 5:30 for dinner. Set in a reclaimed factory building, Zephs' serves American cuisine with a fresh twist; choices may include Moroccan lamb, tomato tart, salt and pepper squid, fresh fruit cobblers, mud cake, and rich custards. Many of the herbs are grown by the owners, and summer diners can enjoy the outdoor patio area. Reservations are necessary.

EATING OUT

Cactus Jack (914-526-2222), 3258 East Main Street, Mohegan Lake; 210 Saw Mill River Road, Elmsford (914-345-3334); 690 Mamaroneck Avenue, Mamaroneck (914-777-1156). ($) Open daily 11:30–10. Southwestern cuisine is served with a Mexican touch. Sample the fajitas, which are excellent, whether you order the steak, shrimp, or chicken.

Cafe Fresco (914-833-2830), 94 Chadsworth Avenue, Larchmont. ($$) Open daily 11:30–9 for lunch and dinner. The eclectic California cuisine has an Italian accent here. Casual dining in a neighborhood café where the staples are pasta, salads of all kinds, sandwiches, and seafood.

Carl's (914-834-1244), 121 Myrtle Boulevard, Larchmont. ($$) Open daily for lunch noon–3; dinner 5–10. Steaks and seafood are served in a casual atmosphere. Try the swordfish or sirloin steak, two of the most popular entrées here.

Heathcote Tavern (914-723-3160), 2 Palmer Avenue, Scarsdale. ($$)

Open daily 6 AM–9 PM. American cuisine is served here, with the emphasis on burgers, salads, sandwiches, and pastas.

✎ **Horsefeathers** (914-631-6606), 94 North Broadway, Tarrytown. ($$) Open daily at 11:30 for lunch and dinner. One of the first "grazing" restaurants in the county, Horsefeathers continues to offer great café food like hamburgers, steaks, and overstuffed sandwiches. The atmosphere is casual and comfortable, and children are welcome.

Louisiana Cajun Cafe (914-674-0706), 25 Cedar Street, Dobbs Ferry. ($$) Open for lunch Monday through Saturday noon–2:30; dinner daily 6–10; Sunday brunch 11–3. The most flavorful Cajun and Creole dishes are served here: Gumbo, red beans and rice, jambalaya, and blackened steak and fish are just some of the dishes that will be prepared to your taste. Live Dixieland band on Saturday night.

Pete's Saloon (914-592-9849), 8 West Main Street, Elmsford. ($$) Open daily 11:30 AM–midnight. This informal eatery serves classic American favorites including a variety of burgers, steaks, sandwiches, and salads. The stuffed pork chops and lemon chicken are two popular entrées. There are over 40 bottled beers available, as well as 9 beers on tap; and there are 30 different single-malt scotches to choose from. Entertainment 5 nights a week starting at 10 or so.

Satsumaya (914-381-0200), 576 Mamaroneck Avenue, Mamaroneck. ($$) Open daily for dinner 5–10; closed Monday. There is a sushi bar at this Japanese restaurant, which serves a variety of tempura and teriyaki selections. The noodle dishes are a specialty of the house.

Susan's (914-737-6624), 12 North Division Street, Peekskill. ($$) Open Tuesday through Saturday for lunch 11:30–3; dinner 5–10. Closed Sunday and Monday. Eclectic international cuisine is served in this informal country bistro. The grilled breast of duck with garlic mashed potaotes, Turkish baked stuffed eggplant, and salmon strudel with spinach and wild rice are just a few of the dinner entrées. All breads and desserts are made fresh daily on the premises.

Sweet Basil Restaurant (914-783-6928), Route 17M, Harriman. ($$) Open Tuesday through Friday for lunch 11:30–2:30; Monday through Saturday for dinner 5–9; Sunday 4–8. Continental cuisine with an Italian flair is served in a country bistro atmosphere. Specialties of the house are veal Luigi, honey-roasted fillet of salmon, and rack of lamb. The signature dessert is the Grand Marnier cheesecake baked in an orange.

Two Moons (914-937-9696), 179 Rectory Street, Port Chester. ($$) Open for lunch Monday through Friday 11:30–3; dinner served daily 5–10. The eclectic decor includes petroglyph-decorated walls with Santa Fe–style ambience. Contemporary American cuisine with a southwestern accent is the fare. Paella, rock shrimp and crab enchilada, and Atlantic salmon with papaya-roasted peppers are a few of the imaginative entrées.

✍ **Underhill's Crossing** (914-337-1200), 74½ Pondfield Road, Bronxville. ($$) Open daily 11:30–10. The eclectic American nouvelle fare ranges from pizza, sandwiches, and burgers to veal, lamb, and salmon entrées. Every dish is prepared to order.

✍ **Watercolor Cafe** (914-834-2213), 2094 Boston Post Road, Larchmont. ($$) Open for lunch Monday through Saturday noon–3:30; dinner served daily from 4:30; Sunday brunch 11–3. This restaurant derives its name from the decor—watercolor paintings by local artists. The contemporary American cuisine includes such intriguing dishes as Hoisin barbecued chicken, crispy angelhair pasta served with basil cream sauce and grilled shrimp, and pecan-crusted salmon.

SPECIAL EVENTS

✍ *May and September:* **Crafts at Lyndhurst** (914-631-4481), Lyndhurst Historic Site, Route 9, Tarrytown. Shows are usually held the third weekend of May and the third weekend of September, Friday 10–5, Saturday 10–6, and Sunday 10–5. Admission fee. This spectacular crafts fair has become a Westchester tradition for more than a decade. Craftspeople from across the United States participate—potters, jewelers, fiber artists, and glassmakers. There's a children's tent with activities for the kids, so parents can shop in the huge tents unimpeded. A tour of the Lyndhurst mansion is available at a discount to those who attend the show. Food vendors offer an array of delicious treats. Be sure to get there early and beat the crowds.

Labor Day–Halloween: **Hudson Heritage Festival** (1-800-833-WCVB). Held throughout Westchester County, this festival celebrates the river and historic heritage of the region. Each river town struts its stuff, with fairs, cruises, and other special events. It's a nice way to enjoy autumn in New York.

Index

Books from The Countryman Press

The alternative to mass-market guides with their homogenized listings, Explorer's Guides focus on independently owned inns, B&Bs, and restaurants, and on family and cultural activities reflecting the character and unique qualities of the area. Explorer's Guides are available for:

- *Maine*, by Christina Tree & Elizabeth Roundy Richards
- *New Hampshire*, by Christina Tree & Christine Hamm
- *Vermont*, by Christina Tree & Peter Jennison
- *Massachusetts: The North Shore, South Coast, Central Massachusetts, and the Berkshires*, by Christina Tree & William Davis
- *Cape Cod, Martha's Vineyard, and Nantucket*, by Kim Grant
- *Connecticut*, by Barnett D. Laschever & Andi Marie Fusco
- *Rhode Island*, by Phyllis Méras & Tom Gannon

A SELECTION OF OUR BOOKS ABOUT NEW YORK

History and Travel
The Other Islands of New York City: A History and Guide

Bicycling
25 Bicycle Tours in the Adirondacks
30 Bicycle Tours in the Finger Lakes Region
25 Bicycle Tours in the Hudson Valley
25 Mountain Bike Tours in the Adirondacks
25 Mountain Bike Tours in the Hudson Valley
The Mountain Biker's Guide to Ski Resorts

Hiking
50 Hikes in the Adirondacks
50 Hikes in Central New York
50 Hikes in Western New York

Walking
Walks & Rambles in Dutchess and Putnam Counties
Walks & Rambles on Long Island
Walks & Rambles in Westchester and Fairfield Counties
Walks & Rambles in the Western Hudson Valley
Walks in Nature's Empire: Exploring the Nature Conservancy's Preserves in New York State

Fishing
Good Fishing in the Adirondacks
Good Fishing in Lake Ontario and Its Tributaries
Mid-Atlantic Trout Streams and Their Hatches

We offer many more books on hiking, fly-fishing, paddling, travel, nature, and other subjects. Our books are available at bookstores and outdoor stores everywhere. For more information or a free catalog, please call 1-800-245-4151 or write to us at The Countryman Press, P.O. Box 748, Woodstock, VT 05091. You can find us on the Internet at www.countrymanpress.com.